S0-EUQ-215

THE AMERICAN COLONIZATION
SOCIETY 1817-1840

AMS PRESS
NEW YORK

Series XXXVII   No. 3

JOHNS HOPKINS UNIVERSITY STUDIES
IN
HISTORICAL AND POLITICAL SCIENCE
Under the Direction of the
Departments of History, Political Economy, and
Political Science

THE AMERICAN COLONIZATION SOCIETY 1817-1840

BY

EARLY LEE FOX, PH.D.
Professor of History in Randolph-Macon College

BALTIMORE
THE JOHNS HOPKINS PRESS
1919

Reprinted from the edition of 1919, Baltimore
First AMS EDITION published 1971
Manufactured in the United States of America

International Standard Book Number: 0-404-00159-9

Library of Congress Number: 71-149687

**AMS PRESS INC.
NEW YORK, N.Y. 10003**

CONTENTS

	PAGE
PREFACE	vii
INTRODUCTION	9
CHAPTER I. The Free Negro and the Slave	13
CHAPTER II. Organization, Purpose, Early Years	46
CHAPTER III. American Colonization and Garrisonian Abolition	125
CHAPTER IV. Colonization and Emancipation	180
CHAPTER V. Colonization and the African Slave Trade	215

PREFACE

The following study was undertaken at the suggestion of Professor John H. Latané, of the Johns Hopkins University. It is a genuine pleasure for me to acknowledge and express my thanks for the interest he has shown at every stage of the work. As a result of his instruction, together with that of Professor J. M. Vincent, also of the Johns Hopkins University, I have come to appreciate, I hope, the importance of a critical evaluation of historical evidence. My thanks are also due those connected with the Manuscripts Division of the Library of Congress, where most of the research work was done, and particularly to Mr. Fitzpatrick, whose courtesy I shall not soon forget. Rev. M. L. Fearnow very kindly read a portion of the manuscript and suggested several changes.

E. L. F.

THE AMERICAN COLONIZATION SOCIETY
1817-1840

INTRODUCTION

It is just a century since a group of men of distinguished talents came together in the city of Washington for an interchange of views on the solution of the negro problem. The result was the organization of the American Colonization Society. From the time of its inception the Society appealed to men in every walk of life and from every section of the Union. The whole movement was in response to a national, not a sectional sentiment. From the day of its birth to the day when, by the proclamation of the president, the slaves in the South were set free, leaders of thought and framers of national policy looked to this organization to save them from what Jefferson had called the fire bell in the night.

Between the Missouri Compromise and John Brown's raid there were few platforms upon which representative men from New England, the West, and the upper South could stand and discuss dispassionately the negro problem. But upon the platform of the Colonizationists they could, and did, stand. On that platform stood Daniel Webster of Massachusetts and William H. Crawford of Georgia, Elisha Whittlesey of Ohio and Theodore Frelinghuysen of New Jersey. There Elijah Paine, that distinguished farmer, jurist, and philanthropist of Vermont, could, in common with his neighbor, Roger M. Sherman of Connecticut, talk with the owner of three hundred slaves, William H. Fitzhugh of Virginia. There stood Francis Scott Key, Charles Fenton Mercer, John Marshall, and James Monroe. There the author of the Olive Branch made common cause with the editor of the North American Review. There James Madison, the father of the Constitution, was of the same mind as was Abraham Lincoln, who stood as the guardian of a national spirit which that time honored instrument had done so much to create.

The organization of the Methodist Church was rent in twain over the question of slavery; but Bishop Beverly Waugh, of the Methodist Episcopal Church, was a Colonizationist in common with Bishop John C. Granberry, of the Southern Methodists; and these made common cause with Bishop Clark of Rhode Island and Bishop Meade of Virginia, both of the Protestant Episcopal Church. Waldo of Massachusetts, and McDonogh of New Orleans, contributed many thousands of dollars for the cause. Presidents McLean of Princeton, Duer of Columbia, Day of Yale, Everett and Sparks of Harvard, were all Colonizationists. Richard Rush, John Eager Howard, Henry Rutgers, John Taylor of Caroline, General George Mason, General Walter Jones, Robert Ralston, Benjamin F. Butler of New York, John Tyler, Henry A. Wise, J. J. Crittenden, Abel P. Upshur, M. C. Perry, and Levi Lincoln, men who thought differently along many lines, all supported the colonization movement.

The decade, 1830–1840, witnessed the development of large areas of the Southwest, and with the economic change came a fundamental change in the point of view of the South toward slavery. Professor Dew's contribution in the "Pro-Slavery Argument" is indicative of a lamentable change that was coming over the mind and conscience of the South. If ever, during the nineteenth century, conditions in the United States called for the leadership of men of foresight and moderation to set forth convincingly the evils of the system that was getting its hold on the South, that time was 1831 and the ten years following. The Colonizationists, both Northern and Southern, attempted to provide just such men and just such leadership. It was with the secret cooperation of the American Colonization Society that Jesse Burton Harrison, a native of Virginia who was then living in New Orleans, contributed to the American Quarterly Review his "Review of the Slave Question," which was intended to counteract the undoubtedly great influence of Professor Dew's argument. Harrison appealed to the Southern States, and particularly Virginia, to throw off that greatest hindrance to economic development. What would have been the result if such a campaign as that begun by Harrison had been allowed to go on unobstructed for a decade or a generation it is not possible to say; but that this was precisely an important part of the program of the Colonizationists will appear in the pages which follow.

To look upon the American Colonization Society as an organization whose success is to be measured solely by the number of shiploads of negroes taken to Africa is to misunderstand the whole movement. Any adequate estimate of the work of Colonizationists must take into account the effect of their program upon the preservation of national unity. And yet, measured concretely, the Colonization Society was a potent factor in securing the emancipation of slaves, thousands of them, and would have secured the liberation of thousands more, had not the rapid expansion of the Southwest, the consequent increased demand for slaves, and the counteracting influences of hostile propagandists brought about the enforcement of hitherto laxly enforced laws and the enactment of more stringent laws prohibiting emancipations.

The influence of the Society in the suppression of the slave trade has, it seems, been entirely overlooked; and yet, there was a time in its history when it probably saved from transportation into slavery no fewer than twenty thousand native Africans a year.

The limitations of both time and space that are necessarily imposed upon one who undertakes to make a study of this character have made it impracticable to present here a complete history of the Colonization Society. That history covers one hundred years; for the Society is still in existence, although, since the close of the Civil War, its influence has been considerably limited and it now undertakes but a very small part of what it once undertook. It has been impracticable here to extend the study even to the opening of the Civil War except in the influence of the Society upon the slave trade and upon emancipations and manumissions. The period covered is limited to the years 1817 to 1840. No one who is even tolerably acquainted with the Society's history after its reorganization in 1839, when it came under the control of the North Middle and New England States, can have the slightest well-founded suspicion that thereafter it pursued a proslavery policy. It has been the chief aim of the writer to set forth unequivocally its aims and purposes prior to that time. The years 1839 and 1840 were years of severe strain upon the Society, and some of the most persistent of its leaders were in low spirits during that time. This will appear at the close of the second chapter. But this by no means signifies that there were not brighter days ahead. Indeed, the Society's resources grew rapidly from 1840 to the very beginning of the Civil War. From 1817 to 1839 Colonizationists looked upon their work chiefly from the point of view of its effect upon the solution of the negro problem in the United States; after 1840 they looked upon it chiefly from the point of view of its effect in building upon the coast of Africa a model negro republic. The object, in this study, has been to set forth fully and completely this first period of its history.

CHAPTER I

THE FREE NEGRO AND THE SLAVE

As late as 1825 New England had not forgotten that she had had a part in the introduction of negro slaves into the Southern States. In that year Daniel Dana, addressing the New Hampshire Auxiliary Colonization Society, said:

> Let us not imagine, for a moment, that we in this Northern clime, are exempt from that enormous guilt, connected with slavery, and the slave-trade, which we are so ready to appropriate to our brethren in distant States. We have no right thus to wash our hands. From *New England* have gone the ships and the sailors that have been polluted with this inhuman traffic. In *New England* are the forges which have framed fetters and manacles for the limbs of unoffending Africans. The iron of *New England* has pierced their anguished souls. In *New England* are found the over-grown fortunes, the proud palaces which have been reared up from the blood and sufferings of these unhappy men. The guilt is strictly national. . . . National, then, let the expiation be. Let us raise up the humbled children of Africa from their dust. . . . Let us send them back to their native land.[1]

Four years later a clergyman from Maine, who hailed the organization of the American Colonization Society as the most promising means of ridding the land of slavery, but whose faith in its efforts was shaken on his hearing that plantation owners who had not set free their slaves were prominent in the movement, made the following confession:

> With many others of the Northern people, I have long entertained erroneous views. I have supposed that slavery was an evil confined merely to the slave-holder himself, and that he might and ought immediately to manumit his slaves. But I am convinced that slavery is a National sin! that we, who are so far removed from the scene of its abominations, partake of its guilt! that it is an evil which is entailed upon the present generation of slave-holders, which they must suffer, whether they will or not; and therefore the North should aid the South, in the expense of emancipating and transporting their slaves back to the land of their fathers.[2]

---
[1] African Repository, vol. i, p. 146.
[2] Ibid., vol. v, pp. 78–80.

Professor Silliman, of Yale, called attention to the fact that had New England, New York, New Jersey, and Pennsylvania been cotton producing States, the slave system would have been fastened on them "to the full extent of profitable employment," and he added:

> Neither can it be denied that the slave trade, for the supply of the South, was carried on by too many persons in the North. . . .
> Slavery is now generally acknowledged, in this country, to be an enormous evil. . . . costly to the proprietor, . . . a source of increasing domestic danger; an insult to the purity of our religion and an outrage on the Majesty of Heaven. This language is not stronger than that which lately resounded in the Capital of Virginia. This is not the proper occasion to discuss the project of the *entire* and *immediate* abolition of slavery; it is enough that it is, at present, impracticable; nor will we take upon us, to reprehend with severity, the intemperate, uncourteous and unchristian language with which the friends of Colonization are from certain [abolition] quarters, assailed through the press. . . . Should their attempt fail, through the unfair and unjust opposition of its enemies, the latter will have much to answer for, to Africa itself, and to the African race in this country, and to the world.[3]

The attitude of the upper South toward the question of negro slavery went through three distinct and important phases from colonial times to the beginning of the Civil War. The period from the beginning to the close of the eighteenth century may be considered approximately the period of the first phase, when the colonies sought from the king relief from the alarming growth of the slave system. Of this period, suffice it here to say that the single colony of Virginia passed twenty-three acts whose object was the suppression of the evils of slavery. All these came to naught as the result of the royal veto.[4] The third period extended from 1835 or 1840 to the beginning of the Civil War. This was the period during which the South was definitely and frankly set on the continuation of the slave system. It was the period between the years 1800, and particularly between 1815, and 1835 or 1840, that claims special attention in this study. If during the first period the evils were clearly anticipated and the system called forth protests, if during the last period the visions of Southerners

---
[3] Ibid., vol. viii, pp. 161–187.
[4] Ibid., 1828, pp. 172–179.

were blurred as a result of a supposed economic self-interest and resentment at the course of radical Abolitionists, during the middle period slavery was looked upon by leaders of thought in the South and in the North as one of the great national problems that pressed for a solution. The American Colonization Society undoubtedly came into being as a result of this point of view. The men who are to be considered its founders recognized in both the free negro and the slave a momentous problem, and the aim of Colonizationists was to find a satisfactory solution of it. The aim of the writer is to present here fairly and fully the nature of that problem.

South Carolina and Georgia, and a large part of Alabama, never engaged with enthusiasm in the work of Colonization. The Southwestern States were but recently admitted into the Union. It was that group of States stretching from, and including, New York at the North, to, and including, North Carolina at the South, and from the Atlantic seaboard to the western limit of Kentucky, that seemed to understand fully the gravity of that problem; yet throughout the first thirty years of the nineteenth century the evils of slavery were admitted by well nigh every State in the Union.

Then, why did not the slaveholding States at this time abolish slavery? Because they did not know how; because the abolition of slavery was the greatest problem the South had ever been called on to face; because no man had suggested a plan that seemed capable of execution. As late as 1828, J. B. Harrison, of Virginia, a man who had traveled a great deal in his State and who spoke with authority, declared: "Almost all masters in Virginia assent to the proposition, that when the slaves can be liberated without danger to ourselves, and to their own advantage, it ought to be done."[5]

As early as 1804, Dr. William Thornton, the versatile and distinguished friend of Washington, wrote: "I condemn not, but feel for the situation of the possessors of slaves.

---

[5] Ibid., 1828, p. 305.

It is a misery entailed on them by those who did not deeply study the laws of humanity, and who depended too implicitly on laws grounded in impolicy and excluding justice."[6] And Gerrit Smith, who later became an ardent Abolitionist, said, in 1828: "I am certainly far from reproaching our slaveholders with the peculiar relation in which they stand towards some of their hapless fellow creatures. It is not the fault of most of those slaveholders. Most of them were born to that relation. Many of them sincerely deplore this part of their inheritance."[7] President Nott, of Union College, said, in 1829: "Our Brethren of the South, have the sympathies, the same moral sentiments, the same love of liberty as ourselves. By them, as by us, slavery is felt to be an evil, a hindrance to our prosperity, and a blot upon our character. But it was in being when they were born and has been forced upon them by a previous generation."[8] In 1827 C. F. Mercer reported for a committee of the House of Representatives, in reply to memorials of the friends of Colonization:

> In many States . . . [the] total number [of slaves] was, as it still continues to be, so great, that universal or general emancipation could not be hazarded, without endangering a convulsion fatal to the peace of society. . . . Nowhere in America . . . has emancipation elevated the colored race to perfect equality with the white; and in many States the disparity is so great that it may be questioned whether the condition of the slave, while protected by his master, however degraded in itself, is not preferable to that of the free negro. [And yet, even in these States,] the principle of voluntary emancipation has operated to a much greater extent than the laws themselves, or the principle of coercion upon the master has ever done, even among those States who had no danger whatever to apprehend from the speedy and universal extension of human liberty.[9]

In a letter received from a gentleman in Massachusetts by the secretary of the Colonization Society in 1826, we find this statement:

> The late, and more frequent emancipations in the middle and southern States, is producing a very happy influence on the public

---
[6] William Thornton Papers, MS., vol. xiv, "Letter to a Friend," 1804.
[7] Letters of American Colonization Society, MS., G. Smith to R. R. Gurley, Nov. 17, 1828.
[8] African Repository, vol. v, pp. 277-278.
[9] 27th Cong., 3d sess., House Report no. 283, pp. 408-414.

mind, generally in this part of the country. They give a spring to public sentiment, and they teach this great lesson, which we northerners are beginning to understand, that many slaveholders retain their slaves not because they love slavery; but because they cannot better the condition of their slaves by emancipating them. . . . The south and the north, I am fully persuaded, after having recently traveled thro' nearly all the states of this happy Union, are approaching every day towards the same views in reference to this whole subject of our African population, both the bond and the free. . . . The influence of your Society on public *sentiment* is the *main* thing. . . .[10]

The following comment appeared in the New York Tract Magazine:

What is the condition and character of those who are emancipated? . . . In general black people gain little, in many instances they are great losers, by emancipation. Law may relieve them from slavery, but laws cannot change their colour.[11]

In 1818, the General Assembly of the Presbyterian Church, at its meeting in Philadelphia, declared:

We do, indeed, tenderly sympathize with those portions of our church and our country, where the evil of slavery has been entailed upon them; where a *great,* and *the most virtuous part* of the *community* abhor slavery, and wish its extermination, as sincerely as any other; but where the number of slaves, their ignorance, and their vicious habits generally, render an immediate and universal emancipation inconsistent, alike, with the safety and happiness of the master and the slave.[12]

A most valuable contribution to the discussion of this whole subject is to be found in a letter from Francis Scott Key to Benjamin Tappan, in 1838. At a general conference of Congregational Churches the question of slavery was up for discussion. It was proposed to appoint a committee to correspond with prominent Southerners, in an effort to find out the true sentiments of that section on the subject of slavery. Tappan put to Key a number of definite questions. Key prefaced his reply by saying that he had been born and reared in Maryland, a slaveholding State, but " No Northern man began the world with more enthusiasm against slavery than I did. For forty years and upwards, I have felt the greatest desire to see Maryland become a free

---

[10] African Repository, vol. ii, pp. 121-122.
[11] Ibid., vol. i, pp. 91-92.
[12] Ibid., vol. i, pp. 272-276.

State, and the strongest conviction that she could become so." For he believed that "no slave State adjacent to a free State can continue so," the superiority of free, over slave, labor being so clearly demonstrated, and the power of public sentiment being so strong that gradual emancipation would always result. He continues:

I have emancipated seven of my slaves. They have done pretty well, and six of them, now alive, are supporting themselves comfortably and creditably. Yet I cannot but see that this is all they are doing now; and, when age and infirmity come upon them, they will probably suffer. It is to be observed, also, that these were selected individuals, who were, with two exceptions, brought up with a view to their being so disposed of, and were made to undergo a probation of a few years in favorable situations, and, when emancipated, were far better fitted for the duties and trials of their new condition than the general mass of slaves. Yet I am still a slaveholder, and could not, without the greatest inhumanity, be otherwise. I own, for instance, an old slave, who has done no work for me for years. I pay his board and other expenses, and cannot believe that I sin in doing so.

The laws of Maryland contain provisions of various kinds, under which slaves, in certain circumstances, are entitled to petition the courts for their freedom. As a lawyer, I always undertook these cases with peculiar zeal, and have been thus instrumental in liberating several large families and many individuals. I cannot remember more than two instances, out of this large number, in which it did not appear that the freedom I so earnestly sought for them was their ruin. It has been so with a very large proportion of all others I have known emancipated.

Tappan's first question was: "Does the opinion generally prevail among the ministers and members of southern churches that slaveholding as practised in this country, is sanctioned by the Word of God? If this is not their opinion, how do they justify themselves in holding slaves?" Key's reply was that he thought that the Bible neither sanctioned slaveholding, *under all circumstances,* nor prohibited slaveholding, *under all circumstances.* The golden rule should be applied in each particular case. He continued:

Hundreds and thousands of Christians, showing in their whole life, undoubted evidences of the faith which they profess, have so applied this rule to their consciences, and so come to this conclusion. Their brethren at the North, knowing nothing of the peculiar circumstances under which they have acted, nor of the care and faithfulness with which they have inquired and decided, call upon them to justify themselves for violating the sanctions of God's Word.

Key pointed out conditions under which slaveholding was in his opinion a duty. For instance, a man inherits, through no fault of his own, an old slave, too old to work or to care for himself. So also, in the case of a slave by nature so indolent and intemperate that without restraint he would be wretched himself and a burden to others. So, too, in the case of a slave purchased in order that he might not be sold in one of the distant States, and thus separated from a wife and family who lived on a neighboring plantation; or, in the case of the purchase by one man of the slave of another, in order to save the slave from cruel and unjust treatment.

Another question put to Key was: "Do professors of religion forfeit their christian character by buying and selling slaves, as they may find it convenient? or do they subject themselves to censure and discipline by any immorality or ill treatment of which they might be guilty towards their slaves?" The reply was:

> The persons among us who buy and sell slaves for profit are never, as I have ever heard or believe, professors of religion. Such conduct, or any immorality or ill treatment towards their slaves, would forfeit their Christian character and privileges, if their minister did his duty. And nothing more disgraces a man, in general estimation, than to be guilty of any immorality or ill treatment towards his slaves.[13]

DeTocqueville, that keen observer of American institutions, expressed sentiments of great value to those who had ears to hear. He demonstrated beyond a doubt, that the abolition of slavery in the South was a far different problem from, and a far graver problem than, its abolition in the North. This was true (1) because the climate of the South was far more favorable to slave labor than the climate of the North; (2) because of the nature of the Northern and of the Southern crops, the former requiring attention only at intervals, the latter requiring almost constant attention; (3) because of the tendency of slavery to move toward the South.

He pointed out the fact that in 1830 there was in Maine

---
[13] Ibid., vol. xv, pp. 113–125.

only one negro for every three hundred of the whites; in Massachusetts one negro for every one hundred; in Virginia forty-two for every one hundred; in South Carolina fifty-five for every one hundred. And his conclusion was that "the most Southern States of the Union cannot abolish slavery without incurring very great danger, which the North had no reason to apprehend when it emancipated its black population." "The Northern States had nothing to fear from the contrast, because in them the blacks were few in number, and the white population was very considerable. But if this faint dawn of freedom were to show two millions of men their true position, the oppressors would have reason to tremble." He disclaimed any sympathy with the principle of negro slavery, but said:

> I am obliged to confess that I do not regard the abolition of slavery as a means of warding off the [to him, inevitable] struggle of the two races in the United States. The negroes may long remain slaves without complaining; but if they are once raised to the level of free men, they will soon revolt at being deprived of all civil rights; and as they cannot become the equals of the whites, they will speedily declare themselves as enemies. In the North everything contributed to the emancipation of the slaves; and slavery was abolished, without placing the free negroes in a position which could become formidable, since their number was too small for them to claim the exercise of their rights. But such is not the case in the South. The question of slavery was a question of commerce and manufacture for the slave-owners in the North; for those of the South, it is a question of life and death.
>
> When I contemplate the condition of the South, I can only discover two alternatives which may be adopted by the white inhabitants of those States; viz., either to emancipate the negroes, and to intermingle with them; or, remaining isolated from them, to keep them in a state of slavery as long as possible. All intermediate measures seem to me likely to terminate, and that shortly, in the most horrible of civil wars, and perhaps in the extirpation of one or other of the two races.[14]

In a memorial from the Colonization Society to Congress in 1819, the following sentiment is expressed:

> If one of these consequences [that is, a consequence of Colonization] shall be the gradual and almost imperceptible removal of a national evil, which all unite in lamenting, and for which, with the most intense, but hitherto hopeless, anxiety the patriots and statesmen of our country have laboured to discover a remedy, who can

---

[14] DeTocqueville, Democracy in America, D. Appleton and Company, ed. of 1904, vol. i, pp. 383-404.

doubt, that of all the things we may be permitted to bequeath to our descendants, this will receive the richest tribute of their thanks and veneration? Your memorialists cannot believe that such an evil, universally acknowledged and deprecated, has been irremovably fixed upon us. Some way will always be opened by Providence, by which a people, desirous of acting justly and benevolently, may be led to the attainment of a meritorious object.[15]

Dr. William Thornton had pointed out clearly in 1804 the seriousness of the problem of the abolition of slavery in the South as compared with its abolition in the North. At that time he said that, in the North, the comparatively few slaves were so distributed among the population that a general emancipation fell but lightly upon each owner; whereas, in the South, "it would perhaps be requiring too much from humanity, to expect those who hold slaves to emancipate them, and thus reduce their own families from affluence to absolute misery. And there is frequently no alternative." He deprecates the evils of slavery, but "it has been not only a query with others, but with myself, whether this partial good does not increase the general evil. . . . Evil therefore rests on evil till a mountain rises whose summit is shadowed by a cloud of sin."[16] And many years later Henry Clay, in a speech on the subject of Abolition petitions, made in the United States Senate, February 7, 1839, estimated the value of property in slaves, in the South, at $1,200,000,000—owned by persons of all classes, those who could afford to emancipate their slaves and very many who could not. Slave property, he said, "is the subject of mortgages, deeds of trust, and family settlements. It has been made the basis of numerous debts contracted upon its faith, and is the sole reliance, in many instances, of creditors within and without the slave States, for the payments of debt due to them."[17]

It is also to be observed that those proprietors who were most anxious to emancipate their slaves were the very ones from whom the slaves received the most consideration. Scores of instances could be noted of the proffer of their

---

[15] Origin, Constitution, and Proceedings, MS., American Colonization Society, vol. i, pp. 127-128.
[16] Thornton Papers.
[17] African Repository, vol. xv, pp. 150-164.

freedom, by such masters, to their slaves, and of the slave's refusal to go free. In succeeding pages of this study instances will also be pointed out of negroes who requested to be purchased by benevolent men. Rev. R. R. Gurley, secretary of the American Colonization Society, tells of an interesting native African sold to a South Carolina slaveholder. The negro's name was Moro; he was educated a Mohammedan.

> About twenty years ago, while scarcely able to express his thoughts intelligently on any subject in the English language, he fled from a severe master in South Carolina, and on his arrival at Fayetteville was seized as a runaway slave, and thrown into jail. His peculiar appearance, inability to converse, and particularly the facility with which he was observed to write a strange language attracted much attention, and induced his present humane and Christian master to take him from prison and finally, at his earnest request, to become his purchaser. His gratitude was boundless, and his joy to be imagined only by him, who has himself been relieved from the iron that enters the soul. Since his residence with General Owen [his purchaser] he has worn no bonds but those of gratitude and affection. . . . Being of a feeble constitution, Moro's duties have been of the lightest kind and he has been treated rather as a friend than a servant. The garden has been to him a place of recreation rather than toil, and the concern is not that he should labor more but less.[18]

There are significant statements in a note, appended by himself, to the will of Reverend Thomas S. Witherspoon, of Alabama:

> It will be plainly seen that my intention is to liberate them [six slaves] by colonizing them in some of the colonies of free blacks. This I would do now, but they utterly refuse to leave me, protesting that they will not leave me until my death. . . . I cannot meet death in peace while the consciousness of the fact is left that these faithful and pious servants are to be left in bondage. I feel that I am responsible to God for them. . . . I am a Presbyterian minister. . . . My slaves I inherited from my father and through my deceased wife, all but one, whom I purchased to keep him with his wife.[19]

It must not be supposed that the upper South was ignorant of the comparative cost of slavery. In a report of the Delaware Auxiliary Colonization Society, in 1825, we find these words: "It [slavery] depreciates our soil, lessens our agricultural revenue, and like the lean kine of Egypt, eats

---
[18] Letters of American Colonization Society, MS., Gurley to Board of Managers, May 21, 1837.
[19] Ibid., J. M. Witherspoon to the President, Dec. 15, 1845.

up the fat of the land. It will hardly admit of a question, but that the Southern section of our country would, in a few years, be richer without one slave, than it is now with 1,600,000."[20] And two years later J. H. B. Latrobe, for many years President of the Colonization Society, declared:

> When white labour becomes so cheap that three men can be hired all the year, and ten at harvest, for less than the families of thirteen working negroes can be supported for (including the services of children), all the twelve months, to do the labour of a farm, these slaves will be the ruin of their possessors. This is coming to pass rapidly, and will be the result of the present state of things and the gradual increase of a white population, before many years, in all those States which do not cultivate rice and cotton—slave labour must be rendered valueless there by competition from the very place we are labouring to build up [Liberia]—cotton and rice cultivated by *free* labour in Africa, ought according to all politico-economical calculations, to undersell the cotton and rice cultivated by *slave* labour to the South; when this is the case, Carolina and her brothers and sisters, or, Carolina and Company, will receive a shock which for some years may prostrate them, but it will be like that weakness which is the immediate effect of a medicine which in the end cures the patient.[21]

In the Virginia Convention of 1829, C. F. Mercer pointed out the fact that, in 1817, the land of Virginia was valued at $206,000,000, while in 1829 the same land was valued at only $96,000,000; and that, while the average value of slaves, in Virginia, was $300 in 1817, the average value, in 1829, was only $150.[22] Henry Clay, for years President of the Society, expressed very clearly his view in 1830. As the population of the United States increased, he predicted, the European would gain ground, numerically, over the negro; hence, white labor would become more abundant. Given enough laborers, free labor is always cheaper than slave labor. Therefore the value of slaves would become smaller and smaller; masters would discourage the raising of negro children; and slavery would become so obviously unprofitable that emancipations would become more and more common. He added:

---
[20] African Repository, vol. i, pp. 343–344.
[21] Letters of American Colonization Society, MS., Latrobe, Jan. 5, 1827.
[22] African Repository, vol. v, p. 377.

What has tended to sustain the price of slaves in the U. S. has been . . . especially the increasing demand for cotton, and the consequent increase of its cultivation. The price of cotton . . . regulates the price of slaves as unerringly as any one subject whatever is regulated by any standard. . . . The adult slaves will, in process of time, sink in value even below $100 each, I have no doubt.[23]

Mrs. Ann R. Page, than whom no more conscientious individual, more consistent opponent of slavery, or more zealous friend of the American Colonization Society lived in the State of Virginia, wrote, in 1831: " The expense of slave estates keeps Virginians, at least many, unable to give freely, unless a new spirit of stronger faith and love could actuate them to deny accustomed self-indulgencies." " If ever I get out of debt, all I hope to want with money is to further its [the American Colonization Society's] plan."[24] In 1834 Garritt Meriweather wrote:

I am a slaveholder and have it in contemplation to liberate several of my slaves, *provided*, they could be removed to Liberia at a cost I could afford. But mine is the common misfortune of most slaveholders—a nominal wealth only; the *shadow* and not the substance, the reality. We may give to Freedom—to Liberia—this delusive property (and I dare say with the majority of masters it would be gain) but here would end the *boon,* for with them could be added no purse, or means of emigration or settlement. There are many, very many, slaveholders, I am sure, who would *cheerfully* relinquish all their slave property to Liberia, could they afford the means of equipment and settlement or temporary maintenance of such manumitted slaves.[25]

The dread of insurrections only added to the problem. In 1791 the slaves of Hayti revolted. For a time the island was without a civil government; and when in 1801 there was an emergence of order, it was in the form of a negro government. In 1800, a negro, Gabriel by name, of Hanover County, Virginia, planned an insurrection. In 1822, Denmark Vesey, of Charleston, was hanged before he was able to execute a plot.[26] In August, 1831, the whole upper South was profoundly moved by the Southampton mas-

---

[23] Ibid., 1830, pp. 1–25.
[24] Letters of American Colonization Society, MS., Mrs. A. R. Page to the Secretary, Millwood, Va., March 26, 1831.
[25] Ibid., Meriweather to Gurley, April 23, 1834.
[26] A. B. Hart, Slavery and Abolition, pp. 157, 163.

sacre. In October of that year, Collin H. Minge, of Virginia, wrote:

> I am . . . sure that there is not an enemy to the cause of Colonization in Virginia at this time. The predictions of Mr. Randolph some years since are now becoming true; the whites are running away from the blacks, the masters from the slaves, in lower Virginia, the place of insurrection. I received an intimation from a gentleman yesterday to go to his house to advize his negroes, 8 in number, most young ones, to embark for Liberia, as he was willing to emancipate them. Our next Legislature I think will do something.[27]

The feeling of alarm that came over one of the counties of Virginia in which negroes were numerous is apparent from a petition signed by one hundred and ninety-five citizens of Northampton County and dated December 6, 1831, just after the Southampton massacre. While it will be evident, from extracts here given, that there was an urgent demand for the removal of the free negro, the demand arose rather from the fear for their personal safety among the citizens than from a desire to perpetuate slavery. The petition in part follows:

> By the last census of the U. States it appears that there are in this county 3573 whites, 3734 slaves, and 1334 free persons of colour. By a comparison with the census of preceding years, it also appears that the proportion of free persons of colour to our white inhabitants is annually increasing. . . . The free persons of colour in Virginia form an anomalous population, standing in a relation to our society, which naturally exposes them to distrust & suspicion. Inferior to the whites in intelligence & information; depraved by the stain which attaches to their colour; excluded from many civil privileges which the humblest white man enjoys, and denied all participation in the government, it would be wholly absurd to expect from them any attachment to our laws & institutions, or any sympathy with our people. On the other hand, the enjoyment of personal freedom is in itself a sufficient mark of distinction between them & our slaves, and elevates them, at least in their own opinion, to a higher condition in life. Standing thus in a middle position between the two extremes of our society and despairing of ever attaining an equality with the higher grade, it is natural that they should connect themselves in feeling & interest, with the slaves among whom many of their domestic ties are formed, and to whom they are bound by the sympathies scarcely less strong, which spring from their common complexion. Independent, therefore, of any particular facts calculated to excite our alarms, the worst evils might justly be apprehended from such an increase of their numbers as would give them confidence in their physical power, while it would enlarge their

---

[27] Letters of American Colonization Society, MS., C. H. Minge to Gurley, Oct. 22, 1831.

means of information, facilitate their intercommunications, and thus add to their capabilities of mischief. Unhappily, however, this is no longer a subject of mere speculation. The scenes which have recently passed around us contain a melancholy & impressive lesson upon the subject, to which the most careless and supine among us cannot be unattentive. The caution which these scenes suggest is of peculiar importance to us. From the number of our free negroes, and from the idle & vicious habits of most of them, we have stronger reason than exists in most of our counties, to suspect dangerous intrigues with our slaves; nor can we be insensible to the great aid which our slaves would derive from that source, in any actual attempts against us.

They therefore appealed to the legislature for permission to borrow $15,000.00, to be repaid by the citizens of the county levying upon themselves a tax equal to the existing State tax. They further resolved: "That our representatives be instructed to vote for every measure, whether of a general or local character, which may have for its object the removal of the free people of colour from the State at large or any part thereof." And the motive is clearly set forth in the concluding portion of the petition: "The evil of which we complain is found to be no longer endurable, without the most serious dangers to the peace & security of our county, & we are willing to rid ourselves of it at every sacrifice & every hazard."[28]

In December of the same year, a member of the Virginia Legislature wrote to the Colonization Society asking whether a very large number of immigrants, such as Virginia might desire to send at once to the Liberian colony, could be received on short notice. He said:

The subject of colonising the free people of colour in this commonwealth, and such of the slaves as their proprietors may voluntarily emancipate, (if indeed it be not made to comprise a scheme of general emancipation,) will be acted upon by the Virginia Legislature during its present session. As a member of that body feeling the liveliest interest in that part of the African race who have residence among us, as well as in the general welfare of our country, upon which they are admitted to be a lamentable burden, it would be highly culpable in me to remain inactive, during the agitation of the subject.

The horrible affair of Southampton has given rise to new and decided feelings in the breasts of Virginians from every part of the State, in regard to the black population. And the friends of

---

[28] Legislative Petitions, MS., Dec. 6, 1831, Virginia State Library.

Colonization, (I had almost said, of emancipation) may now find willing and anxious agents, to push to the utmost practicable extent their philanthropic wishes.

The following January he wrote:

> The committee to which was referred the subject of the free people of colour was organized on Monday last, and have proceeded to discuss some of the delicate questions relating to it. Upon one point there is no difference of opinion; I mean as to the expediency of adopting a scheme *at once* for the removal of the free people of colour, and such of the other class as their proprietors may voluntarily manumit. Thus far the people are prepared to go, as shewn in their accumulated memorials from every portion of the State. Many are for going much farther, and comprehending the whole black class in a system of gradual reduction. . . . The Legislature are certainly ready to make the most ample appropriation, efficiently to carry through the first named object. Different sums are mentioned, from 100,000 to 300,000 dollars annually. . . .[29]

Opinion in the border slave States at this time undoubtedly was: (1) the abolition of slavery, if practicable, consistently with the safety of the whites and the welfare of the blacks, was desirable; (2) any scheme of immediate and unconditional emancipation was wholly impracticable; (3) the tendency among newly emancipated negroes was to incite the slaves to revolt; (4) emancipated negroes, as a class, had not been benefited, but, on the contrary, had been actually the losers by the fact of emancipation. The opinion was widespread in the whole South that if the time ever came when two races, as distinct as the white and the black, occupied the same territory, and were numerically not greatly unequal, a war of extermination was almost inevitable. It has been seen that DeTocqueville held distinctly to this view and, although he was altogether an opponent of the principle of slavery, the only suggestions he had to offer to the South were amalgamation with the blacks, and a continuance of the system of slavery as long as possible. To look for amalgamation was to look for the mountains to remove themselves; and yet, up to a period as late as 1840, the leaders of thought, except in the Southeastern States, were far from willing to admit that the other was the only alternative.

---
[29] Letters of American Colonization Society, MS., C. S. Carter, Dec. 22, 1831; Jan. 6, 1832.

Not long after the organization of the Colonization Society, Dr. William Thornton expressed the conviction that there "never could exist a sincere union between the whites and the blacks, even on admitting the latter to the rights of freemen."[30] In 1827, Clay asked:

> What is the true nature of the evil of the existence of a portion of the African race in our population? It is not that there are *some*, but that there are so *many* among us of a different caste, of a different physical, if not moral, constitution, who never could amalgamate with the great body of our population.... Any project, therefore, by which, in a material degree, the dangerous element in the general mass, can be diminished or rendered stationary, deserves deliberate consideration.[31]

Jonathan Mayhew Wainwright, in 1829, asked a similar question:

> What is to be done with our rapidly increasing coloured population? Any one who can think, and compute numbers, and who will look at our censuses of population, must be convinced that the reply to this inquiry should call forth all the wisdom, foresight, patriotism, and benevolence of our whole country. A refuge must be prepared for these people.[32]

W. M. Atkinson, one of the most prominent Colonizationists in the State of Virginia, said:

> . On one point we differ *toto caelo*—I have no doubt that emancipation without emigration, would utterly ruin the State. I further believe that it would end in the extermination of the one race or the other—and if so, I do not doubt it would be the African. Hence I must oppose it, everywhere, and by all gentlemanly and Christian means. Hence, too, one reason of my zeal for colonization, as indispensable to that other indispensable measure [emancipation].
> I succeeded today in obtaining a decree for the emancipation of Elder's slaves, but his cause will go to the court of appeals.[33]

In 1830, the Senate of Massachusetts, in a resolution highly commendatory of the Colonization project, stated: "In those States where slavery is tolerated, as well as in the others, where it has ceased to exist, the dangers and difficulties, emanating from the great and increasing numbers of free persons of colour, had long been the subjects of

---

[30] African Repository, vol. i, pp. 87–88.
[31] Ibid., vol. ii, pp. 334–345.
[32] Letters of American Colonization Society, MS., Wainwright to Gurley, Jan. 5, 1829.
[33] Ibid., Atkinson to Gurley, Nov. 10, 1831.

deep individual solicitude and inquiry, and of numerous legislative enactments."[34] In 1839 Clay declared:

> In the slave States the alternative is, that the white man must govern the black, or the black govern the white. In several of these States the number of slaves is greater than that of the white population. An immediate abolition of slavery in them, as these ultra-abolitionists propose would be followed by a desperate struggle for immediate ascendancy of the black race over the white race, or rather it would be followed by instantaneous collisions between the two races, which would break out into a civil war that would end in the extermination or subjugation of the one race or the other.[35]

This alarm at the rapid increase of the free negro population was an important cause of enactments of slaveholding States prohibiting emancipations. Within a fortnight of the organization of the Colonization Society, a memorial was presented to Congress, by its Board of Managers, in which this rapid increase was remarked on in the following words: "The evil has become so apparent, and the necessity for a remedy so palpable, that some of the most considerable of the slaveholding States, have been induced to impose restraints upon the practice of emancipation, by annexing conditions, which have no effect but to transfer the evil from one State to another."[36] In reply to memorials from Colonizationists, the Legislature of Virginia stated:

> The extent of this evil [the increase in the number of free negroes] may be fairly estimated, by a reference to our Statute book. The laws intended either to prevent or to limit its effects, are of a character, which nothing, but the extreme necessity of the case, could ever justify, to a community of republicans; and the obligation to resort to them, is sufficient to command the serious attention of every enlightened patriot.
> To considerations such as these, may be traced the policy first resorted to by the Legislature of Virginia in 1805, of arresting the progress of emancipation, by requiring the speedy removal from the State, of all to whom its privileges might be extended.[37]

In an address before the New Hampshire Colonization Society, Daniel Dana said:

> It is a fact, given us on the most unquestionable authority, that there are now in the Southern States of our Union, hundreds, and

---
[34] African Repository, vol. vi, pp. 144-147.
[35] Ibid., vol. xv, pp. 50-64.
[36] Origin, Constitution, and Proceedings, American Colonization Society, MS., pp. 13-19.
[37] African Repository, vol. v, pp. 50-55.

even thousands of proprietors, who would gladly give liberty to their slaves, but are deterred by the apprehension of doing injury to their country, and perhaps to the slaves themselves. It is a fact that in the States of Maryland and Virginia alone, there were fifteen years since, 63,000 free people of colour. It is likewise a fact, that within a few years past, more than 500 slaves have been emancipated, in the State of Virginia, by only three proprietors. Indeed, so prevalent has been the disposition of Southern proprietors, for many years, to give liberty to their slaves, that this condition of things has excited a serious alarm. The legislatures of several States have interposed their authority, and prohibited the emancipation of slaves, except on the condition of their being transferred to some other State.[38]

The House of Representatives of Maryland, in 1831, passed the following resolutions:

That as philanthropists and lovers of freedom, we deplore the existence of slavery amongst us, and would use our utmost exertions to ameliorate its condition, yet we consider the unrestricted power of manumission as fraught with ultimate evils of a more dangerous tendency than the circumstance of slavery alone, and that any act, having for its object the mitigation of these joint evils, not inconsistent with other paramount considerations, would be worthy the attention and deliberation of the representatives of a free, liberal-minded and enlightened people.

Resolved, That we consider the colonization of free people of colour in Africa as the commencement of a system, by which, if judicious encouragement be afforded, these evils may be measurably diminished.[39]

It is a significant fact, however, that these individual and legislative objections to the right of emancipation were confined to cases in which the emancipated remained within the limits of the State. In explanation of this fact, students of slavery have urged that the real reasons behind such objections was either the desire of pro-slavery men to "boost" the price of slaves by reducing to a minimum the competition of free-negro labor, or the fear, among the slaveholders, that an increasing free negro element was dangerous to the security of their slave property. Undoubtedly both of these explanations contain an element of truth; but there is abundant evidence to show that the leading single cause of this widespread attitude was the deliberate and firm conviction that the free negro was a source, and a most

---

[38] Ibid., vol. i, p. 144.
[39] Ibid., vol. vii, p. 30.

fruitful source, of lawlessness and crime, of social and political insecurity. The degrading influence of, and the degraded condition of, the free negro were recognized and remarked upon from every quarter of the Union. It was not a sectional opinion; it was a national one. Of this important free negro problem DeTocqueville writes:

> Whoever has inhabited the United States must have perceived that in those parts of the Union in which the negroes are no longer slaves, they have in nowise drawn nearer to the whites. On the contrary, the prejudice of the race appears to be stronger in the States which have abolished slavery than in those where it still exists; and nowhere is it so intolerant as in those States where servitude never has been known. The electoral franchise has been conferred upon the negroes in almost all the States in which slavery has been abolished; but if they come forward to vote, their lives are in danger. . . . The gates of Heaven are not closed against these unhappy beings; but their inferiority is continued to the very confines of the other world; when the negro is defunct, his bones are cast aside, and the distinction of condition prevails even in the equality of death.
> In the South, where slavery still exists, the negroes are kept less carefully apart; they sometimes share the labour and the exertions of the whites; the whites consent to intermix with them to a certain extent, and although the legislation treats them more harshly the habits of the people are more tolerant and compassionate. . . . Thus it is, in the United States, that the prejudice which repels the negroes seems to increase in proportion as they are emancipated, and inequality is sanctioned by the manners while it is effaced from the laws of the country.[40]

Memorialists from the Richmond and Manchester Auxiliary Colonization Society, about 1825, called attention to the fact that of 37,000 free negroes in Virginia, not two hundred were proprietors of land.[41] About the same time the New York Tract Magazine stated:

> Free blacks are collected in large towns and cities, where a great portion of them are found in the abodes of poverty and vice, and become the tenants of poor houses and prisons. As a proof . . . the following striking fact has been mentioned. The State of Pennsylvania, before the last census, had a population of upwards of 800,000; the number of free blacks was about 26,000, and yet one half of the convicts in the State prison were free blacks.[42]

The Charlottesville, Virginia, Central Gazette declared: "that slavery is unjust by the laws of nature, is a truth

---

[40] DeTocqueville, vol. i, p. 383 ff.
[41] African Repository, vol. i, p. 67.
[42] Ibid., vol. i, pp. 91–92.

which every man derives directly from the infallible oracles of his own conscientious convictions," and at the same time it declared that the emancipation of the slaves, without their removal from the State, " would be pernicious."[43] In 1827, a citizen of Chillicothe wrote: " In most of the towns of Ohio, there are a number of free blacks, who with few exceptions, are little less than a nuisance and their numbers are every year increasing by immigration, as well as other causes. All of the whites would willingly do something to free themselves from this evil.[44]

Gerrit Smith, who had thought of establishing a school for free negroes, " so that they might take knowledge and Christianity to the natives of Africa," announced, in 1827:

> I am recently getting off this scheme. The turn that *negro-learning* takes in this country is not always favorable. It is certainly not so with the editors of the Freedom's Journal, a paper I was at first disposed to patronize and which I still take. . . . My heart is fully set on discharging the patriotic duty of contributing to relieve our country of its black population.[45]

A Virginia clergyman, writing to the Colonization Society in 1829, states:

> Having formerly set free a number of coloured people who are now vagabonds, I have done them no profit, but injured society. For this there is no remedy, as I have no control over them. Those still in my possession, I cannot conscientiously emancipate, unless they shall be removed by the Society to Liberia. A list of six, which I wish transferred to the Colony, was last fall furnished to the Society, and entered upon its books. I wish them to be called for, as I am old, and desire the business may be completed before I quit my earthly station.[46]

In 1829 the President of Union College stated:

> Our manumitted bondmen have remained already to the third and fourth, as they will to the thousandth generation—a distinct, a degraded, and a wretched race. When therefore the fetters, whether gradually or suddenly, shall be stricken off, and stricken off they will be, from those accumulating millions yet to be born in bondage, it is evident that this land, unless some outlet be provided, will be flooded with a population as useless as it will be wretched; a

---

[43] Ibid., vol. i, p. 215 ff.
[44] Letters of American Colonization Society, MS., Wm. Graham to Gurley, Feb. 10, 1827.
[45] Ibid., G. Smith to Gurley, Oct. 10, 1827.
[46] African Repository, vol. v, pp. 177-178.

population which, with every increase, will detract from our strength, and only add to our numbers, our pauperism and our crimes. Whether bond or free, their presence will be forever a calamity. Why, then, in the name of God, should we hesitate to encourage their departure?[47]

Arthur Tappan, soon to be a disciple of William Lloyd Garrison, had, himself, experienced a problem whose solution evidently gave him concern; although, had he been a Southerner, he would doubtless have quietly added another item to his account for incidental expenses. Slave traders had brought to America and sold two brothers, the sons of Prince Abduhl Rahhahman, a native African prince. These had secured their freedom and were, at the time Tappan wrote, in New York, being cared for by Tappan himself.

> I feel it to be incumbent on me to advise with the managers of your Society before sending the children of Prince Abduhl Rahhahman to Norfolk [to be transported to Africa], respecting the single son. Without any motive that we discover, having a sufficiency of food, etc., he has been guilty of stealing some poultry and has been liberated from prison, ... by his brother's borrowing and paying a sum of money. I can regard this as no less than an indication of a thievish propensity that will be likely to show itself whenever a good opportunity offers.[48]

Of this class of persons, Henry Clay said: "They are not slaves, yet they are not free.—The laws, it is true, proclaim them free; but prejudices, more powerful than laws, deny them the privileges of freemen. ... They crowd our large cities ... where those who addict themselves to vice can best practice and conceal their crimes." He also called attention to the adoption, by the city of Cincinnati, of measures to expel all "who could not give guaranties of their good behavior."[49] President Duer, of Columbia, said of the free blacks:

> Their numbers are constantly increasing in a formidable ratio. At the South they are looked upon with suspicion, and almost with abhorrence. At the North they are regarded as an inferior caste, and consequently deprived of every incentive to virtuous action. ... Conscious that they can never surmount these barriers, they natu-

---
[47] Ibid., vol. v, pp. 277-278.
[48] Letters of American Colonization Society, MS., Tappan to Gurley, Sept. 11, 1830.
[49] African Repository, March, 1830, pp. 1-25.

rally become improvident—and from improvidence the descent is easy to recklessness, profligacy, and crime. To the fidelity of this inference our criminal calendar bears melancholy witness. Comparing the relative proportions of white and colored population in our State, more than nine-tenths of those who are arraigned at our police establishments and courts of sessions, and who occupy the cells of our bridewells, penitentiaries, and State prisons, are, we are constrained to say, of the latter description.[50]

Reverend William Meade, later Bishop of Virginia, the first agent of the Colonization Society and a man who, though by no means wealthy, gave hundreds of dollars to the cause, and who hated the system of slavery as sincerely as did any son of New England, and said of it that it is "one of the most deadly evils that ever afflicted a nation," wrote, in 1832:

I have thought, read, conversed, written, and spoken much on this subject for the last fifteen years. I have travelled through all the length and breadth of our land, and witnessed the condition of the negroes, bond and free; conversed fully with them, their owners, and their philanthropic friends; and every year only rivets the conviction more deeply in my mind, that to do them real good they must be separated from those of a different color.[51]

C. F. Mercer, for a committee of the House of Representatives, at Washington, replied to memorials from the friends of Colonization, presented in 1827. He called attention to the fact that one of the important results of the large number and the degraded condition of the free blacks in the South, was to impose further restraints upon the practice of emancipation.[52]

Reverend William Henry Foote wrote of the free colored population of Hampshire County, Virginia, now West Virginia: "They are here a miserable race. . . . I have a number of colored members in my church (about 30) and only two are free, and they are old. The slaves are better in every respect. And in sending to Africa I should from this region prefer for the good of the Colony a manumitted

---

[50] Letters of American Colonization Society, MS., Duer to Gurley, Dec. 10, 1831.
[51] African Repository, vol. viii, pp. 86–87; Letters of American Colonization Society, MS., Meade to Samuel Wilkeson, Dec. 14, 1839.
[52] 27th Cong., 3d sess., H. Rept. no. 283, pp. 408–414.

black to one of these already free or born free."[53] In 1836, Citizens of Dauphin County, Pennsylvania, petitioning Congress in behalf of Colonization, spoke in no uncertain tones of the unworthiness and degradation of the free negro population.[54] Judge Samuel Wilkeson, of New York, later general agent for the Colonization Society, wrote to Lewis Sheridan, a free negro of respectability, a very successful farmer of North Carolina, and himself the owner of nineteen slaves:

> The high character which you have acquired in North Carolina, for moral worth and mercantile ability, might be regarded as evidence that the colored man stands on ground equally elevated as the white man, making allowance only for the difference of education, and political condition. . . . Feeling a great desire for the elevation of the colored man, I embraced every opportunity by several visits to the Southern and Southwestern States of making myself acquainted with the condition of both slaves and free people of colour, and their susceptibility of elevation in this country. . . . I am satisfied that the coloured man is as capable of acquiring trades as the white man, and that the reason he is so seldom found in the Middle and Eastern States carrying on mechanic business, is not for want of ability to acquire the knowledge and skill, but on account of the difficulties and discouragements incident to his condition. . . . The merchant will not employ them as clerks; the mechanic will not employ them as journeymen; should he perchance find such employment, he applies for board and is refused—other workmen will not eat with him; thus he meets at the very outset in life with difficulties which he cannot surmount.

Wilkeson proposed that he should be one of ten men to organize a ship line between the United States and Liberia to be turned over to free negroes in order to give them encouragement in their mercantile ambitions.[55]

A free negro from South Carolina had been induced to go to the North. Writing to friends in his native city, he requested the names of the members of the State Legislature, in order that he might urge them to repeal the law forbidding free blacks to come into the State, for he desired to return. He says:

> Although I have visited almost every city and town, from Charleston, South Carolina, to Portland, Maine, I can find no such home

---
[53] Letters of American Colonization Society, MS., Foote to Gurley, Sept. 19, 1833.
[54] African Repository, vol. xii, pp. 82-85.
[55] Ibid., vol. xiv, pp. 58-60.

and no such respectable body of colored people, as I left in my native city Charleston. The law in my adopted city, Philadelphia, when applied to colored people, in opposition to white people, is not as good as in Charleston, unless the former has respectable white witness to sustain it. . . . All the advantage that I see by living in Philadelphia is, that if my family is sick, I can send for a doctor at any time of the night without a ticket.[56]

And the following extract from Marville H. Smith's letter seems to bear out the assertion of De Tocqueville, that the free negro was nowhere so badly treated as in those parts of the Union in which slavery never existed. Smith was a free negro who acted as the spokesman for a group of eighteen, who had gone to Illinois.

We are ready to start from Shawneetown at any moment, and wish the time to come as soon as possible [the time to go to Liberia]; for though we are free in name we are not free in fact. We are in as bad, or worse condition than the slaves of which you speak, being compelled to leave the State, or give security, and those of the whites who would befriend us are debarred by the fear of public opinion. If only those who deserve such treatment, if any do, were the only ones to suffer we should be content; but on the contrary, if one misbehaves, all the colored people in the neighborhood are the sufferers, and that frequently by unlawful means; dragged from our beds at the hour of midnight, stripped naked, in presence of our children and wives, by a set of men alike lost to mercy, decency and Christianity, and flogged till they are satisfied, before we know for what; and when we are informed, it is probably the first time we heard of the offence. Such is our situation and such the condition from which your Society can extricate us. We deem it worse than slavery. We say again we wish to go to Liberia, and if no way else is provided, we had as lief soon *indent* ourselves to the Society for *life* for our passage, so we can live among our own color. Let me know as soon as possible, whether you can help us, and how soon, and how much.[57]

Roger M. Sherman, of Connecticut, said of the emancipated slave: "He is liable to be taken and sold again into slavery, unless removed from the State. Remove him to a free State, and he is cut off from the hopes of any political standing and condemned, by the unalterable usages of society, to a state of degradation."[58] Edward Everett described their condition as one of "disability, discourage-

---

[56] Ibid., vol. xv, pp. 178–180.
[57] Ibid., vol. xviii, p. 221.
[58] Ibid., vol. xx, pp. 294–296.

ment, and hardship."[59] Reverend John Orcutt, of Connecticut, a traveling agent of the Society, reported:

> Not only are free negroes forbidden to come into Indiana by express statute, but it is made a penal offense for a white person to induce such immigration. . . . When a State constitution was adopted in Oregon, four-fifths of the electors said by their vote we will not have slavery! and they also said by about the same majority, "we will have no free negroes!" Illinois too, has a similar prohibitory law against free negroes. . . . Already in the Eastern States, the black man finds himself on equal footing with the whites *nowhere*, except in the State prisons, where he is on the same level, and fully represented! No wonder that some of the free colored people at the North should begin to inquire with solicitude what they shall do. I saw several at the West who said, "We must go somewhere!"[60]

Up to 1830 the opinion prevailed throughout the United States, unless, indeed, we except Georgia and South Carolina, that, both for the sake of the free and unhampered development of his possibilities, and for the purpose of stimulating more frequent emancipations, the free negro must be sent to a home without the limits of any one of the States.[61] And scores of slaveholders after 1817 offered liberty to their slaves on the condition of their willingness to emigrate to Liberia. John A. Dix, speaking before the New York State Colonization Society, in 1830, said: "The mass of crime committed by Africans is greater, in proportion to numbers, in the non-slaveholding than in the slaveholding States; and as a rule the degree of comfort enjoyed by them is inferior. This is not an argument in favor of slavery; but it is an unanswerable argument in favor of rendering emancipation and colonization co-extensive with each other."[62]

---

[59] Address at Annual Meeting, American Colonization Society, Jan. 18, 1853.
[60] Minutes of Board of Directors of American Colonization Society, MS., Jan. 16, 1861.
[61] Origin, Constitution, and Proceedings of American Colonization Society, MS., vol. i, pp. 120-121; vol. i, pp. 127-128; African Repository, vol. i, p. 89, reprint from the Albany Argus; vol. i, p. 182 ff., reprint from Niles Register; vol. i, p. 285; vol. v, p. 4, speech of Clay before the Kentucky Colonization Society, Dec. 17, 1829; vol. v, pp. 50-55; vol. vi, pp. 144-147; vol. xiii, p. 38; vol. xxi, pp. 145-149; 27th Cong., 3d sess., H. Rept. No. 283, passim.
[62] African Repository, vol. vi, pp. 163-169.

One or two quotations, from many that could be given, will illustrate the point of view from which a large class of Southern slaveholders looked at the problem of emancipation. Reverend C. J. Gibson wrote from Petersburg, Virginia:

I have belonging to me two families of servants, whom I am anxious to emancipate, if, by any means, I can settle them in Liberia. The duties of the Holy Ministry, . . ., render me utterly unfit to be a faithful Christian Master and incline me to desire this step for the benefit of my own highest interests and those of my sacred office. At the same time, I feel bound to consult the best good of my servants, and in releasing them from my care, to place them in a situation, where the blessings of freedom may *really* be enjoyed. This, I am very sure, cannot be found in our own country, and I am therefore determined not to free them unless they can be sent to Africa.[63]

It will not be without interest or profit to read the following letter from an unlearned Southern slaveholder:

Dear Sir at the Death of my Father I inherited a Negro boy by Name (Moses) from his Est. and by Misfortunes and the Imprudence of my Youth I had to sell him Some year or two after which Time. I sought and found the Lord precious to my Immortal Soul Soon after this Happy Change the Grace of God began to Shed Light upon my mind I read the Holy Laws of God and found therein this Command do to Others as you would Others Should do to you I then began to Ask My Self if I had of been Moses' Slave and he my Master if I would have had him to of Sold me to a man who would have kept me in Slavery all my days on Earth and Perhaps without the Comforts of Life and in Perfect Ignorance and degradation. I readily answered the Question and determined by the Help of God to buy Moses if ever I Got able if he would agree to go to the Colony Settled on the Shores of Africa I was at that Time Very Poor as to this World's Goods I however went to work and after some Years Toil I found I had the means to Buy Moses I saw him and Talked with him about going to Africa and he declined I then Told him I would leave him to consider on the Subject and when ever he got his Consent to go I would buy him but that I would buy him on No Other Terms as I did not wish to own any Slaves Some Year or two pass'd by when Early one Morning Moses made his appearance at my door and Told he wanted me to buy him I ask'd him if he had Consented to go to the Colony he said if I would buy him he would go but he had rather Stay with me I told him I would only buy him on the Conditions he would go to the Colony (and then bought him he was then Quite a Prayerless Wicked Man I thought it would be best for him that I would keep him a year or two and try by the assistance of the Lord to be Instrumental in his Salvation in 12 or 18 Months after he Profess'd

---

[63] Letters of American Colonization Society, MS., Gibson to Gurley, Jan. 26, 1844.

the Religion of the Savior Since which Time say 12 or 18 Months he has to all Human Appearance been a Very Pious Man and I do hope and think he is now traveling that Road that Leads to the fair Climes of Immortal Joys. I have been Striving in my poor way to do my duty to this poor Coloured Man the Time has Arrived when I think I ought to send him on to the Colony and although he is a poor Colour'd Man I feel distress at Parting with him but a sense of my duty urges me and I now wish to get Some Instruction and assistance from You by what Vessel I can send him and from what place and at What Time will it start and for what Settlement I want him Carried to a Healthy Settlement what Implements is necessary and what Kind of Clotheing and how Shall I get him to the place where the Vessel is to Sail from and to whom Shall I direct him to be put in the Care of and what Shall I do with the Money I give him to Carry with him Your kind Instruction in this Matter will Very Much Oblige yours with Much esteem
SAMUEL O. MOON.[64]

A Kentucky slaveholder, whose slaves had been left behind, when a vessel sailed with emigrants to Liberia wrote to the Colonization Society: "*I cannot be a slaveholder.* I must get rid of my slaves in some way. To set them free in Kentucky I *cannot* and will not. I fear I shall have to adopt the *revolting* expedient of *selling;* I dread this but I must do something."[65] W. M. Atkinson, of Virginia, believed that, because of the necessity of preserving the safety of the whites, Virginia would never give up slavery unless provision should be made for the removal of the blacks.[66] A similar opinion was expressed by General Bayly, of the same State.[67]

The idea of the colonization of the negro sprang full grown from the brain of no individual. Henry Clay thought that it was the product, not of the minds of men, but of the very requirements of the times, because it was "an obvious remedy." As early as 1773 a correspondence was begun between Doctor Samuel Hopkins, of Rhode Island, and Reverend Ezra Stiles, later President of Yale College. Hopkins desired to send two or three negroes of Rhode Island to the coast of Guinea. Stiles thought that not fewer than thirty or forty could be profitably sent. The

---

[64] Ibid., Moon to Gurley, August 17, 1835.
[65] Ibid., Triplett to W. McLain, Jan. 16, 1846.
[66] Ibid., Atkinson to Gurley, Sept. 27, 1831.
[67] African Repository, vol. xiv, pp. 119-120.

purpose of these men, however, was purely missionary; they did not discuss the desirability of transporting the free colored population back to their native land, although it is evident that Doctor Stiles thought one effect of such a settlement on the coast of Africa might be to have some influence in putting an end to the African slave trade.[68] The Revolutionary War cut short all hopes of carrying out these plans. In 1777 a committee of the Virginia Legislature, of which Jefferson was chairman, proposed the gradual emancipation of slaves, and, at the same time, their exportation.[69]

There can be no doubt that between 1785 and 1817, Doctor William Thornton exerted a powerful influence in favor of colonization. He was in correspondence with British leaders in the movement for the transportation of their blacks, and which, under the direction of Granville Sharpe and others, resulted in the establishment of the British colony of Sierra Leone on the West coast of Africa. In an undated letter "To the Black Inhabitants of Pennsylvania, assembled at one of their stated meetings in Philadelphia," he wrote:

> It is in contemplation by the English to make a free settlement of Blacks on the Coast of Africa, which they have already begun. ... They are desirous of knowing if any of the Blacks of this country be willing to return to that Region which their fathers originally possessed, and finding many in Boston, Providence and Rhode Island very anxious of embarking for Africa, wish also to be informed if any of the Blacks in Pennsylvania are inclined to settle there.[70]

Indeed, soon after the preliminary meeting which resulted in the organization of the American Colonization Society, Thornton wrote to Henry Clay that, during the winter of 1786–87, while traveling in Rhode Island and Massachusetts, he found many free blacks and became deeply interested in them. He had already corresponded with friends, members of the Sierra Leone Society, and he became anxious to know whether the free blacks of those two States desired

---

[68] Literary Diary of Ezra Stiles, vol. i, pp. 363-364.
[69] African Colonization, "An Inquiry into the Origin, Plan, and Prospects of the American Colonization Society," p. 4.
[70] Thornton Papers, MS., vol. xiv. Pages not numbered.

to be transported to the British Colony. He had a meeting called, at which hundreds of that class were present, and he was later informed by them that 2,000 of them would go. The Massachusetts Legislature seemed interested, and many members promised liberal aid, until they heard that he proposed to settle the emigrants under British protection. They desired the settlement to be made "in the most southern part of the back country between the whites and Indians." To this scheme Thornton objected.[71] Thornton assures us, however, that about the year 1788, "the Americans in New England were desirous of sending all the free blacks from that country, and offered ships and every necessary for their support."[72] Thornton himself at one time had made many preparations to go to Africa to superintend such a colony; but his plan did not materialize.[73] Doctor Hopkins, whose letter to Stiles is quoted above, was, in 1789, in correspondence with Thornton on the subject of colonization; and in 1791 he made an effort to secure the incorporation of the Connecticut Emancipation Society, one of whose objects was the colonization of free blacks.[74]

In December, 1800, the Virginia Legislature requested Governor Monroe to correspond with the President of the United States "on the subject of purchasing lands without the limits of this State," whither obnoxious persons might be sent. This resolution was called forth by a conspiracy of slaves in or near Richmond. By law the conspirators were guilty of a capital offence; but the Legislature proposed transportation, as an act of clemency. This correspondence was productive of no material results. But the following year the Legislature directed the Governor to continue the correspondence, suggesting this time that it might be desirable to locate a colony outside the limits of the United States, a view in which President Jefferson fully

---

[71] Ibid., vol. xiv, letter to Clay, no date.
[72] Ibid., vol. xiv, no name, no date.
[73] Letters of American Colonization Society, MS., Mrs. Anna M. Thornton, Jan. 18, 1831.
[74] Half-Century Memorial, American Colonization Society, 1867, pp. 62–65.

concurred. The essential difference between these two Virginia resolutions was that the first contemplated merely the establishment of a penal colony, while the second proposed to provide an outlet for the whole of the free black population, and to provide for those who desired to emancipate their slaves an opportunity to do so without danger to the State. President Jefferson corresponded, though without success, with the British authorities regarding the incorporation of the free blacks of this country into the Sierra Leone colony.[75]

Samuel J. Mills of Connecticut, deservedly called the father of the foreign missionary enterprise in the United States, came to the conclusion, after a tour of the Southwestern part of the United States, that "we must save the negroes, or the negroes will ruin us." He thought the South at that time so well disposed towards the negro as to be willing to enter heartily into a colonization scheme.[76]

Paul Cuffee, a negro sea captain, a resident of Massachusetts, and the son of a native African who had been sold into slavery but who had later secured his own freedom, transported from the United States to Africa thirty-eight persons of color, probably the first company of negro emigrants whose object was resettlement in the land from which they or their fathers had come. The expense of the voyage, nearly $4000, was borne by Cuffee himself and the negroes were taken for settlement to the Sierra Leone colony. From the point of view of actual accomplishment the name of Paul Cuffee must find a place on the list of those whose efforts and whose views made possible the organization of the American Colonization Society, although his company set sail in 1815, almost two years before the formal organization of the American Colonization Society, and the voyage was undertaken upon Cuffee's personal responsibility and

---

[75] Mathew Carey, Reflections, p. 6; Half-Century Memorial, American Colonization Society, 1867, pp. 62–65.
[76] Half-Century Memorial, American Colonization Society, 1867, pp. 66–68.

without cooperation or help from either the government or any philanthropic association.[77]

Reverend Robert Finley of New Jersey has generally been considered the father of the American Colonization Society. If by this it is meant that he, more than any other man, brought about the meeting which resulted in the organization of that Society, no violence is done to truth; although it could with equal justice and probably more accuracy be said that the Society was the result of the efforts of Thornton, Mills, and Finley, north of Mason and Dixon's line, and of Charles Fenton Mercer, Francis Scott Key, and E. B. Caldwell, south of that line.

At least as early as February, 1815, Finley had become deeply interested in the organization of a colonization movement. He talked of colonization, wrote of colonization, made a visit to Washington in the interest of colonization, and led in the movement which resulted in a public meeting at Princeton in furtherance of the plan. But while he had been at work in New Jersey, Mercer had not been idle in Virginia. Each, it seems, worked at this time independently of the other. Mercer had been elected a member of the Virginia Legislature. He had learned of the two resolutions passed by that body on the subject of colonization, in 1800 and 1802—both passed under a pledge of secrecy. Mercer was not under this pledge, and he published abroad the action taken at that time. A new interest was aroused. He secured the passage of a resolution which met, in most respects, the views of Doctor Finley. This resolution was passed in the Senate with but one dissenting vote, and in the House by a vote of 132 to 14.[78] The governor was thereby instructed to correspond with the President of the United States for the purpose of obtaining territory upon the coast of Africa, or upon the shore of the North Pacific, or at some other place, "to serve as an asylum for such

---

[77] J. W. Lugenbeel, Sketch of the History of Liberia, MS.
[78] Half-Century Memorial, American Colonization Society, 1867, pp. 68–71; Carey, Reflections, p. 6; African Colonization, "An Inquiry into the Origin, Plan, and Prospects of the American Colonization Society," pp. 4–5.

persons of colour as are now free, and may desire the same, and for those who may hereafter be emancipated within this commonwealth."[79] While Finley and Mercer worked in New Jersey and Virginia, Key was at work in Maryland, and Doctor E. B. Caldwell, a brother-in-law of Finley, was busy in the District of Columbia; and when it was proposed to hold a meeting in Washington, December 21, 1816, the leaders were thoroughly interested and, to a degree at least, the public mind had been prepared.

And now by way of summary. In 1815 New England recognized the evil of slavery to be a national evil. New England felt the responsibility of helping, not driving, the South to get rid of that institution. Cooperation, not antagonism, was to be the means employed by each section in its relations with the other. To the upper South slavery was a *problem,* because it had grown to be one of those underlying bases in the economic life of the South; because its immediate abolition would mean, in many cases, a sudden change from affluence to poverty; because it was sincerely believed that the sudden emancipation of many thousands of slaves in the South would be an added cruelty to the class of improvident free negroes; because of the very fact that the liberation of one slave meant the addition of one free negro. For the free negro was also a problem. He was a problem because of the instances in the mind of every tolerably read Southerner, of outrages and insurrections of the blacks against the whites, in countries in which the population of each was not greatly unequal; because of the opinion that prevailed in every part of the Union that the negro could never rise to the limit of his possibilities so long as he remained in this country; because in his degraded condition he was a source of danger, only and always, to the community in which he lived. These were the problems, and together they made up the great negro problem of that time. There were four solutions proposed: (1) the immediate and unconditional abolition of slavery; (2) the perpetuation of slavery as long as possible; (3) the policy

---

[79] *African Repository,* vol. i, pp. 249–251.

of non-interference with the natural course of events; (4) colonization.

The first of these proposed solutions was supposed to be, and was, utterly impracticable, the paramount importance of the preservation of the Union from a dissolution, either actual or seriously attempted, being at once taken for granted. For it is utterly impossible to reconcile with the statements of either the leaders or the leading opponents of Garrisonian Abolition the statement of Professor A. B. Hart that "it must not be supposed that . . . even the [anti-slavery] agitators realized that slavery had the latent power of dividing the Union and bringing about civil war." Time and again they were warned of just this latent power; and the Garrisonians expressed their satisfaction with the result, should that result be even the dissolution of the Union.

The second proposed solution was as impracticable as the first. The institution of slavery was doomed to die. The question of prime importance was, not whether or not slavery could continue to exist as a system, but what form its destruction should take. The Garrisonians and the cotton gin had not yet filled the upper South with a lingering wish that it might survive, and a lingering hope that it would. In 1815, the leaders of thought in the upper South were definitely set against the second proposed solution.

The third was so seldom advocated by men of pronounced influence, that a consideration of its merits is unnecessary, in this study.

Unquestionably, the one supposed solution to which the leaders of thought in every part of the Union, except possibly the extreme South, turned was that of colonization. The free negro would be transported to the land whence his fathers came; the danger from the alarming increase in the free negro population would vanish as ghosts vanish with the coming of the morning; slaveholders could then safely and gradually emancipate their slaves, and the negro problem would be solved. And now let us consider the channel through which the experiment was made.

CHAPTER II

Organization, Purpose, and Early Years of the American Colonization Society

As a result of the efforts of the brothers-in-law, Rev. Robert Finley of New Jersey, and Dr. E. B. Caldwell of Washington, a meeting was held in that city December 16, 1816. The general purpose was the discussion of negro colonization. Bushrod Washington presided, and among the speakers were Henry Clay and John Randolph of Roanoke. Five days later a second meeting was held, presided over by Clay. Among resolutions adopted, the following is of interest:

> The situation of the free people of colour in the United States has been the subject of anxious solicitude, with many of our most distinguished citizens, from the first existence of our country as an independent nation; but the great difficulty and embarrassment attending the establishment of an infant nation when first struggling into existence, and the subsequent great convulsions of Europe have hitherto prevented any great national effort to provide a remedy for the evils existing or apprehended. The present period seems peculiarly auspicious to invite attention to this important subject, and gives a well grounded hope of success. The nations of Europe are hushed into peace; unexampled efforts are making in various parts of the world to diffuse knowledge, civilization, and the influence of the Christian religion.... Desirous of aiding in the great cause of philanthropy, and of promoting the prosperity and happiness of our country, it is recommended by this meeting, to form an association or Society for the purpose of giving aid and assisting in the colonization of the free people of colour in the United States.[1]

E. B. Caldwell, John Randolph, Richard Rush, Gen. Walter Jones, Francis Scott Key, Robert Wright, James H. Blake, and John Peter were appointed to present a memorial to Congress, requesting federal aid in procuring territory in Africa or elsewhere for the carrying out of their design; Key, Washington, Caldwell, James Breckenridge,

---

[1] Origin, Constitution, and Proceedings of American Colonization Society, MS., vol. i, pp. 1-3.

Gen. Walter Jones, Rush, and W. G. D. Worthington were appointed to prepare a constitution and rules.

At a third meeting, December 28, there was adopted a constitution, in which the sole object of the organization was stated to be "to promote and execute a plan for colonizing (with their consent) the Free People of Colour residing in our country, in Africa, or such other place as Congress shall deem most expedient. And the society shall act to effect this object, in cooperation with the General Government, and such of the States as may adopt regulations upon the subject."[2] A president, eight vice-presidents, a secretary, a treasurer, and a recorder were to be chosen. A board of managers, composed of these officers and twelve other members of the Society, was to constitute the central organization. Societies organized in the United States, working with the same object as that of the parent Society, and contributing to the funds of the central treasury, were to be considered auxiliary to it.

A great deal has been written regarding the ulterior motives of those who in its early days controlled the Society. Yet, even during the bitter decade from 1830 to 1840, The Liberator admitted many a time the sincerity of motive and the nobility of design of those whose active interest brought the Colonization Society into being. The quarrel was not brought about, it was said, because the movement had been dug up out of the miry clay; it was rather because it had cast itself down from the height on which it was born. It will, therefore, be safe to assume that those leaders who have left behind them a record of the motives of both themselves and their coadjutors, have spoken from their hearts.

No more credible witnesses could be found to represent respectively, the northern and southern portions of the Middle Atlantic States than Robert Finley, of New Jersey, and William H. Fitzhugh, of Virginia. Finley, whose State was not burdened with the problem of slavery, looked at the Society from the point of view of the welfare of the

---
[2] Ibid., vol. i, pp. 4-9.

free negro. Fitzhugh, a splendid example of the influential Virginia slaveholder, the owner of three hundred slaves who were by his will emancipated and offered special inducements if they would consent to go to Liberia, heartily and sincerely opposed human slavery, and yet, with others, saw that an epidemic of smallpox could not be relieved by abusive letters to the victims by a member of the health board. The South, to him and to others, was rather another Prometheus Bound, waiting for a deliverer. He saw that the abolition of slavery, if it was to come peaceably, must come gradually; that unconditional and immediate abolition would be accompanied by a national upheaval and a radical readjustment. Of Finley's motive, he himself wrote in 1815:

> The longer I live to see the wretchedness of men, the more I admire the virtue of those who devise, and with patience labor to execute, plans for the relief of the wretched. On this subject, the state of the *free blacks* has very much occupied my mind. Their number increases greatly, and their wretchedness too, as appears to me. Everything connected with their condition, including their color, is against them; nor is there much prospect that their state can ever be greatly ameliorated, while they continue among us. Could not the rich and benevolent devise means to form a Colony on some part of the Coast of Africa, similar to the one at Sierra Leone, which might gradually induce many free blacks to go and settle, devising for them the means of getting there, and of protection and support till they were established.[3]

Fitzhugh wrote in 1826:

> Our design was, by providing an asylum on the coast of Africa, and furnishing the necessary facilities for removal to the people of colour, to induce the voluntary emigration of that portion of them already free, and to throw open to individuals and the States a wider door for voluntary and legal emancipation. The operation, we were aware, must be—and, for the interests of our country, ought to be gradual. But we entertained a hope, founded on our knowledge of the interests as well as the feelings of the South, that this operation, properly conducted, would, *in the end*, remove from our country every vestige of domestic slavery, without a single violation of individual wishes or individual rights.[4]

Reverend William Meade, later bishop of Virginia, who was the first agent of the Society, and to whom slavery was

---
[3] North American Review, vol. xxxv, p. 119.
[4] African Repository, vol. ii, pp. 254–256.

an "accursed evil," said in 1825 that, in addition to the purpose of the leaders in the colonization movement, as stated in the constitution, the Society

> hopes to show to the pious and benevolent how and where they may accomplish a wish near and dear to many hearts, which is now impossible; it hopes to point out to our several legislatures, and even to the august council of this great nation, a way by which, with safety and advantage, they may henceforth encourage and facilitate that system of emancipation which they have almost forbidden.[5]

As early as 1819 such formidable opposition had reared its head, from extremists of both the pro-slavery and the anti-slavery parties, that the managers of the Society officially denied that their design was either " to rivet the chains of servitude " upon the negroes at the South, or "to invade the rights of private property, secured by the constitution and laws of the several slave-holding States."[6] Indeed, it is a significant fact, and worthy of note at this point, that during the whole period from 1820 to the issuance, by Abraham Lincoln, of the Proclamation of Emancipation, the bitterest opponents Colonization had were those strange bedfellows—New England and South Carolina. If the opposition from New England was more pronounced than that of the Carolinians it was largely because of the fact that the former was better organized. It is very probable that never, in any section, did Colonization have so few friends as in South Carolina and Georgia. Again and again the Society was called upon to repeat its original denial, and always with as little effect.

The reason is obvious. Colonization was essentially a moderate, a middle-State movement, counting among its supporters the moderate men of every part of the Union. The idea that called it forth was a middle-State idea. Extremists of the far North and the far South were unable to enter into its feelings. As is likely to be the case in all compromise movements, extremists on either side magnified possible objections into actually base designs. The whole

---
[5] Ibid., vol. i, pp. 147–150.
[6] Origin, Constitution, and Proceedings of American Colonization Society, MS., vol. i, pp. 65–74.

history of Colonization contains conclusive evidence that those leaders who actually directed the affairs of the organization, where they deviated at all from the design of the Society, as expressed in its constitution, deviated consistently on the side of emancipation. If those who hesitate to admit the purity of their designs would go to the trouble of investigating the evidence that remains, they would probably accept the defense of the Board of Managers in 1823, that "they have persevered, confident that their motives will one day be duly appreciated, and trusting their cause to the ruler of the world."[7]

Sentiments of friends and leaders, and reasons given by individuals for favoring the Colonization scheme, cover a wide range—from that of Gerrit Smith, who said, while yet a member of the Colonization Society, "We are all abolitionists at the north,"[8] to that of a friend from Canton, Ohio: "Among the multitude carried away by the floods of abolitionism, I remain an unwavering friend of the Colonization *mode,* of abolishing slavery in the United States,"[9] and to that of the Albany Argus:

> It seems to be the middle ground, upon which the several interests throughout the country, in relation to slavery, can meet and act together. It appears, indeed, to be the only feasible mode by which we can remove that stigma, as well as danger from among us. . . . Gradual emancipation . . ., under the advantages of a free government, formed, in their native land, by their own hands . . . is the only rational scheme of relieving them from the bondage of their present condition.[10]

But those who desire to consult a proslavery collection of letters could not profitably spend their time among the records of the American Colonization Society, where, of many thousands of letters, probably not a dozen, written prior to 1846, attempted a defence of the principle of slavery.

The organization of the Society was completed January 1, 1817, when Judge Bushrod Washington was elected

---
[7] Ibid., vol. i, pp. 199-200.
[8] Letters of American Colonization Society, MS., G. Smith to Walter Lourie, Albany, N. Y., Dec. 31, 1834.
[9] Ibid., Geo. Sheldon to Gurley, Canton, Ohio, Aug. 2, 1836.
[10] African Repository, vol. i, p. 89.

President, the following being elected Vice-Presidents: William H. Crawford of Georgia; Henry Clay of Kentucky; William Phillips of Massachusetts; Col. Henry Rutgers of New York; John E. Howard, Samuel Smith, and John C. Herbert, all of Maryland; John Taylor of Caroline, in Virginia; Gen. Andrew Jackson of Tennessee; Robert Ralston of Pennsylvania, and Richard Rush, of the same State; General John Mason of the District of Columbia, and Rev. Robert Finley of New Jersey. The foregoing, with E. B. Caldwell, Secretary, W. G. D. Worthington, Recorder, David English, Treasurer, and Francis Scott Key, Gen. Walter Jones, John Laird, Rev. James Laurie, Rev. Stephen B. Balch, Rev. Obadiah B. Brown, James H. Blake, John Peter, Edmund J. Lee, William Thornton, Jacob Hoffman and Henry Carroll constituted the Board of Managers. On the list of first contributors to the efforts of the Society appear the signatures, among others, of Henry Clay, John Randolph of Roanoke, William Thornton, Daniel Webster, William Dudly Diggs, Samuel J. Mills, Richard Bland Lee, John Taylor of Caroline and Bushrod Washington.[11]

Within a fortnight of the organization of the Society, a memorial was presented to both Houses of Congress, calling attention to the condition and prospects of the free colored population, calling attention also to the fact that, in order to safeguard themselves against what might prove dire consequences, important slaveholding States had adopted measures to restrict the further growth of the evil, by the enactment of laws prohibiting emancipations within the State. The memorialists consider the right of emancipating slaves "a right which benevolent or conscientious proprietors had long enjoyed under all the sanctions of positive law, and of ancient usage," and suggest as a more satisfactory solution of the problem, that adequate provision be made for the establishment of such a colony as the Society later established. The subject of the colonization of Africa was presented in its varied aspects: as a movement for ridding the

---

[11] Original List of Subscribers, MS.

United States of a separate caste or class, dangerous to the peace and safety of the country; as an important factor in the elevation of the free negro, who, it was believed, could never rise to his possibilities in the United States; as an instrument for the spread of civilization in Africa, and as promising much as a missionary enterprise. Pickering, for the House Committee on the Slave Trade, reported favorably, urging that the free negro, when colonized, should be sent where he would never provoke friction with the whites. Africa was considered the most desirable place for the realization of this object. The committee expressed its belief that the civilized powers should engage and assent to "the perfect neutrality of the colony." It was believed that arrangements might be made, whereby the colony might be incorporated with that at Sierra Leone. A resolution, not acted on at that session of Congress, was recommended, directing that the United States open negotiations with other powers for the abolition of the slave trade, and with Great Britain for the reception into Sierra Leone of "such of the free people of color of the United States as, with their own consent, shall be carried thither." In case no such arrangement could be made, it was recommended that the United States should seek to obtain from Great Britain and the other maritime powers a guarantee of "permanent neutrality for the formation of such a colony."[12]

In October, a committee was appointed to interview President Monroe who, during the whole term of his presidency, actively cooperated with the Society.[13] In November, Rev. Samuel J. Mills and Ebenezer Burgess were appointed the Society's first agents to Africa. They were directed to go by way of England and secure there such information as they could, that would be helpful in the selection of territory favorable for the proposed colony.

---

[12] 27th Cong., 3d Sess., H. Rept., no. 283, pp. 208-213. J. P. Kennedy's Report. This is a most valuable document on colonization and the slave trade. By some, it was considered the most important House Report of the session.

[13] Journal of Board of Managers of American Colonization Society, MS., October, 1817.

From there, they were to proceed to the West Coast of Africa for the purpose of exploration and of ascertaining the best situation for the establishment of such a colony as the Society contemplated. They were to observe the climate, soil, etc., of such parts of the coast as they visited, "as it is in contemplation to turn the attention of the new colonists mostly to agriculture."[14] On the return voyage Mills died.

At the annual meeting, January 1, 1818, President Washington reported a growing interest in every part of the Union in favor of the Society; also a respectable subscription from a "small but opulent society of slave-holders in Virginia." Further, it was stated:

> Should it [the Society] lead as we may fairly hope it will, to the slow but gradual abolition of slavery, it will wipe from our political institutions the only blot which stains them; and in palliation of which, we shall not be at liberty to plead the excuse of moral necessity, until we have honestly exerted all the means which we possess for its extinction.[15]

During this first year, also, auxiliary societies had been formed in Baltimore, Philadelphia, New York, Virginia, and Ohio.[16]

Already, by 1819, one happy result of the Society's efforts was seen in an act passed by the State of Georgia. It was an act providing for the disposal of slaves illegally imported into the State. Such slaves, if captured, were to be considered the property of the State and were to be sold at auction, provided that, in case the Colonization Society agreed to transport such negroes to such foreign colony as the Society might have established, the negroes, after payment by the Society of all expenses incurred by the State in connection with them, were to be transferred to the Society.[17] This was the beginning of a crusade against the African slave-trade, and from this time until that trade had ceased,

---

[14] Minutes of Board of Managers of American Colonization Society, MS., Nov. 5, 1817.
[15] Origin, Constitution, and Proceedings of American Colonization Society, MS., vol. i, pp. 20–23.
[16] Ibid., vol. i, pp. 23–30.
[17] Ibid., vol. i, pp. 65–74.

the Society's existence would have been amply justified if it had accomplished nothing beyond its influence against that inhuman traffic. It is believed that Charles Fenton Mercer, "the Wilberforce of America," was inspired by his interest in African colonization to wage, in Congress, a warfare against the African slave trade such as was waged by no other American. The Anti-Slave-Trade Act of 1819 was the outcome of a memorial from the Board of Managers of the Colonization Society.[13] In the annual report of the Board of Managers, 1819, the efforts of the managers are stated to be directed to "the happiness of the free people of colour and the reduction of the number of slaves in America."[19]

In January, 1819, a letter from the Colonization Society was presented in the House of Representatives. The efforts of the Society in sending out Mills and Burgess were noted, and it was stated that, although the Society owed its origin to philanthropic individuals, its purposes could not be satisfactorily realized and its success could not be complete unless it had the support of the Federal government.[20] Probably the greatest single disappointment the Society ever experienced was in the continued refusal of the Federal government to appropriate funds for the carrying out of the chief purpose of the Society; the transportation and settlement of free persons of color on the west coast of Africa. Year after year memorials were presented; year after year favorable reports were read from House committees to which the memorials were referred; and year after year Congress refused to make an appropriation. There can be no doubt that when the Society was formed, it looked to the Federal government for aid in its undertaking.[21]

This disposition to leave the Society to work out its own program and collect, as best it could, the funds that were

---

[18] Ibid., vol. i, p. 88.
[19] Ibid., vol. i, pp. 65-74.
[20] 27th Cong., 3d Sess., H. Rept. no. 283, pp. 223-225.
[21] Origin, Constitution, and Proceedings of American Colonization Society, MS. See Original Constitution.

necessary, was not shared by President Monroe. When the Anti-Slave-Trade Act of 1819 was passed, he construed it liberally and, in cooperation with the managers of the Colonization Society, sent out Agents of the United States to select on the west African coast a territory on which recaptured Africans might be landed and cared for by the government.[22] The first material result of this cooperation was the chartering, in 1820, of the Elizabeth by the government, and her departure from New York with Rev. Samuel Bacon and John P. Bankson, government agents, Samuel C. Crozer, agent for the Colonization Society, and eighty-odd free negroes. Going by way of Sierra Leone, the company landed on Sherbro Island where, by the first of June, the three agents and twenty-four of the settlers had died.[23]

So much has been said of the unhealthfulness of the territory to which the Society's first negroes were sent, that it will be fitting here to record the facts as they were presented by the colonial agents. As years added to the experience of those who directed the settlement, it was observed that the cases of African fever through which most of the immigrants passed were less frequent and less violent among those who arrived during the dry than among those who arrived during the rainy season. But this lesson had to be learned and, although the Abolitionists of the Garrisonian school and their apologists have depicted in glowing terms the wretchedness of the free negro, "expatriated" and sent off, out of the way, to die of African fever, it is yet true that if the number of deaths among the Liberian colonists be compared with the number of deaths among the settlers of either Virginia or Plymouth, the comparison is highly favorable to the Liberians and the Colonization Society, and this notwithstanding the fact that the African colonists as a class were imprudent in observing even the essentials of personal hygiene.[24] They insisted on eating, when they should have abstained from food. They

---
[22] 27th Cong., 3d Sess., H. Rept. no. 283, p. 2.
[23] Lugenbeel.
[24] African Repository, vol. xv, p. 306.

exposed themselves needlessly and carelessly and, in spite of the most earnest efforts on the part of the Society and its physicians in the colony, the death-rate figures were eagerly used to stir up opposition among the New Englanders.

In 1832 the Board of Managers went carefully into a consideration of the actual number of deaths, the causes of death, and the possibility of decreasing materially the death-rate. A committee appointed for that purpose reported that since 1820, twenty-two expeditions had gone out from the United States to Liberia. On the first eighteen of these, 1487 emigrants had been transported. Of these, two hundred and thirty had died from diseases of acclimation, from fever and diseases consequent upon it. The conclusion reached was that the three most fruitful causes of death were, in descending order: (1) the transportation to Africa of persons who had become accustomed to the high or mountainous country in the United States, (2) the settlement of immigrants too close to the coast and in the heart of the malarial district, (3) the arrival of immigrants at the wrong time of the year. While, of those persons who left the high, and non-malarial sections of the United States, one out of every two and one-fourth died; of those who left the malarial sections of the United States, only one out of every twenty-seven died. Of those landed at Monrovia, a settlement in the malarial section, one out of every five died; while, of those landed at Caldwell, further from the coast and having a greater elevation, one in every fourteen died. Of those transported to Liberia during the rainy season, one out of every four and one-third died; while, of those transported during the dry season, only one out of every six and two-thirds died.[25]

Thereafter, the Society used every reasonable precaution within its power to prevent sickness, to care for those who were sick, and to cut down the death-rate—and with success.

---

[25] Minutes Board of Managers of American Colonization Society, MS., May 7, 1832, vol. ii, p. 273 ff.

But there can be no doubt that the climate was much more severe in its effects upon the health of the white man than upon that of the black. Indeed, every white agent who went out, from the first expedition until the independence of the Republic of Liberia was declared, took his life in his hands and knew very well that the odds were greatly against not only his health, but his life. Mills, Bacon, Crozer, Bankson, Andrews, Winns and his wife, Randall, Anderson, Skinner and his wife, Ashmun and his wife, Buchanan— heroes and heroines these—and Ashmun and Buchanan the greatest of them. Men and women who, like these, lay down their lives voluntarily upon the altar of service, are not to be charged with selfishness or the desire to perpetuate a system against which they spoke and labored eloquently.

The sending of expeditions and the sustenance of emigrants required funds. How were the finances to be provided and the enthusiasm spread? The President had gone as far as he could, in keeping with the law of 1819, in cooperation with the Society. By that law, his efforts were confined to the suppression of the slave-trade. No direct appropriation could be secured from Congress. The result was that for many years, indeed, during the whole period covered in this study, the important sources of revenue were: (1) a national system of agencies, (2) receipts from auxiliary societies, (3) bequests and legacies, (4) State appropriations, (5) collections taken by ministers in churches on the Fourth of July each year.

As early as March, 1819, the Managers appointed thirteen agents whose duty it was to collect funds and arouse interest throughout the Union. Among these were General Walter Jones, C. F. Mercer, William H. Fitzhugh, and Francis Scott Key. But the first important general agent of the Society was Rev. William Meade. The origin of the agency is interesting. William H. Crawford, who was presiding at a meeting of the Managers, in April, 1819, called attention to an advertisement he had found in a Georgia newspaper. Thirty or forty negroes had been illegally imported into the State. The law of the State required that they should be sold at auction, unless, by a provision already referred to, they could be taken over by the Colonization Society, and transported to Africa. Meade was at once sent to Georgia to make an effort to save the negroes from slavery.

In May, Meade reported that the Governor had agreed to postpone the sale and "afforded me an opportunity of seeking among the humane and generous of this southern country, the means of their redemption."[26] In June he reported that arrangements had been made, by which the negroes were to be turned over to the Society. "Some who had but little hope of our general enterprize declared their willingness to contribute for the ransome of these; and a few who intended to have become the purchasers at this sale, expressed a pleasure at the thought of their restoration to Africa, and proved their sincerity by uniting with the Society at Milledgeville." Under the direction of the most prominent citizens of the State, he had formed three auxiliary societies. At Augusta and Savannah he found similar good feeling toward the Society. Of the negroes at Charleston he says: "their attendance in the church where I was invited to officiate, (and it was the same, I was told, in all the others,) was truly grateful to the soul of the Christian. The aisles and other places in the church set apart for them, were filled with young and old, decently dressed and many of them having their prayer books, and joining in all the responses of the church. I must also beg leave to add a general remark concerning the whole Southern country, in which I am justified by the repeated assurances of the most pious and benevolent that the condition of the negroes is greatly ameliorated in every respect. As to food, raiment, houses, labour, and correction, there is yearly less and less over which religion and humanity must lament." At Georgetown he saw "eight or ten of the most

---

[26] Minutes Board of Managers of American Colonization Society, MS., April 7, 1819; May 4, 1819.

wealthy and influential, and obtained assurances of their cordial co-operation." At Fayetteville "all the citizens prepared for co-operation. I had only to go to their houses and take down their names."

At Raleigh he found "the same unanimity of sentiment. The supreme court being in session, many of the judges and lawyers were collected from the different parts of the State, who cordially joined in the Society, and testified to the general prevalence of good will to it throughout the State. At a meeting for forming a constitution, the highest talents, authorities, and wealth of the State were present, and unanimously sanctioned the measure." From Raleigh, he went to Chapel Hill, the seat of the State University. It was commencement time, and ministers, trustees, and other persons of influence were assembled. "I was happy to find the same feeling here, and that a small society had already been formed." For his agency as a whole, he reported six organized, and ten or twelve prospective, societies. He had secured, in about two months time, subscriptions amounting to between seven and eight thousand dollars. He reported that his success in raising funds would have been greater, but for the fact that "the pecuniary distress is, by universal consent, greater than ever was known. . . . I was told a hundred times that no other cause but this would elicit anything." Of the general feeling in regard to the Society, he reported "a conviction that unless a great alteration takes place; or I have been misinformed, it will meet with a liberal support."[27] During the early years of the Society, Rev. William Meade also undertook a local agency in his own county in the Valley of Virginia. He secured subscriptions amounting to almost seven thousand dollars there, his own near relatives contributing, with himself, seventeen hundred dollars.[28]

In 1825 William H. Fitzhugh, of Virginia, was appointed to go through the Middle Atlantic and New England States

---
[27] Ibid., Report of Meade, June 21, 1819.
[28] African Repository, vol. i, pp. 146-147.

in the interests of the Society. Theodore Frelinghuysen, of New Jersey, received an appointment in 1828, as did also Rev. Leonard Bacon, of Connecticut.[29] In 1830, the Managers resolved to appoint a permanent agent for the New England States, "who by correspondence, the establishment of auxiliary societies, and an attendance upon the Legislatures of those States shall awaken a more general and active interest in the object and augment the funds of the Society." Whenever desirable agents could be obtained general agencies were created for the lower Middle States, the upper Middle States, the New England States, the Western States, the Southern States, and the Southwestern States. During the years 1838 to 1845 these agencies were by far the most important source of revenue that the Society had.

Thousands of dollars were annually turned over to the funds of the parent Society by the various State and county societies. The organization toward which the Society worked, in its earlier years, was, (1) the parent organization, (2) a State auxiliary society in every State of the Union, (3) societies auxiliary to the State societies, in every county of every State. There was a time when the number of auxiliary societies was about one hundred and fifty.[30]

Of these, special mention should be made of the Vermont Society, over which the venerable Elijah Paine presided for many years; the Massachusetts Society, among whose foremost members were Joseph Tracy and Simon Greenleaf; the Connecticut Society, with Leonard Bacon, Roger M. Sherman and Governor Tomlinson;[31] the New York Society, which for years was favored with the services of Dr. Alexander Proudfit and President Duer of Columbia, and which received liberal support from Benjamin F. Butler and, until about 1835, from the philanthropist, Gerrit

---
[29] Board of Managers of American Colonization Society, MS., Sept. 5, 1828.
[30] For lists of the auxiliary societies see appendices to the annual reports of the American Colonization Society.
[31] African Repository, vol. v, p. 93.

Smith; the New Jersey Society, with Judge Halsey a leading spirit; the Young Men's Society of Philadelphia, which at times was almost completely under the dominance of that quaint, queer, irrepressible Quaker, Elliot Cresson, who whether at home, or in England, or in Mississippi, or in Vermont, never failed to impress his hearers with his untiring energy, and oftentimes with his utter disagreement with Garrison as to the method of ridding the land of slavery, although he was as anxious as Garrison to get rid of the whole system; the Maryland Society, that counted among its leaders Key, C. C. Harper, John E. Howard, and J. H. B. Latrobe; the Virginia Society, whose President in 1833 was John Marshall, and among whose twelve Vice-Presidents were John Tyler, James Madison, James Pleasants, Hugh Nelson, William H. Broadnax, William Maxwell, and Abel P. Upshur;[32] the Loudoun County (Virginia) Society, one of whose Presidents was James Monroe; the Petersburg (Virginia) Society, in which John Early, later a bishop in the Southern Methodist Church, was for years a most active member; also the Societies of Kentucky, Ohio, Louisiana, and Mississippi, the last two of which, for some years, exerted an influence that brought about the liberation of hundreds of slaves, that established a separate settlement at Sinoe in the Liberian country, and counted among their members and leaders, John Ker, John McDonogh, William Winans, and Zebulun Butler. In 1824 there were only twenty auxiliary societies; two years later there were forty-six. From this time the number grew rapidly.[33] By 1838, it seems, auxiliary societies had been organized in every State and Territory in the Union, except Rhode Island, South Carolina, Arkansas, and Michigan.[34]

Another source of revenue was the subscription of large sums by philanthropists throughout the Union. Mercer was one of the earliest contributors of this class. About 1821 he pledged himself to be responsible for the collection

[32] Ibid., vol. ix, pp. 24-25.
[33] Ibid., vol. i, p. 347.
[34] Ibid., vol. xiv, p. 100.

of $5000, with which to begin the active operations of the Society, he to be personally liable for that amount if he failed to secure it by solicitation.[35] Gerrit Smith, later Abolitionist, proposed, in 1828, that friends of the Society contribute $100 per year for ten years. The plan became well known as the Gerrit Smith plan. Of $54,000 contributed on this plan, the New England States gave $9000, New York, Pennsylvania, New Jersey and Delaware $14,000, Maryland and the District of Columbia, $4000; the South $26,000, and the Northwest $1000.[36] One of the contributors on this plan was Gerrit Smith; another, Mathew Carey, also Theodore Frelinghuysen, John McDonogh of New Orleans, John H. Cocke of Virginia, and Courtlandt Van Rensaelaer of New York. J. H. McClure, of Kentucky, gave $1000 per year for ten years. George Hargraves of Georgia, and John Marshall of Virginia gave $500 each.[37] Gerrit Smith contributed, besides his contribution on the Gerrit Smith plan, $5000, when the Society reached a period of extreme need.[38] Judge Workman of New Orleans left, by will, to the Society $10,000. Colonel Rutgers of New York left $1000. "Two Friends" in Georgia left $500 each.[39] Childers of Mississippi left a sum which was estimated to be about $30,000.[40] James Madison left $2000 and also the proceeds from the sale of a grist mill and lot.[41] Daniel Waldo and his wife of Boston gave $24,000 in 1845.[42]

Soon after the Southampton Insurrection in 1831, and due in large measure to the alarm that was excited by it, the Maryland Legislature provided for an appropriation total-

---

[35] Fragment in Gurley's handwriting, MS., in which is copied a letter from C. F. Mercer.
[36] Life Members, MS.
[37] Letters of American Colonization Society, MS., Hargraves to Treasurer, Augusta, Ga., June 9, 1833; African Repository, vol. ix, p. 364.
[38] African Repository, vol. ix, p. 364.
[39] Ibid., vol. viii, p. 366.
[40] Letters of American Colonization Society, MS., Gurley to P. R. Fendall, July 16, 1836.
[41] African Repository, vol. xii, p. 237.
[42] Letters to American Colonization Society, MS., Joseph Tracy to McLain, Boston, Sept. 5, 1845.

ing $200,000, payable in instalments each year. Because of the independent action of the Maryland Society, the parent organization was deprived of this source of revenue.[43] At about the same time, the Virginia Legislature made an appropriation of $90,000, though certain restrictions as to its application made it almost useless for the purposes of the Society.[44] In 1850 the Legislature of the same State appropriated $30,000 per year for five years, on condition that the negroes for whose transportation the fund was to provide were free at the time of the passage of the act, were residents of Virginia, and had already been transported when application was made for the payment of the amount appropriated for such transportation.[45] In addition to these sources of revenue John McDonogh, by will, left to the Society $25,000 annually,[46] and David Hunt of Mississippi left to it $45,000.[47]

The fifth source of revenue, and it was much more than a mere source of revenue, was the annual Fourth of July collection taken up in churches in almost every part of the Union. In these days, when a most important new light has been thrown upon the forces that have cooperated in the making of history; when, particularly in the study of that generation from 1830 to 1860—a time pregnant with problems and with possibilities, and with historical interpretations—the economic interpretation is monopolizing interest, it has become habitual with students of history to speak and write in terms of cotton production, the cotton gin, the expanding Southwest, and so on. There is very much truth in this from the point of view of the South. But, from the point of view of the North, that busy decade from 1835 to 1845 was the battleground between public

---

[43] African Repository, vol. viii, p. 61.
[44] Letters of American Colonization Society, F. Knight to Dr. A. Cummings, vol. iii, no. 738, Aug. 17, 1840.
[45] Journal of Executive Committee of American Colonization Society, 1845-54, March 16, 1850, pp. 139-141.
[46] Journal of Board of Directors of American Colonization Society, MS., Jan. 23, 1851, vol. iv, pp. 90-91.
[47] Ibid., vol. iv, p. 271.

opinion, so-called, and that opinion moulded by the active and lay ministry, meaning by the lay ministry that body of educational and philanthropic men who, from lecture room or counting house, cooperated with the Christian ministry in forming a distinctly church sentiment. At the beginning of that decade the ministry was leading public sentiment; at the end of it public sentiment was leading the ministry. This is altogether obvious from the correspondence preserved by the Society.

From the organization of the Society in 1817 to the early thirties, the ministry all over New England cooperated splendidly with the Colonization managers, preached annual sermons on Colonization, on or near the Fourth of July, and contributed to the Washington office annually thousands of dollars. At their general conferences and associations they passed with great unanimity resolutions commendatory of the Society, and urged a continuance of the July sermons and collections. Beginning with the thirties, church doors in New England and in many parts of the West were closed to Colonization lecturers and agents, and the reason given, in scores of cases, was not an objection of the minister himself, but his fear that his membership would be displeased if he allowed the use of his pulpit to Colonizationist lecturers. From 1817 to 1830 cooperation and collections from the pew in the New England States were important contributions to the early success of the enterprise.

Among the contributors to the Colonization treasury must be mentioned also the Society of Friends, particularly the Friends of North Carolina who, though comparatively poor, contributed very liberally to the transportation of free negroes. As early as 1820, they paid over to the Society eight hundred dollars.[48] In 1827 they again contributed the same amount.[49] Between 1825 and 1830, Masonic

---

[48] Journal of Board of Managers of American Colonization Society, MS., May 30, 1820.
[49] African Repository, vol. ii, p. 351; Journal of Board of Managers of American Colonization Society, MS., Feb. 12, 1827.

Lodge chapters in Maryland, Pennsylvania, Maine, Massachusetts, Columbus and Woodville, Mississippi, also sent in contributions.[50]

But to return to our narrative of the Society's operations. In 1820, the fifteen Vice-Presidents were equally divided between the States south of the border States, the border States, and the States north of those States, five being elected from Georgia, Tennessee, and Virginia; five from Kentucky, the District of Columbia, and Maryland, and five from Pennsylvania, New Jersey, New York, and Massachusetts.[51] Of the funds received by the Society by the time the Elizabeth sailed for Africa, out of a total of $14,031.50, the States north of the border States had contributed $2664.67, the District of Columbia and Maryland had contributed $8466.58, and the States south of the border States had contributed $2900.25.[52] If those who already believed that the Society was an organization gotten up by slaveholders for the purpose of getting rid of the free negro, and thereby increasing the value of the slaves that they desired to sell further South, had taken the trouble to think upon these figures, they would have seen that Virginia, the State, above all others, to which their views might have been expected to apply, was sending in contributions that were just about equal to those that came from the States in which slavery had already been abolished; and that the movement was a national, not a sectional one, although its vital energy undoubtedly did come from the middle-State section.

Even before the Elizabeth sailed, the managers went carefully into the question of the practicability of their scheme. They considered the "marrow" of the arguments against colonization to be whether or not the colony proposed could receive and subsist, or the Society transport, all the free

---

[50] African Repository, vol. ii, p. 353; Letters of American Colonization Society, Apr. 21, 1827, May 21, 1827, May 24, 1827.
[51] Origin, Constitution, and Proceedings of American Colonization Society, MS., vol. i, pp. 118–119.
[52] Ibid., vol. i, pp. 150–151.

negroes from the United States. They realized that the colony could not receive, in any one year, more immigrants than could be provided for by the annual surplus products of the colony, including importations. They doubted whether the Society, unaided by the resources of the State or Federal governments, could transport the annual increase in the free negro population, about 5000. But with such governmental aid, they were sure of the success of their undertaking. At any rate, they said, whether accompanied by complete or only partial success, the movement could not but have the most salutary results. As was said at the time:

> Although it is believed, and is, indeed, too obvious to require proof, that the colonization of the free people of colour, alone, would not only tend to civilise Africa; to abolish the slave trade; and greatly to advance their own happiness; but to promote that, also, of the other classes of society, the proprietors and their slaves, yet the hope of the gradual and utter abolition of slavery, in a manner consistent with the rights, interests, and happiness of society, ought never to be abandoned.[53]

If Ohio, with one crop only a year, could add on an average 26,000 a year to her population, could not the west coast of Africa, with two crops a year and a perpetual summer, sustain an average immigration of 5000 from the United States? Indeed, ought it not to be able to sustain the whole of the annual increase of the negro population of the United States, free and slave, which amounted to 40,000? If only the movement would receive cordial support, between America and Africa an interchange of useful articles would take the place of trade in human beings, and

> new forms of Government, modelled after those which constitute the pride and boast of America, will attest the extent of their obligations to their former masters, and myriads of freemen, while they course the margin of the Gambia, the Senegal, the Congo, and the Niger, will sing, in the language which records the constitution, laws, and history of America, hymns of praise to the common parent of man.[54]

But these high hopes were disturbed, and it was a gloomy day among the Managers when, in October, 1820, they dis-

---
[53] Ibid., vol. i, pp. 106–107.
[54] Ibid., vol. i, pp. 107–115.

cussed the prospects for colonization in the light of the distressing news that had come of the large number of deaths among the emigrants carried over by the Elizabeth. If there was much likelihood that these conditions would continue, they had no doubt that their efforts on the west coast of Africa ought to be given up without delay. But the experiment had not been made under favorable conditions. The vessel had landed during the unhealthful, rainy season. The landing and settlement had been made at a most undesirable location. Diseases had been contracted on the vessel during the voyage. Besides, there were many applicants who were not only ready but anxious to go. The decision was that they must continue the experiment.[55]

Nothing daunted, therefore, by reports from the first expedition, the United States Government chartered the Nautilus, and she sailed from Norfolk early in 1821, and towards the latter part of March, the same year, the U. S. Schooner Augusta sailed. In the Nautilus went about thirty emigrants who, with a number of those who had been transported in the Elizabeth, were received into Sierra Leone. With these two expeditions went Messrs. Andrews, Winn, Bacon, Wittberger, and Mrs. Winn, agents for the Government and the Society. By the beginning of autumn, Andrews and Mr. and Mrs. Winn had died.[56]

Late in 1821 Dr. Eli Ayres, as principal agent for the Society, arrived at Sierra Leone, and Captain R. F. Stockton arrived in the U. S. Schooner Alligator. December 11, Ayres and Stockton anchored off Cape Mesurado, or Montserado, and in exchange for gunpowder, tobacco, muskets, iron pots, beads, looking-glasses, pipes, cotton, etc., secured a title deed to a valuable tract of land which was the nucleus of what is now the Republic of Liberia.[57] It seems that the

---

[55] Journal of Board of Managers of American Colonization Society, MS., October 16, 1820; Origin, Constitution and Proceedings of American Colonization Society, MS., vol. i, pp. 131-149.
[56] Lugenbeel; African Repository, vol. i, pp. 3-4; Origin, Constitution, and Proceedings of American Colonization Society, MS., vol. i, pp. 168-194.
[57] Lugenbeel.

land was never ceded either to the United States Government or to the Colonization Society. It was ceded to Captain Stockton and Dr. Ayres " to have and to hold the said premises for the use of these said [negroes] citizens of America."[58] The territory was a trust, and was from the first so considered by the Managers of the Society. From the first, they looked to the time when the colony they should plant would be able to stand alone, a model republic for the African to admire and, perhaps some day, imitate. Ayres then returned to Sierra Leone and prepared to plant the emigrants on the newly ceded territory. By April, 1822, this had been done.[59] At the beginning of summer Dr. Ayres left Africa for America, and put one of the colonists, Elijah Johnson, in charge of the settlement.

In August of this year, the brig Strong arrived from Baltimore with immigrants, a cargo of provisions, and Jehudi Ashmun, a name that must ever remain first in importance among the early white men who went to Africa to help establish the Society's colony. An indiscretion on the part of the colonists who had settled at Montserado, arising from a wrong interpretation of some of the acts of the native tribes, and the inability of the natives to appreciate fully their obligation to respect the deed of cession which they had made over to Dr. Ayres and Captain Stockton, caused hard feeling between the colonists and the natives. Ashmun saw at once that he must look for friction, and he lost no time in putting the settlement in a condition of military defence for the protection of the settlers who were then living at Montserado. Several attacks were made by the natives, but altogether without success. The defeated natives acquiesced in the occupation of the land they had ceded to the agents.[60] April 25, 1822, the American flag was for the first time hoisted on Cape Montserado.

By 1823 the Managers of the Society had become again

---
[58] Half-Century Memorial of American Colonization Society, 1867, p. 83.
[59] Lugenbeel.
[60] Ibid.

very hopeful of the success of colonization on the West Coast of Africa. They reported about a hundred and thirty settlers at that time living at the Society's settlement, a regularly planned town, and great improvement in the health of the colonists, although Mrs. Ashmun had died since her arrival in Africa. They noted a rapidly growing desire among the free negroes of America to emigrate to the settlement, and

when they reflect upon the frequency of manumissions, wherever the law has imposed no restrictions, when they consider the power of example . . ., and especially when they recollect the institutions of their country, and the light of the age, they are induced to expect that, should prosperity attend the colony, thousands now in servitude amongst us will one day be freemen in the land of their ancestors.[61]

Dr. Ayres, who had returned to Africa after his visit to the United States, was instructed to negotiate with the native kings for a "much larger extent of country than we now possess on that continent."[62] An appeal went out from the Managers for more funds to meet the opportunities that were dawning upon the enterprise. They appealed for the means to send emigrants in sufficient numbers to render their presence along the coast a "security from the intrigues of slave traders," and to protect the settlements from the "cupidity of neighboring tribes." Also, "abundant information has been laid before the Board . . . to warrant the declaration that numerous slave holders would send, some a portion, and others the whole of their slaves to the colony, as soon as they are convinced that the colony is prepared for their reception, and that their condition would be improved by the removal."[63]

In view of the often repeated charge made by the ultra-abolitionists that, between the African fever and the barbarity of the native tribes, the Society was sacrificing the

---

[61] Origin, Constitution, and Proceedings of American Colonization Society, MS., vol. i, pp. 198-221, Sixth Annual Report of the Board of Managers, 1823.
[62] Minutes of Board of Managers of American Colonization Society, MS., March 28, 1823.
[63] Ibid., June 4, 1823.

American free negro for its own selfish and unworthy aims, it will be not without interest to call attention to a report of the Managers, early in 1824. Since the origin of the Society, two hundred and twenty-five emigrants had sailed for the African coast. The number in the colony at the time of the report was one hundred and forty, a number of those missing having gone to Sierra Leone to live; several had returned to the United States, and only forty deaths had been reported. Of these forty, twenty-two were passengers on the Elizabeth. Only four deaths had resulted from conflicts with the natives; two had been drowned, one had died of old age, one died through his own rashness, and four were children under four years of age.[64] Indeed, the Managers thought this a very hopeful beginning, and others evidently agreed with them, for the Presbyterian Synods of Philadelphia and Virginia had approved the efforts of the Society, as had also the General Convention of the Protestant Episcopal Church, the first two, unanimously. And as for the possibility of securing emigrants, it was the opinion of the Board that "the means will never equal the demand for transportation."[65]

The Managers, who had again memorialized Congress in 1822, urging further restrictive measures against the African slave trade,[66] adopted the recommendations of a committee appointed to consider the advisability of requesting further aid from Congress. The committee expressed the opinion that " it [the scheme of colonization] is well known to be far too great, to be sensibly affected by any resources which an association of individuals can command. To the nation, and to the nation alone, must we look for adequate means of accomplishing such a work." It was recommended that Congress be asked to take under its protection the colony already planted, to provide appropriations for its development, to make further purchases of territory, to

---

[64] Origin, Constitution, and Proceedings of American Colonization Society, MS., vol. i, pp. 231–232.
[65] Ibid., vol. i, pp. 244–253.
[66] Ibid., vol. i, p. 182.

supply it with a force adequate for its military defence, and to enact regulations for its temporary government. It was also recommended to petition Congress to incorporate the Society in the District of Columbia.[67] The petition that resulted went the way of all other petitions whose aim was to secure direct financial aid from Congress.

At the annual meeting in February, 1824, on the motion of General Robert G. Harper, the territory that had been secured was named Liberia, and the settlement made was named after the President of the United States, Monrovia. Early in this year a remonstrance from the Liberian settlements reached the officers of the Society. Although great care was taken to send out to the settlement only those who were believed to be desirable immigrants, the government of the Liberians by direction of the Society soon began to present added problems. Dissatisfaction among the few settlers had reached such a point that four documents and a special agent were sent to Liberia before the colonial agent was able to restore peace and order. The settlers complained, first, that lots had not been distributed to immigrants in accordance with instructions of the Board of Managers; second, that it was impracticable for settlers to obey the regulations requiring them to erect, each on his lot, a dwelling, within two years of his selection of the lot; third, that, because of the return of Dr. Ayres to the United States, the Managers evidently intended to abandon the settlers in a strange land; fourth, that certain settlers were being discriminated against, by the government, in favor of other settlers; and finally, that they were dissatisfied with the agents. The reply of the Managers is conclusive and sets forth beyond doubt the fact that the complaints were founded upon ignorance of the facts, although it is probably true that no adequate instructions and no definite and detailed scheme had ever been sent out to the agent for the government of the colony. Direct, and probably useful advice was given in the following words:

---

[67] Ibid., vol. i, pp. 272-276.

Let us not be misunderstood. . . . It is our intention now and all times to distinguish between the industrious, the provident, the orderly and useful citizens—and those who are lazy, disorderly, and hurtful to the settlement. We wish it to be explicitly understood, that we will not extend . . . indulgence to the lazy and the disorderly. . . . It would give us great pleasure if we had the means to extend our supplies to those who would properly value and make good use of them. We have begged through the country—we have begged of Congress and of the State Legislatures—we are constantly begging and contributing ourselves. You receive all the benefit of it. Those who are not satisfied with this, will be satisfied with nothing.[68]

During the disorders in the colony, the Society's agent was insulted and abused, public authority was defied, and an armed force had taken possession of, and robbed, the public storehouse, and the Managers, in an address to the Citizens of Liberia, say: "This is the very conduct repeatedly predicted by our opponents; we have been told over and over again that you would not submit to any law or government without an armed force; we have constantly repelled these reproaches on your character as unjust; what shall we now say?" The address was characterized by firmness, but also by kindness; and it was rather by an appeal to their reason than by threats of punishment that the Managers called upon the colonists to submit to rightful authority and settle their differences.[69] In their general instructions to the colonial agent, Mr. Ashmun, the Managers speak of the "wicked combination and disgraceful proceedings of Lot Carey and others. . . ." "Such proceedings, if repeated, must inevitably lead to the destruction of the Colony." The mildest punishment consistent with the reestablishment of order was to be inflicted; the arms were to be taken away from those who had had a part in the rioting; civil officers, among the offenders, were to have their commissions revoked. Carey, himself a minister, was to abstain from the further exercise of his ministerial function "till time and circumstances shall have evidenced the deepness and sincerity of his repentance."[70]

---

[68] Minutes of Board of Managers of American Colonization Society, MS., March 20, 1824.
[69] Ibid., March 20, 1824.
[70] Ibid., vol. i, p. 201.

In private instructions, the agent was criticised for not having promptly resisted the first expression of "insolent and abusive language" toward him; and he was instructed: ". . . keep your arms by you, or near you. Never continue altercation, where there are symptoms of passion. . . . Stop the rations of every one who refuses to labour in the public service according to their oaths and engagements. If this will not do they must be banished." He was instructed to be as "mild, calm, steady, firm," as was consistent with the necessities of the case.[71]

In addition to these efforts to bring peace to Monrovia, the Managers sent out a special agent to examine and report on the prospects of the colony. The man selected was Rev. Ralph Randolph Gurley, a graduate of Yale and a native of Connecticut who, in 1822, began a connection with the central office of the American Colonization Society, where he gained a reputation as editor and orator that was not only coextensive with the limits of the Union, but that extended to England and Scotland. From 1822 to 1840 he did more than any other single man connected with the Society—and many men thought, as much as almost any half dozen men—to keep open the avenues of thought and sympathy and cooperation between the biggest and best of men in every part of the Union. Utterly unlike in their private practices, what Henry Clay was in the Halls of Congress, Gurley was to Colonization, essentially a peacemaker and a lover of the Union. Those who, following Garrison and his partisans, charge the colonization movement with being a move to rivet the chains of the slaves, and base their contention upon the fact that every President of the Society, from its organization to near the opening of the Civil War, was a holder of slaves, must be ignorant of the fact that Gurley's influence during those years of his active leadership was so much greater, in molding the policies of the Society, than that of any of these presidents, that it would be ridiculous to compare it with the influence of any, or all, of them.

---

[71] Ibid., April 1, 1824.

Elliot Cresson, one of the most persistent Colonizationists in the history of the Society, used to call the second President, Charles Carroll of Carrollton, "The Great Incubus." Those who would understand the platform of the Colonization movement must consult, not the list of slaveholding presidents who were the official heads of the organization, although, with the possible exception of Carroll, not a president of the Society has ever been a proponent of slavery, notwithstanding the fact that the first four of them were holders of negro slaves (and the two phrases are by no means synonymous to those who realize that slavery was a problem), but the secretaries and the boards of managers and directors, for these were the molders of policy. During those years of bitter struggle, between 1830 and 1840, Gurley stands out as the great Colonizationist. He was the one man who held in the hollow of his hand the confidence of moderate men throughout the United States, on the subject of slavery. He was undoubtedly a poor guardian of the Society's exchequer. He wrought mightily with the pen and played havoc with the purse. But of all the charges that were made against him by extremists in England and America, not one has resulted in his conviction at the bar of public opinion. When he was superseded, a nation-wide protest, but a protest particularly from the South, went up. While Garrison was actively and consciously engaged in pulling the Union to pieces, Gurley was traveling from North to South, from East to West, observing the results of radicalism and dreading the aftermath. An accurate biography of Gurley would throw a new and not favorable light upon the results of Garrisonism.

This man was about to perform his first important service to the cause of Colonization. He met Ashmun at the Cape Verde Islands, whither the latter had been compelled to go, for rest and recuperation, and the two proceeded to Liberia. After ten days, Gurley left for America, leaving Ashmun commissions which, like his own, were from both the Government and the Society.[72] When Gurley presented to the

---

[72] Lugenbeel.

Managers his proposed constitution for the government of the colony, it was received with disappointment. "The Board think it much too complicated and intricate for the simplicity of a few settlers. . . . We wish the settlement founded in republican simplicity and Christian plainness—all unnecessary offices and dignities and official titles ought to be avoided."[73] But after six months' experiment, the instrument had proved so satisfactory that the Board withdrew its objection and officially approved it.[74] In his report to the Managers, Gurley expressed great satisfaction with the location of the settlement, the fertility of the soil, the health of the colonists, their general intelligence, their Sunday Schools. He was convinced, however, that the government was too feeble, and that several recent decisions of the Board had been received with dissatisfaction among the colonists. He noted the need for medicines, agricultural implements, etc.[75]

The years 1825–1830 were years of rapid progress and expansion of the colonization scheme in the United States. The few settlers who began to return exerted an influence favorable to the spread of sentiment among the blacks in favor of emigration,[76] though some who returned opposed the colony. The opportunities of the Society, during this whole period, far exceeded its ability to take advantage of them. It was unable to afford the means of transportation for those who applied for passage. It did a great service in bringing about an interchange of views between leading men in the South Middle States and the New England States by sending such men as Charles Fenton Mercer and J. B. Harrison to meet with the legislature and to converse privately with leaders in New York and the New England

---

[73] Minutes of Board of Managers of American Colonization Society, MS., Nov. 13, 1824.
[74] Ibid., May 18, 1825.
[75] Origin, Constitution, and Proceedings of American Colonization Society, MS., vol. i, p. 277 ff.
[76] Minutes of Board of Managers of American Colonization Society, MS., Dec. 22, 1825.

States.[77] Memorials were presented to legislatures of the several States, asking their approbation of the objects of the Society and their pecuniary support.[78] The Society enlisted important workers when it adopted the suggestion of J. H. B. Latrobe, that the ladies of the Union be invited to organize female societies " for the purpose of aiding in the collection of funds by procuring donations, holding fairs, etc., etc.—that this be put into the form of a resolution, prefaced by some general remarks—'female sensibility—sympathy'—etc. etc. etc. and then published as a circular." It also sought to make the means that it had count for most in the colony, by refusing to transport to Africa any free negro over fifty years of age, unless he was a member of a family that was emigrating to Liberia; and by refusing, except in extreme cases, to give more than six months' subsistence to colonists after their arrival at the settlement.[79]

At the annual meeting in 1827, Henry Clay made an important speech, voicing the disappointment that was felt by the managers at the continued refusal of Congress to appropriate funds for the cause. He was sure that the Society had been organized merely as a pioneer in the work, and conscious of its inability to carry out its program without the support of Federal or State governments, or both. He realized that assistance had been denied it largely because it had been compelled to stand between two violent cross-fires of public criticism.

> According to one (that rash class which, without a due estimate of the fatal consequence, would forthwith issue a decree of general, immediate, and indiscriminate emancipation) it was a scheme of the slaveholder to perpetuate slavery. The other, (that class which believes slavery a blessing, and which trembles with aspen sensibility at the appearance of the most distant and ideal danger to the tenure by which that description of property is held,) declared it a contrivance to let loose on society all the slaves of the country. . . .

He believed that, hereafter, the population of the United States would duplicate itself not oftener than once in every

---

[77] Ibid., May 10, 1825; Jan. 24, 1828.
[78] Ibid., Mar. 4, 1825; Sept. 24, 1827.
[79] Ibid., Jan. 12, 1829; Sept. 24, 1829.

thirty-three years. If, during the next period of duplication, he said, "the capital of the African stock could be kept down, or stationary, whilst that of European origin should be left to an unobstructed increase, the result, at the end of the term, would be most propitious," and at the end of two terms, would leave the proportion of black to white approximately one to twenty. Now, he thought it practicable to transport the annual increase of the whole colored population, slave and free, estimated by him to be about 52,000. The total expense of sending this increase to Africa, each year, would be $1,040,000 and 65,000 tons of shipping. Is that, considering the magnitude of the object,

> beyond the ability of this country? . . . If I could only be instrumental in ridding of this foul blot [slavery] that revered State that gave me birth, or that of not less beloved State which kindly adopted me as her own, I would not exchange the proud satisfaction which I should enjoy, for the honor of all the triumphs ever decreed to the most successful conqueror.

Of the opponents of colonization he said:

> If they succeed, they must go back to the era of our liberty and independence, and muzzle the cannon which thunders its annual joyous return. They must revive the slave trade with all its train of atrocities. . . . They must arrest the career of South American deliverance from thraldom. They must blow out the moral lights around us, and extinguish that greatest torch of all which America presents to a benighted world, pointing the way to their rights, their liberties, and their happiness. . . . Then, and not till then, . . . can you perpetuate slavery, and repress all sympathies and all humane and benevolent efforts among freemen, in behalf of the unhappy portion of our race who are doomed to bondage.

Of the future of the Society he says, "I boldly and confidently anticipate success."[80]

The managers undoubtedly felt that, if the North was opposed to slavery, and if it regarded the presence of the free blacks as a source of weakness and of danger to the Union, and if the slaveholder was expected to offer his slaves their freedom, they ought to be able to hope confidently for liberal contributions from the Middle and New England States. But despite a rapidly growing sentiment favorable to the Society, despite active cooperation between

---

[80] *African Repository*, vol. ii, pp. 334-345.

the Secretary of the Navy and the Board of Managers, and despite the hopeful future that seemed to be opening upon Liberia, contributions from New England were distinctly disappointing.[81] Expeditions had to be delayed or omitted and negroes who desired passage had to be refused, although the Society did not give up hope of providing necessary funds, until it had appealed for aid, not only through the ordinary channels, but through the churches, State Legislatures, and Masonic Orders.[82] In 1829 the Managers publicly announced that the need for funds was "never so urgent as at present. Large drafts have come on us from the Colony, and it is all-important that our funds should be greatly increased, and that speedily."

If it be asked, why did not New England and why did not Congress grant to the Society the funds that it certainly needed, and without which it was unable to work most effectively, and the lack of which was the most important cause of the small number of emigrants transported to Liberia and a very important cause of the comparatively small number, not nearly so inconsiderable as is generally supposed, of slaves whose liberation it secured, the answer is not obvious. Perhaps the most satisfactory method of getting at the root of the matter will be to survey the progress of public sentiment, on the subject of colonization, from 1820 to 1830.

In 1818 the aims and efforts of the Society were approved by the General Assembly of the Presbyterian Church; also by the Society of Friends of Greensboro, North Carolina; by the Synod of Virginia; and by the General Association of Massachusetts.[83] Again in 1823, and again in 1826, the General Assembly of the Presbyterian Church reiterated its

---

[81] Origin, Constitution, and Proceedings of American Colonization Society, MS., Annual Report, 1825; Minutes of Board of Managers of American Colonization Society, MS., vol. i, pp. 358, 359, 369, 383, 462, 466, 468, 483.
[82] Minutes of Board of Managers of American Colonization Society, MS., vol. i, pp. 372, 374, 410, 428, 429, 430, 463, 504, 516, 561, 664, 665; African Repository, vol. v, p. 128.
[83] 27th Cong., 3d sess., H. Rept. no. 283, pp. 421-422, "Relating to African Colonization, etc.," MS.

approval of the work of the Society, as did the General Synod of the Dutch Reformed Church, and the Episcopal Convention of Virginia.[84] Before 1826 and again, between 1826 and 1830, the General Conference of the Methodist Church had approved the scheme; likewise, the Baptist General Convention.[85] In 1827 it was heartily endorsed by the Massachusetts and the Connecticut Conventions of Congregational Clergy, and by the Ohio Methodist District Conference.[86] But the talented and well known Samuel M. Worcester, college professor, senator, clergyman, and writer, called attention to a significant fact, in his correpondence with the Society:

> There is another difficulty, which you will find opposing your efforts in this Commonwealth. It arises from the state of religious parties. The Orthodox and Unitarians seldom unite in the promotion of a benevolent object. Now it happens, that almost all our leading political men are Unitarians. It is not to be disguised that the influence of these men is wanted to give a State Society Auxiliary to the A. C. S. a certain kind of popularity. At the same time the orthodox are the people on whom you are to rely for efficient and permanent patronage. Whether the two parties can be brought to act in concert in regard to Colonization, is I think a hard question.[87]

Prior to 1826 the legislatures of Virginia, Maryland, Tennessee, Ohio, New Jersey, Connecticut, Rhode Island and Indiana had officially approved the colonization project as carried on by the Society.[88] In 1827 Vermont and Kentucky expressed themselves, through their legislatures, favorable to the Society, as did Ohio, and Kentucky again, in 1828; Pennsylvania and Indiana, in 1829; Massachusetts, in 1831; and New York and Maryland, in 1832. The Delaware Legislature likewise gave its approval.[89] The reso-

---

[84] African Repository, vol. i, p. 125; Minutes of Board of Managers of American Colonization Society, MS., June 2, 1823; 27th Cong., 3d sess.., H. Rept. no. 283, pp. 421-422.
[85] African Repository, vol. i, pp. 343-344; Letters of American Colonization Society, MS., Martin Ruter to Gurley, Cincinnati, Ohio, June 27, 1828.
[86] African Repository, vol. iii, pp. 118-120.
[87] Letters of American Colonization Society, MS., Worcester, Amherst College, Nov. 16, 1829.
[88] African Repository, vol. i, pp. 343-344.
[89] 27th Cong., 3d sess., H. Rept. no. 283, pp. 926-936.

lution of the Massachusetts Legislature was in the following words: "That the Legislature of Massachusetts view with great interest the efforts made by the American Colonization Society in establishing an asylum on the Coast of Africa for the free people of color of the United States; and that, in the opinion of this Legislature, it is a subject eminently deserving the attention and aid of Congress, so far as shall be consistent with the powers of Congress, the rights of the several States of the Union, and the rights of the individuals who are the objects of those efforts." The Pennsylvania Legislature declared, "Their removal [that of the free people of color] from among us would not only be beneficial to them, but highly auspicious to the best interests of our country." The Indiana Legislature expressed "unqualified approbation."

As to public sentiment in the Middle and New England States, David Hale, of the New York Journal of Commerce, said: "So far as I have been able to understand public sentiment here, it is entirely (among evangelical Christians at least) in favor of the Society, and its objects are believed to be attainable. The principal thing to be established, I think, is a firm conviction that the affairs of the Society are always judiciously managed. It has been thought that there was in some instances a want of system and order."[90] One of the Society's agents in Vermont reported: "There is a very general impression in these States that we are coming up to the work about as fast as could be expected and that the Southern States are not doing their part."[91] Theodore Frelinghuysen wrote, of New Jersey: "Public feeling is against us—it regards the scheme as visionary—and nothing but an experiment conducted upon decided and liberal principles will correct the views of the great majority of our citizens."[92] Jared Sparks said: "The cause is one of great importance, and cannot be supported with too much zeal or force."[93] The editor of the Vermont Chronicle thought:

---
[90] Letters of American Colonization Society, MS., Sept. 7, 1826.
[91] Ibid., Myron Tracy to Gurley, Hartford, Conn., October 3, 1826.
[92] Ibid., Frelinghuysen, Newark, N. J., Feb. 3, 1827.
[93] Ibid., Sparks to Gurley, 1827.

"There is not, we believe, another benevolent enterprise on earth, so well calculated to secure the favorable opinion and enlist the hearty good will of all men, as is this, when its objects and bearings are fully understood."[94] The Connecticut society reported, in 1829: "Only one opinion is expressed among our citizens, and that opinion is unqualified approbation."[95]

From the South, particularly the lower South, reports were not so favorable. A South Carolinian wrote in 1827: "I am truly sorry I cannot procure more friends and aid to the Society. I am however determined to persevere, under the belief that opposition will give way to information. This however is the great difficulty. The press, in the State, is mostly against the Society. Things in its favor are uniformly excluded and things against it are spread abroad."[96] Rev. William Winans, a prominent Mississippi Methodist preacher and an agent of the Society, wrote: "I am persuaded that the efforts of an agent would be of vast importance: but the selection must be judicious."[97] Clergymen from South Carolina and Georgia reported much hostility to the Society in those States.[98]

Of sentiment in Ohio, one of the general agents of the Society, whose territory included that State, reported very favorably.[99] Another agent, reporting from the same State, said:

> Among the members, we number the Governor, Auditor and Treasurer of the State, Speaker of the Senate, a considerable number of Senators and Representatives, respectable and influential citizens. But sir, though the attempt will doubtless be triumphant, I frankly confess, that I have met strong opposition, resulting from ignorance of the nature and design of the A. C. Soc. The great, popular objection is, that it is a scheme of slaveholders, to strengthen the bonds of slavery, by the removal of the free blacks. You may say that I have the means, at once of refuting these ungenerous slan-

---
[94] African Repository, vol. iv, p. 142.
[95] Ibid., vol. v, p. 121.
[96] Letters of American Colonization Society, MS., H. McMellan, of South Carolina, Feb. 23, 1827.
[97] Ibid., Winans, Centreville, Miss., Feb. 27, 1827.
[99] Letters of American Colonization Society, MS., Canton, Ohio, B. O. Peers to Gurley, Nov. 1, 1826.

ders; but, sir, this is hard to accomplish, however ample the means, when men will neither hear nor read and are pertinaceously wedded to their errors. The cause however, gains ground very obviously and will achieve a general conquest. It is the cause of justice, of humanity, of God, and shall prevail.[100]

Few men in Virginia were more competent than W. M. Atkinson, of Petersburg, to give an accurate report of sentiment in that State. In 1827 he was greatly discouraged, for the success of the Society in its operations in the South. He said:

> To see a people to whom I am thus closely bound by ties of affection, differing from me, on any question so important and so interesting as this, would of itself be painful. But there is another and a more legitimate source of painful feeling. One of the strongest recommendations of the Colon. Soc. in my eyes, has always been the *indirect* but powerful influence which I thought it would exert on the very existence of that fell destroyer of the prosperity and the morals, of our land, slavery. I hoped it would do this by keeping the public mind fixed on the subject, and by showing the practicability of removing the unhappy race . . . to the land of their fathers, whilst it carefully avoided touching those points, which could not even be discussed without awakening the most unkind and bitter feelings. Hence I regarded every friend gained by the Society in the larger slaveholding States as equal to two friends in any other region. . . . Now I have seen with deep regret that the enemies of the Society in this part of Virginia, (and I fear it is the case throughout the Southeastern States,) are increasing in number and violence. . . . Do you desire to know the cause? So far as I can judge, (and I have used all the means in my power to learn the true reason,) it is the application *made last winter and it is supposed to be renewed next winter, to Congress for aid.* The people of this region, at least an overwhelming majority of them, believe that Congress have no power to grant that aid. I will not stop to ask whether their opinions are right or wrong. . . . It is sufficient that they do hold these opinions—and furthermore, if upon any topic they would watch with double jealously the movements of Congress, it is upon such as are in the most distant manner connected with our black population. . . . I feel constrained to express the opinion that if the Managers and the Society do persevere in making their application to Congress they do it at the cost of alienating almost all their friends in the Southern Atlantic States. Hence they must lose not only whatever pecuniary aid they have expected from this quarter, but they must abandon forever the hope, of operating on the public mind in the manner above hinted, so as ultimately to exert a powerful influence on the total voluntary abolition of slavery.[101]

Yet General John H. Cocke, a prominent figure in the colonization cause, wrote more hopefully of Virginia. He

---
[100] Ibid., Rev. M. Henkle, Columbus, Ohio, Jan. 4, 1827.
[101] Ibid., Atkinson to Gurley, Petersburg, Va., July 4, 1827.

thought the cause was gaining ground, although he thought that political agitation had done it injury in certain parts of the State.[102]

The fact is that it was a very difficult matter to keep the colonization movement entirely distinct from the discussions during political campaigns. This was true, not because Colonization leaders sought to work through the channels of political parties, but because Colonization was too meaty a bone, over which political aspirants could harangue, to be entirely ignored. In January, 1827, Latrobe wrote:

> Clay I see has been helping himself to a ride on our shoulders—but as he has no doubt been of service to us, I will not scrutinize too closely into his motives. . . . Weems [a Maryland Congressman, who insisted on favoring Colonization, in spite of his unpopularity and his inability to ride like a Clay] is an ass, aye, a very ass.[103]

Of the public men of Virginia who, in 1827, opposed the Society, William B. Giles stands out prominently. William Maxwell, prominent in Virginia as college president, legislator, and Colonizationist, wrote:

> I cannot tell you what you are to think of our Virginia Assembly, for I really don't know what to think of them myself. They certainly seem to hang back most shabbily in this great business of our Society. But the truth is, I suppose, they are many of them still wofully ignorant of the whole nature and progress of our engagement, and I have had some proof of it that would amuse and amaze and distress you all together.

But he thinks that at the next session of the legislature:

> We shall be able to obtain an act that will please you—Governor Giles notwithstanding.
> I should have liked hugely to have taken this political mountebank in hand, as you wish me to do; but have been restrained from meddling with him for two or three weighty reasons. In the first place his [policies] are such tissues of nonsense and paganism that they can do no harm, I think, except with incurables. 2ly, he is such a prince of hoaxers, and has such power of misleading the simple, and all who are willing enough to be duped by him, that I do not think it would be good policy to irritate [him into] more active hostility against our scheme if we can help it. . . . and lastly, I am more and more satisfied that it is our duty to pursue this great subject with the tone and spirit of the gospel in meekness instruct-

---

[102] Ibid., Cocke to Gurley, Fluvanna County, Va., July 7, 1827.
[103] Ibid., Latrobe to Gurley, Baltimore, Jan. 27, 1827.

ing them that oppose themselves if peradventure God will give them grace to the acknowledging of the truth. So I shall let him alone, for the present at least—and especially since he is become (by a fantastic revolution of the wheel of fortune) our Governor elect!— for which I am most heartily sorry of course.[104]

William M. Blackford, the most important Colonizationist living in Fredericksburg, Virginia, wrote, in 1828:

I cannot forbear congratulating you on the active hostility to our scheme of the miserable wretch now at the head of affairs in Virginia. The suicidal infelicity of his arguments is never dangerous to any cause but the one he supports. I know of several who have become friends simply because Giles is an enemy. Any scheme of benevolence within the level of his comprehension or approbation, would be received with suspicion—and *e converso* his denunciation received as highest praise and commendation.

I have reason to believe that a great change is about to take place in Virginia—she will I have no doubt become decidedly the advocate of colonization. The coming year (in which the question of convention will be settled) is big with her fate.

I cannot omit to state, as an evidence of the progress of our cause, that the announcement of our intention to have a public address excited no other feeling than that of approbation, whereas, had anyone attempted some 8 or 10 years ago to make a speech on the subject, he would in all probability have been mobbed.[105]

It was significant that the legislature refused to consider resolutions hostile to the Society, submitted by the Giles party.[106]

During the years 1827-1829, the Society was viewed, at least in some of the Northern and Western States, as a part of the Clay machine. Clay had supported it so consistently that it was brought into every contest in which he was a leading character. And even today, his support of it will be by many considered a support purely for party purposes. And yet Clay's support of colonization was the logical outcome of his whole political course, and any other position would have been inconsistent with the public policy of the man.

If now it be asked again, why did not Congress appropriate funds to carry on the work of the Society, the answer may be somewhat simplified by this discussion of the state

---

[104] Ibid., Wm. Maxwell to American Colonization Society, MS., Norfolk, Va., Feb. 24, 1827.
[105] Ibid., Blackford to Gurley, Feb. 26, 1828.
[106] Ibid., D. J. Burr, Richmond, Va., to Gurley, March 10, 1828.

of public opinion in the different sections of the Union. The congressmen from South Carolina and Georgia would not support such an appropriation because South Carolina and Georgia were wedded to the system of slavery, and looked upon the Society as a form of New England abolitionism.[107] The hostility was made all the more pronounced by the fact that the political acrobats made capital of the opposition and used it as a favorite issue. They associated it, in their campaigns, with the tariff and internal improvements. Charles Coatesworth Pinckney who, ten years before, had been one of the most liberal contributors in Charleston to the Society, was now in 1830 calling the scheme both cruel and absurd. The editor of the official journal of the Society sized up the situation in these two Southern States as follows:

> Voluntary emancipation begins to follow in the train of Colonization, and the advocates of perpetual slavery are indignant at witnessing in effectual operation, a scheme which permits better men than themselves to exercise without restraint the purest and the noblest feelings of our nature.[108]

The opposition in Virginia, and doubtless in North Carolina, was not from the enemies, but from the friends of colonization. Even William H. Fitzhugh had declared that, firm as he was in his advocacy of the colonization scheme, and favorable as he was to asking for an appropriation for it from Congress, he would actively oppose such an appropriation if he thought it was not in keeping with the spirit of the Constitution to grant it. It was undoubtedly the belief in Virginia and, at least to a considerable extent, in North Carolina, that such an appropriation was not warranted by that instrument. The view of Atkinson, a leader in the colonization movement in Virginia, has already been set forth. Rev. John Cooke of Hanover County, Virginia,

---

[107] Ibid., Rev. Wm. Meade, Feb. 21, 1827; S. K. Talmage to Gurley, Augusta, Ga., May 29, 1829; Rev. B. M. Palmer, Charleston, S. C., Aug. 4, 1830; African Repository, vol. i, pp. 161-164, 180-191; vol. ii, pp. 22-23; vol. iii, p. 172 ff.; vol. ix, pp. 228-229; vol. vi, p. 193 ff.; Minutes of Board of Managers of American Colonization Society, Apr. 25, 1831.

[108] African Repository, vol. vi, pp. 193-209.

had been requested to distribute memorials praying for aid for the Society from Congress. His reply was: "Even those who have reflected on the subject and are favorably disposed towards it, are generally opposed to Congress interfering. I am rather afraid that, with their present limited knowledge of the subject, their many mistaken views of it, and the morbid state of feeling that exists about here respecting the assumptions and implied powers of the General Government, it will be dangerous to offer the memorial for signatures."[109]

Probably the most powerful, or at least the most influential, argument that was made against federal appropriation in aid of the Society, was that contained in a report, presented by Senator L. W. Tazewell, of Virginia, in reply to many memorials asking that the Society receive federal aid. The burden of the argument was the unconstitutionality of appropriating federal revenue for the purposes proposed; the unconstitutionality of holding as a dependency a colony that, from its very position, could never become an integral part of the American system and that, therefore, was not contemplated by the fathers of the Constitution; the danger involved in any effort, on the part of the Federal Government "to intrude itself within the limits of the States, for the purpose of withdrawing from them, an important portion of their population"; and the probability that such a move would soon result in the Federal Government being called upon by the States to pay "something like an equivalent for the slaves, in order to obtain their manumission."[110]

Nor were these constitutional scruples confined to those who lived in Virginia. Gerrit Smith himself doubted the power of the Federal Government to make appropriations for this purpose.[111] And he said of the Van Buren men in the New York Legislature, that they were as full of consti-

---

[109] Letters of American Colonization Society, MS., Rev. John Cooke, Hanover County, Va., Feb. 9, 1827.
[110] African Repository, vol. iii, pp. 161–172.
[111] Letters of American Colonization Society, MS., G. Smith, Jan. 5, 1830.

tutional scruples as the South Carolinians were.[112] When, in 1835, Clay made another attempt in the Senate, Maxwell thought that if the Virginia Legislature failed to take action favorable to the Society, it would be because of the effort made in the federal body.[113] An agent of the Society wrote in 1837:

> I have just come from Mr. Ritchie's office, where I found him engaged in writing an article, calculated to do away in a great degree the good effect of what he has said before; and all drawn forth by the discussion in Congress. . . . It is a matter of universal regret among our friends here that Mr. Clay moved the subject in Congress.[114]

Among those Virginia colonizationists who did not agree with their colonization brethren of the strict construction school were John Marshall and James Madison. On this point they were both prepared to admit the power of the Federal Government to offer aid, it seems. But they thought the most unobjectionable scheme, and the one most likely to overcome popular prejudice, was that proposed by Rufus King in the United States Senate, February 18, 1825:

> That, as the portion of the existing funded debt of the United States, for the payment of which the public land of the United States is pledged, shall have been paid off, then and thenceforth, the whole of the public land of the United States, with the net proceeds of all future sales thereof, shall constitute and form a fund, which is hereby appropriated, and the faith of the United States is hereby pledged, that the said fund shall be inviolably applied to aid the emancipation of such slaves, within any of the United States, and to aid the removal of such slaves, and the removal of such free persons of color, in any of the said States, as by the laws of the States respectively may be allowed to be emancipated, or removed, to any territory or country without the limits of the United States of America.

Of this plan Marshall said:

> It is undoubtedly of great importance to retain the countenance and protection of the general government. . . . The power of the government to afford this aid is not, I believe, contested. I regret that its power to grant pecuniary aid is not equally free from question. On this subject I have thought and still think that the proposition made by Mr. King in the Senate is the most unexceptionable and the most effective that can be devised.[115]

---

[112] Ibid., Smith to Gurley, April 16, 1832.
[113] Ibid., Rev. C. W. Andrews to Gurley, Richmond, Feb. 1, 1836.
[114] Ibid., Rev. C. W. Andrews, Richmond, Feb. 1, 1837.
[115] Ibid., Marshall to Gurley, Richmond, Va., December 13, 1831.

Mr. Madison favored, likewise, the plan of Mr. King. "I am aware," he said, "of the constitutional obstacle which has presented itself; but if the general will be reconciled to an application of the territorial fund to the removal of the colored population, a grant to Congress of the necessary authority, would be carried with little delay through the forms of the constitution."[116]

The active and open opposition of the States of the Southeast, the constitutional objections that prevailed in other of the Southern States, and in some of the Middle States, and the various local opinions that predominated in portions of New England and the Western States, such objections, for instance, as the doubt of the practicability of the scheme; the belief that pervaded many localities that the Society's chief purpose was to increase the value of slaves; and the feeling, now becoming deeply rooted, that the remedy for slavery was immediate emancipation rather than settlement on the coast of Africa—these causes are sufficient to explain why the Society was unable to secure from Congress direct appropriations in aid of colonization.

And so the Society was forced to depend, at the time of its greatest promise, upon the contributions voluntarily sent in. The amount contributed from the year 1820 to the end of 1830 was $112,842.89. The amount of the expenditures during the same period was $106,367.72. The number of emigrants transported to Liberia was 1430. The total cost, per emigrant, including in this amount not only the transportation and subsistence expenses, but also salaries paid to officers of the Society both in the United States and Liberia, the support of public schools, buildings, presents to native kings, fortifications, expenses of court house and jail in the colony, expenses of opening roads, and founding settlements, was $74.38.[117] In spite of the criticism of the Abolitionists that the public was being imposed upon by men who used too large a part of the contributions in the payment of

---

[116] African Repository, vol. xiv, pp. 305-306.
[117] Minutes of Board of Managers of American Colonization Society, MS., Feb. 20, 1834.

office salaries, it is difficult to see how so much could have been done with the expenditure of so limited an amount.

The expeditions of emigrants between 1820 and the end of 1830 are as follows, with number of emigrants, by States:[118]

Year.	Vessel.	Va.	N.C.	S.C.	Ga.	Md.	D.C.	N.Y.	R.I.	Tenn.	Miss.	Pa.	Total.
1820	Elizabeth	9				2	2	41				32	86
1821	Nautilus	24				8							32
1822	Strong					26						10	36
1823	Oswego	17				24						19	60
1424	Cyrus	103											103
"	Fidelity					4						1	5
1825	Hunter	48	17				1						66
1826	Vine									32			33[a]
"	Indian Chief	18	118			12							148
1827	Doris	8	74			10							92
"	"	22				65		15					104[b]
"	Randolph				26								26
1828	Nautilus	7	145			12							164
1829	Harriet	132	1			17							150
1830	Liberia	45	1							10		1	58[c]
"	Montgomery	30	2		30	7	1						70
"	Carolinian	78	1	9	9		1				8		106
"	Valador	39	41										81[d]
Totals.	18	580	400	26	39	196	4	57	32	10	8	63	1,420

[a] One also from Massachusetts.
[b] Two from Delaware.
[c] One from Connecticut.
[d] One from Alabama.

Prior to 1827 the emigrants transported were nearly all free negroes; after that time, many of them were recently emancipated slaves and, in very many cases, slaves who had been emancipated or manumitted for the express purpose of removal and who would not have been given their liberty had it not been for the Colonization Society.[119]

If the Society had had the financial support of the federal

---

[118] African Repository, vol. x, p. 292. It will be noted that the total number of emigrants here given is 1420, whereas the number reported by the Board is 1430. The cause of the discrepancy is not apparent.
[119] Lugenbeel.

government, there is no doubt that its operations would have been greatly enlarged and that the number of slaves liberated would have reached far into the thousands. At this time, as at every other time, up to the proclamation of emancipation, the active directors of the Society, the agents, the colonial agents and governors, and the active members in every part of the Union were opponents of slavery, and looked forward, some of them, to its comparatively speedy, and by far the larger number of them, to its ultimate, abolition. Fearing the increase of the free negro population, the legislatures had passed laws restricting very materially the right to emancipate slaves. Indeed, emancipation, without the removal from the State of those emancipated, was made a violation of the law. And yet, the emancipations went on in the Southern tier of the Middle Atlantic States, and there is no telling how far it would have gone had the Society's efforts not been circumscribed by the limitation of its resources. Monroe told Elliott Cresson that he believed the Society could secure the emancipation of ten thousand slaves in the single State of Virginia if it would send them to Liberia. Undoubtedly the Society was favorably known in every part of the Union in 1829, although its friends were comparatively few in Georgia and South Carolina.

It was just at this hour of triumph and of promise that there arose, in the North and West, the most virulent, needless, and unscrupulous opposition the Society was ever called on to face. And this was but one of several causes of the difficulties it had to encounter between 1831 and 1839. The Abolition offensive, the secession of auxiliary societies, financial difficulties, distress in the colony, and a reorganization of the Society—these are the topics of real importance that ought to be discussed, in a study of its operations.

Opposition from the Garrisonians was like a bolt from the blue. Garrison himself began life a friend of the Society. Arthur Tappan, James G. Birney, who was for months one of its active agents, Gerrit Smith, who gave thousands of dollars to the Society before the time of his defection—all these were Colonizationists before they were Abolitionists. Garrison had addressed a Boston audience in a speech favoring colonization; it was while he was working for the Society, not after he went over to the Garrisonians, that Birney decided to give up his slaves; Gerrit Smith, up to 1835, thought that the Society was not only not pro-slavery, but that it stressed emancipation too consistently to retain the active cooperation of the South. And when these men ceased to be Colonizationists, they did so, not because they had discovered some ulterior and hidden, or dishonorable motive. The swan songs of Birney and Smith, each requiring a considerable part of the issue of the Liberator in which it appeared, were very frank disavowals of the discovery of such motives. The opprobrium and the charges were evolutions, largely of Garrison's mind. The General Assembly of the Presbyterian Church in 1830, with but four dissenting votes recommended the taking of Fourth of July collections for the objects of the Society.[120] John A. Dix of New York wrote, in the same year: "The current of opinion is with the Institution; and it will be borne on to the fulfilment of its object."[121] Thomas Clarkson, of England, wrote:

> For myself I am free to confess, that of all the things that have been going on in our favor since 1787, when the abolition of the slave trade was first seriously proposed; that which is now going on in the United States is the most important. It surpasses everything which has yet occurred. No sooner had your Colony been established on Cape Mesurado, than there appeared to be a disposition among the owners of slaves in the U. S. to give them freedom voluntarily without compensation and to allow them to be sent to the land of their ancestors. To me this is truly astonishing.[122]

Wilberforce wrote: "You have gladdened my heart by convincing me, that sanguine as had been my hopes of the happy effects to be produced by your Institution, all my anticipations are scanty and cold compared with the reality."[123]

---

[120] African Repository, vol. vi, p. 91.
[121] Ibid., vol. vi, pp. 163-169.
[122] Letters of American Colonization Society, MS., London, Oct. 6, 1831. E. Cresson to Gurley.
[123] Ibid., Cresson to Gurley, Nov. 29, 1831.

The whole State of Virginia was deeply stirred by the Southampton Insurrection, as was also at least one neighboring State, Maryland, and the cause was greatly revived.[124] In the midst of Garrison's tirades, George Bancroft and Governor Levi Lincoln, of Massachusetts, were both friends of the Society.[125] An agent of the Society, traveling by a circuitous route from New York to Maine, had conversed with editors, clergymen, and others acquainted with public sentiment. He reported that he had talked with from ninety to one hundred editors. Of these, only four expressed hostility to the Society, one of the four being the editor of the Liberator. More than nine-tenths of these editors expressed friendly feeling towards the Society. He had talked with more than three hundred clergymen, only three of whom expressed hostility to it. He quoted very favorable resolutions passed by the Methodist District Conference of Penobscot District, of the Baptist Convention of Maine, and of the Baptist Convention of Massachusetts.[126] R. H. Toler, editor of the Lynchburg Virginian, wrote: "Among the people of this section of country, there is very little opposition felt or manifested to the scheme of African Colonization. Men, of all creeds in politics and of all sects in religion, cooperate in advancing its interests."[127] Of the Valley of Virginia, William C. Matthews wrote: "As far as I know, throughout all this valley, there is an almost universal feeling in favor of your American Colonization Society."[128]

And yet Gurley, the Society's secretary, writing from Richmond, Virginia, where he had gone during the meeting of the legislature, wrote to a member of the Board of

---

[124] Ibid., Atkinson to Gurley, Petersburg, Va., Sept. 10, 1831; Benjamin Brand to Gurley, Richmond, Va., Oct. 5, 1831; Brand to Gurley, Richmond, Va., Oct. 8, 1831; Gen. John H. Cocke, Sr., to Gurley, Steamboat on Chester Ricer, Oct. 7, 1831; D. J. Burr, Richmond, Va., Oct. 17, 1831; Wm. Maxwell, Nov. 30, 1831.
[125] African Repository, vol. ix, p. 24.
[126] Letters of American Colonization Society, MS., Wm. L. Stone, N. Y., Apr. 19, 1833.
[127] Ibid., Toler to Gurley, Lynchburg, Va., Aug. 22, 1833.
[128] Ibid., W. C. Matthews, Martinsburg, Va., Aug. 13, 1833.

Managers of the Society: "We can account for the course of the Legislature only by supposing either that *professions* of regard for colonization have been insincere—that abolitionism has alienated the members from colonization—or that they have changed their principles and go for perpetual slavery—something may be owing to each of these supposed facts."[129] To him who is tolerably acquainted with Virginia history, the statement of Toler and that of Gurley are full of significance. An extract from a letter of William H. Fitzhugh to the Society in 1829 will throw much light on these statements. Fitzhugh was at that time a member of the Virginia legislature.

> We have no chance to do anything for the Col. Soc. this winter, nor indeed ever again, till our representation [the representation of Eastern and Western Virginia, in the Legislature] is equalized. The present is the ablest legislature I have ever seen assembled here; and it is also completely drilled for party purposes. On the subject of the Col. Soc. we can carry with us the representatives of a majority of the people; but the lower country, by its excess of representation, can control all our movements. We have just concluded one of the most protracted as well as able debates I have ever heard, on the subject of South Carolina opposition to the tariff . . . one of the majority acknowledged, in debate, his belief that these were the last resolutions in favor of State rights that would ever be passed. My own opinion is that the effect of the convention will be to revolutionize the politics of Virginia entirely—"a consummation most devoutly to be wished."[130]

From these statements and from very many others that might be added, it is evident that the legislature of Virginia did not represent the public opinion of the entire State, but only of the Eastern section of the State. If, as the Abolitionists were just at this time charging, the Colonization Society was an invention of slaveholders and, of course primarily Virginia slaveholders, to increase the value of their slaves, eastern Virginia sentiment would have been more favorable than western Virginia sentiment towards the Colonization Society. Western Virginia was certainly in no mood to be foremost in favoring an organization gotten up by the slave owners of the eastern counties

---

[129] Ibid., Gurley to Joseph Gales, Richmond, Va., March 16, 1837.
[130] Ibid., Fitzhugh to Gurley, Richmond, Feb. 22, 1829.

94   THE AMERICAN COLONIZATION SOCIETY

for their own pecuniary profit. The opposition between these two sections was active and the hostility acute,[131] and particularly in the attitude each took towards the question of slavery. The fact that it was the legislature that held back and the western part of the State that urged support of the Society, is very important evidence that Garrison's accusations were baseless.

In the West Clay, of Kentucky, and Elisha Whittlesey, were probably the most influential of all the Colonizationists. In the Southwest, there was zealous support of the Society. Hundreds of slaves were given over to it for transportation to the Colony. The Presbytery of Mississippi, in 1833, passed resolutions expressing "unabated confidence in the principles and plans of the American Colonization Society . . . and once more recommend it cordially to their congregations."[132] But in South Carolina and Georgia, opposition was still pronounced.[133] Y. S. Grimke wrote from Charleston: "Let me advise for your sakes and for the sake of the Union, that until this crisis be past you do not send an agent at all, not even to explain your views to the colored people,—so as to encourage them to emigrate."

It was just at this time, when sentiment was very favorable to the Colonization scheme, and when the charges made by Garrison and his coadjutors were utterly out of place and uncalled for, that the storm of that radical leader broke upon the Society. An account of that opposition will receive more attention hereafter. It is enough, here, to say that Secretary Gurley, writing from New York in 1834 declared: "The Abolitionists are certainly gaining ground, and will carry a large portion of the North with them unless we can find agents of zeal and talent to defend the cause in this part of the country."[134] In 1835 he thought there were

---

[131] C. H. Ambler, Sectionalism in Virginia, passim.
[132] Letters of American Colonization Society, MS., Pine Grove, Miss., Feb. 23, 1834.
[133] Ibid., J. Corning to Gurley, Charleston, S. C., Feb. 10, 1831; Grimke to Gurley, Charleston, S. C., May 17, 1831; African Repository, vol. xiii, pp. 201-206.
[134] Letters of American Colonization Society, MS., Gurley to Gales, N. Y., Apr. 8, 1834.

nearly a dozen weekly newspapers, besides many other periodicals, "in great part devoted to the work of destroying the influence of this Society."[135] And the influence that resulted from the Abolition crusade was great and immediate, as will appear from a letter from the New England philanthropist, Thomas H. Gallaudet: "But *in confidence,* I must tell you, that the Col. cause must recede in its influence in New England, unless it is made to operate, (and *avowedly so by* those who advocate it here), as one of the means for the abolition of slavery."[136] At a later time the Society regained some of the ground it had lost in New England; but for approximately ten years it was almost impotent in that section.

Another difficulty was the secession of auxiliary societies. During the decade from 1830 to 1840, the Maryland, Pennsylvania, New York, Mississippi, and Louisiana societies adopted policies either partially or entirely independent of the parent organization. The Maryland Society was the first to assume an independent course, and its independence was practically complete. It established a settlement of its own at Cape Palmas, miles south of the older settlements; the Pennsylvania and New York societies established a settlement at Bassa Cove, between Monrovia and Cape Palmas; the Mississippi and Louisiana societies established a settlemet at Sinou. Eventually all these societies were restored to their auxiliary relation; but during the period of their independent action they were a source of weakness to the parent Society. With all their good wishes at the parting, they invariably competed with the activities of the older organization. Not only so; but they almost nullified the efforts of the Society to raise funds in territory over which they claimed jurisdiction. They also sent out their own expeditions and controlled their own policies, which sometimes fell short of the requirements of wisdom.

For instance, the Pennsylvania society, mindful of the

---
[135] Ibid., Gurley, Washington, D. C., Mar. 23, 1835.
[136] Ibid., Gallaudet to Gurley, Hartford, Conn., July 5, 1838.

origin of the Keystone colony, established a settlement on peace principles, forbidding the possession or use of arms therein. The result was that the Africans made an attack which proved so disastrous that the surviving settlers had to be taken to a protected settlement. Furthermore, so long as the parent Society was able to hold together the auxiliaries, it was able to unify the aims and feelings of organizations widely separated, in distance and also in the environment of opinion in which they lived. Numerous societies under a common head would entertain, in general, a common opinion and have common aims. Hardly had the Maryland Society seceded before its policy began to differ from that of the American Colonization Society. And after the withdrawal, for many, though not all, purposes, of the Pennsylvania and New York Societies, they immediately began to approximate more and more closely the moderate Abolitionists of the North. Separate action on the part of these organizations was a severe blow to the parent society, and for years a large part of its energy was directed to the restoration of auxiliary relations.

The movement for separate action, on the part of the Maryland Society began, it seems, early in 1831. Various causes have been given for the action that was then taken. Elliot Cresson, whose zeal for Colonization was equaled only by his exaggerated views of the business inefficiency of the Board of Managers of the parent Society, declared that the reason back of Maryland's defection was her distrust of the Board's ability to handle properly the funds— not the dishonesty but the business incompetency of it.[137] And it is certainly true that after repeated meetings in an attempt to adjust satisfactorily the differences that had arisen, for the Board of Managers saw in Maryland's action the setting of a precedent that was likely to rise to plague them, the point upon which negotiations were finally broken off was in the discussion upon the disposition of funds re-

---

[137] Ibid., Cresson, Philadelphia, Pa., Apr. 12, 1831.

ceived into the Maryland treasury.[138] The position of the Maryland Society was stated by J. H. B. Latrobe: "We agree to make regular returns of our receipts and expenditures to you and to bear the expences of our colonists in Africa; but not a voice was heard in favor of paying or placing to your credit one penny of our funds gross or surplus."[139] By a committee of the Maryland Society it was urged that the State could never be rid of the incubus of the free negro population until a State organization, prepared to take a more aggressive part in the accomplishment of its purpose than a mere auxiliary to a national organization could take, was put into operation. The situation of the State and her peculiar problem made necessary, they said, a separate organization.[140] What these peculiar conditions were was set forth as follows, by Latrobe, in a private letter to Gurley in 1834.

To prove Colonization, two things had to be established. The first, that colonies of colored people, capable of self-defence, self support, and self government could be founded on the coast of Africa. Second, that by means of these colonies, slave-holding States could be made free States. The first was proved by you. *The second remains to be proved.* Upon proof of the second now hangs the whole system. The first step to be taken to prove it, is to get a slave-holding State to determine to make the experiment. This, which, three years ago, was hardly within the range of any reasonable probability, has been done; and Maryland is now striving to establish the second branch of the proposition, and to prove that, by means of colonies on the coast of Africa, a slaveholding State may be made a free State.

Now, it appears to the Board of Managers, that the success of Maryland will have such all powerful effect upon Virginia, Kentucky, Tennessee, and North Carolina, that the whole influence of the friends of colonization, everywhere, ought to be devoted to her aid. If colonization, they think, were to stand still, in every other State, until Maryland succeeded in her undertaking, yet provided she did succeed, no mischief would be done, but, on the contrary, all the assistance that had been given her would be amply compensated by the then omnipotent influence of her example.[141]

---

[138] Minutes of Board of Managers of American Colonization Society, MS., Apr. 4, 1831.
[139] Letters to American Colonization Society, MS., Latrobe to Gurley, Baltimore, Md., Mar. 30, 1831.
[140] Minutes of Board of Managers of American Colonization Society, MS., Apr. 4, 1831.
[141] Letters of American Colonization Society, MS., Baltimore, Md., Latrobe to Gurley, December 29, 1834.

The Board of Managers made a very earnest attempt to dissuade the Maryland Society from independent action. They called attention to the fact that the views of Colonizationists in different parts of the country had already begun to vary widely, and "the friends of the cause are beginning to operate in their several ways, a multiplicity of interests will engender collision of views and of vital interests. Hence it becomes and continues of paramount importance that some salutary control should be concentrated in the Parent Society."[142] In a continuation of the policy of separate action the parent society would be rendered utterly impotent, for not only would each of the Southern States pursuing that policy, act upon its own local views, but the Northern States Societies, seeing that there was no central control and no uniformity of policy, would discontinue their support. And yet, with the most forceful protest it could make, the parent society saw that there was no means of compelling the Maryland Society to continue its auxiliary relation, and its attitude was that of a willingness to surrender every point at issue, except the vital one of dependence. Even this the Maryland Society compelled it to give up also; and from 1833 the active operations of the two societies were entirely separate, the Cape Palmas settlement and territory comprising about one thousand square miles in the southern part of Liberia. Here Maryland sent her emigrants and established them under laws which entirely excluded ardent spirits from the settlement.[143] Within the next five years the Maryland Society sent out nine expeditions.[144]

In November, 1833, requests came from the Philadelphia and New York societies for permission to act with a considerable degree of independence. They desired to establish jointly in Liberia settlers taken out and governed, in Africa, almost entirely by themselves. The shadow, but

---
[142] Minutes of Board of Managers of American Colonization Society, MS., April 4, 1831.
[143] African Repository, vol. xvii, pp. 184-186.
[144] Ibid., vol. xiv, p. 33 ff.

not the substance, of the auxiliary relation was to continue as heretofore. Undoubtedly the most energetic and persistent agitator for this independent relation was the Philadelphian, Elliot Cresson, one of the most zealous partizans and certainly the most belligerent Friend the Society ever had. His reasons for desiring independence, he said, were: (1) the inefficient management of the parent Board of Managers, and (2) the unsatisfactory colonial governor recently appointed and sent out.[145] Also, there is no doubt that Cresson was anxious for the establishment, upon Quaker principles, of a settlement whose name should be Penn, or Benezet. Other reasons doubtless were, the comparative inactivity of the parent Society in sending out emigrants during 1833, arising from a want of funds; also the delivery of several speeches at the annual meeting, which did not meet with the entire approval of the New York or Philadelphia delegates. Also, there is no doubt that the charge of Cresson against the colonial governor or agent was general in the North Middle States.[146]

Gurley wrote from Philadelphia, where he went in 1835, in an effort to reconcile the differences between the Philadelphia and New York Societies, on the one hand, and the parent society, on the other, suggesting that the demand for independent action had arisen from (1) "the general sentiment of the friends of colonization at the North demanding that colonization societies should be *avowedly* and *decidedly* hostile to slavery," and (2) "a distrust in the management of the Board at Washington utterly destructive to its influence as the exclusive director of the funds."[147] Indeed, by 1834, there was excited in the Northern colonization societies a strong, and almost uncontrollable, tendency toward aggressive action on the subject of slavery,[148] and the danger undoubtedly was, not that the Society would tend to

---
[145] Letters of American Colonization Society, MS., Cresson, Philadelphia, Nov. 20, 1833.
[146] Ibid., Confidential, Gurley, Philadelphia, Apr. 1, 1834.
[147] Ibid., Gurley to Board of Managers, Philadelphia, May 1, 1835.
[148] Ibid., Gurley to Fendall, New York, May 31, 1834.

perpetuate slavery, but that it was rushing into such radical action that it would lose once and forever the cooperation of the slaveholding border States. And yet, it was just at this time that The Liberator was spreading throughout New England the "facts" about the Society, that it was a device of the slaveholders to rivet the chains of their slaves! The truth is that The Liberator lived on sectionalism; the Colonization Society would have been killed by it.

The effort of Gurley in this crisis was to inject, by cooperation, the anti-slavery spirit of the North into the South and bring about, by peaceable means, the gradual abolition of slavery. This danger of a division among the societies, so decided as to result, in all likelihood, in a separate organization of the northern group of the Middle and the New England States, and the resultant alienation of the South from the whole movement, was foreseen and dreaded by the Board of Managers. "As the population to be especially benefitted by this Society mostly reside at the South, . . ., it is of extreme importance, that the people of the North should remain united with those of the South, in the plans and measures that may be devised and executed for their good."[149] But it was again as it had been in the case of the Maryland Society. The parent society could argue and urge but it could not force the Philadelphia and New York Societies to continue their former relations. As Gurley wrote: "If we cannot have things as we would, we must do the best we can." The result was a compromise, but a compromise in which the associated societies got practically all that they asked for. In July, 1834, preparations were being made to send to their colony at Bassa Cove one hundred slaves liberated by Dr. Hawes, of Virginia. The parent board commented: "it now presents the community with the spectacle of more than one hundred freemen, who, but for it, would still have been slaves. And one hundred more are waiting merely till the parent board, or its auxil-

---

[149] Minutes of Board of Managers of American Colonization Society, MS., July 3, 1834.

iaries, possess the means to place them as freemen in the same company."[150]

As Cresson had been the guiding spirit in the restlessness of the Northern societies in their relations with the parent body, so, it seems, Robert S. Finley, a son of the Rev. Robert Finley, who had a leading part in the organization of the Society, was stirring up the Southwest. Of the two men Gurley wrote: "Finley and Cresson both, are excentric and erratic, but will not fail to stir the elements in their course." And if he said of Cresson, "I have just seen Mr. Cresson and heard only complaints from him for three hours," he could have said the same thing in reference to the directness, if not the duration, of Mr. Finley's remarks. There is some probability that the desire of the Louisiana and Mississippi societies for independent action, resulted more directly from the efforts of Mr. Finley, but also more or less remotely from the encouragement they received from both Latrobe and Cresson.[151] The relations between the Mississippi and Louisiana Societies, after they withdrew from the status of purely auxiliary societies, were still far from independent, and were of comparatively short duration.

So far was the American Colonization Society from being the creature of, and under the dominance of, the Maryland and Virginia slaveholder, we have seen that Maryland established an altogether distinct settlement; and in 1838 the Virginia Society was on the verge of following the example of her sister State. At the annual meeting of that year a motion, made by the Attorney-General of the State, Sidney S. Baxter, to recommend to the Board of Managers the establishment of an independent colony in Liberia, was carried, though the Board of Managers did not act favorably upon the recommendation.[152]

A third difficulty that the Society had to face during this

---
[150] Ibid., July 3, 1834.
[151] Letters of American Colonization Society, MS., Gurley to Gales, Natchez, Miss., May 9, 1836; Gurley to Fendall, May 11, 1836; May 16, 1836; June 3, 1836.
[152] African Repository, vol. xiv, p. 120.

eventful decade was the financial embarrassment in which it found itself. There was hardly a time, before the Civil War, when the Society's opportunities were not limited by its means. But it usually managed to keep its head above water by refusing to allow its expenditures to exceed its revenue. In 1834 the treasury was empty and thousands of dollars were due, and there was nothing with which to pay. The receipts for the three years, 1831, 1832, and 1833 were $105,606.69; the expenditures, $115,349.91, leaving a deficit for those years of nearly $10,000.00. The number of emigrants transported during the same period was 1339.[153] The receipts, which had never been as much as $20,000.00 prior to 1830, were $26,583.51 that year; and by 1834, they had mounted to $51,662.95. But in 1838 they were only $11,597.[154] Of its receipts in 1835, $4079.95 had been secured as donations; in 1838, the donations amounted to only $2,438.73.[155] The hard times of 1837 doubtless had much to do with the decreasing revenue of the Society during the last years of the decade.

And this was not all. The ruinous practice of purchasing provisions in Liberia on credit, and paying for them by writing drafts on the Board of Managers; the very unsatisfactory and loose condition in which the accounts were kept; the accumulation of accounts, and hence debts with the Liberian merchants, of which the Managers were ignorant; and the want of care and economy in Liberia were among the causes of a debt which the Board estimated, in 1834, to be between $45,000 and $50,000, and which was later estimated to be some ten to twenty thousand dollars in excess of that amount.[156]

How are we to explain this debt? Of the several con-

[153] Minutes of Board of Managers of American Colonization Society, MS., Feb. 20, 1834.
[154] Ibid., Feb. 20, 1834; African Repository, vol. xii, p. 28; vol. xv, p. 18.
[155] African Repository, vol. xii, p. 28; vol. xv, p. 18.
[156] Minutes of Board of Managers of American Colonization Society, MS., Feb. 20, 1834; Letters of American Colonization Society, MS., Wilkeson to John Ker, July 25, 1830, no. 680.

tributing causes, the most important, in all probability, were the hard times of the decade and the absence of men of business ability and experience on the Board of Managers. There has been found no evidence whatever that any of these men were guilty of personal profit. Even The Liberator, which exulted in the debt, could make good no charge of dishonesty against the managers. But it was a wise warning that Cresson, himself a successful business man, gave, as early as 1831, when he said: "Your Board are so terribly afraid of DEBT, that to save incurring $1000 *now,* they subject themselves to two alternatives—starving the emigrants, or being drawn on for $5000 [bye] and bye."[157]

Provisions should have been purchased in the United States, where they could be purchased for a reasonable sum, and the Board should have kept itself regularly informed of the amount of the drafts it would be called upon to pay, if, indeed, it allowed the drawing of drafts without its own consent. It should have refused to pay drafts for which properly signed vouchers did not appear. These things it failed to do and, beginning about 1832, its financial difficulties began to grow more and more serious. By 1833 its drafts were being protested and soon its credit was destroyed.[158] It was too late to correct the mischief already done, but the Managers made an effort to introduce a more businesslike system for the future. A salaried treasurer was appointed, and he was to be at all times strictly accountable to the Board.[159]

At the annual meeting of the Society in 1833, its Managers were called upon to submit a "full and detailed statement" of the origin, rise, and present condition of the debt. Its reply was a very frank statement of the facts above set

---

[157] Letters of American Colonization Society, MS., Cresson to Gurley, Philadelphia, Apr. 12, 1831.
[158] Ibid., Gurley to Fendall, New York, June 19, 1833; T. W. Blight and Gerard, Philadelphia, June 19, 1833.
[159] Minutes of Board of Managers of American Colonization Society, MS., Aug. 12, 1833.

forth. The opportunities were so great in 1832, it was stated, and the tendency of the Society had been so evidently to bring about the suppression of the slave trade, the enlightenment and civilizing of Africa, the removal of the "positive impediments to the free exercise of the right to emancipate slaves," and to transport to a land where he could be not only physically but also mentally and spiritually free, the "free" man of the United States, that the Managers had been led to undertake too much, and with too little means or opportunity for supervision. To correct the trouble, it was proposed (1) to enlarge the powers of the colonial council, so that the colonists might select their own officers, make their own laws, and bear the expense of their own government; (2) to offer stock on a loan of $50,000 and provide a sinking fund to relieve them from their present embarrassment.[160]

Early in 1834 Dr. Mechlin, the colonial agent, resigned.[161] Whether true or false, there had been reports that in the colony he had been guilty of profligacy.[162] And the Managers subsequently reported on his agency with anything but praise. Many of the items in his report were left unexplained. Since 1830 over 1800 gallons of brandy, whiskey, and rum had been purchased in the colony, most of it, they believed, by Mechlin himself, and used in the trade with the natives. Against this practice the Board entered a solemn protest.[163] Whatever blame for the very poor state of the Society's finances is placed upon the Board of Managers, and it would do violence to the truth to try to relieve them of a considerable responsibility for it, that blame must be shared also by the colonial agent, for his administration was exceedingly unbusinesslike. The Springfield Republican probably named the chief causes of the financial difficulty:

---

[160] Ibid., Feb. 20, 1834.
[161] Ibid., Mar. 6, 1834.
[162] Letters of American Colonization Society, MS., Confidential, Gurley to Gales, Philadelphia, April 1, 1834.
[163] Minutes of Board of Managers of American Colonization Society, MS., July 24, 1834.

(1) the Liberian merchants, in charging exorbitant profits upon stores furnished the colonists, and to an amount far beyond the expectation of the Managers, (2) the large emigration of colonists in 1832, when the Society was already beginning to be in debt, (3) the want of practical, businesslike management and supervision on the part of the Managers.[164]

As a part of the Board's policy of retrenchment to rid it of the debt was the reduction in number of expeditions of emigrants to the colony. But this step was opposed by the Society's Northern friends, who thought that under no circumstances should economy follow that channel. The result was that some refused to give, so long as emigrants were refused transportation, and that which the Board had supposed would result in a saving really resulted in cutting off a portion of its revenue. In the annual meeting of 1835, the New York delegation made it very plain that they were dissatisfied with the business administration of the Managers.[165] And yet the funds of the parent Board were being still further reduced by the fact that the New York and Pennsylvania Societies, in their comparative independence, were collecting funds in the Kentucky and Tennessee country. It was this that called forth the following remonstrance from the Board:

If, in the opinion of auxiliary societies . . . the Parent Board, after a toilsome, gratuitous, and measurably successful service of eighteen years resulting in the establishment of a Christian Republic on a heathen shore, can now be dispensed with advantageously to the cause for which it has made such heavy personal sacrifices, and encountered so many obstacles, it would willingly retire from its trust . . . ; but . . . if the continuance of the Parent Society be desirable, its efficiency ought to be unimpaired; and . . . in the deliberate judgment of this Board, the separate, independent action of auxiliary societies must inevitably lessen the resources of the Parent Institution, and its importance in the public eye; . . . and finally make the system itself a victim to multiplied objects and disconnected operations.[166]

From this date until the reorganization of the Society in

---
[164] Springfield Republican, May 17, 1834.
[165] African Repository, vol. xi, pp. 44–45.
[166] Minutes of Board of Managers of American Colonization Society, MS., May 12, 1836.

1839, the relations between the parent Society and the associated Pennsylvania and New York Societies were peculiarly exasperating to the parent Board. Extraordinary bills were presented to it by those societies, on the one hand; and on the other, those societies which had, at the time of the agreement on the independent relations that the two societies should enjoy, pledged to pay over to the parent treasury annually a per cent of their receipts, failed to meet their obligations to the parent Board.[167] The result of the disagreement was a request by the Pennsylvania Society for the reorganization of the Society.[168] The meeting that resulted made proposals which were very similar to the changes actually made at the annual meeting, in 1839.

The unusually small revenue of the Society in 1838 is to be accounted for not only by the circumstances to which reference has been made, but also to the great scarcity of money after the panic of 1837. The first speech Clay made, as President of the Society, January, 1836—the preceding presidents of the Society having been, with the dates of their election: Judge Bushrod Washington, Jan. 1st, 1817; Charles Carroll of Carrollton, Jan. 18th, 1830; James Madison, Jan. 20th, 1833—set forth clearly the fact that the Society had not yet given up hope of aid from the Federal Government, and that a further application might be expected in the time of the Society's need.[169]

But the most interesting effort to bolster up the financial affairs of the Society was an appeal to the people of the United States, signed by sixty-six leading men of the country, and resulting from a meeting held in May, 1838. Among the signers were C. F. Mercer; Governor Levi Lincoln of Massachusetts; John H. Prentiss, the editor; Samuel Wilkeson, New York pioneer and one of the founders of Buffalo; Charles C. Strattan, later governor of New Jersey; Ex-Governor Samuel L. Southard, who was at one

---

[167] Ibid., Apr. 6, 1837; Sept. 28, 1837; Dec. 27, 1837; June 15, 1838; Oct. 16, 1838.
[168] Ibid., 1838, passim.
[169] African Repository, vol. xiv, pp. 17-18; vol. xix, p. 369.

time Secretary of the Navy, and served in many important offices, State and Federal; James Murry Mason, author of the Fugitive Slave Law of 1850; William C. Rives, United States Senator and Minister to France; William Maxwell, college president, editor, lawyer, and member of the legislature; Henry Clay, John Pope, of Kentucky, a president pro tempore of the United States Senate; Governor and Congressman John Chambers, of Kentucky; John J. Crittenden, twice attorney-general and a United States Senator; Elisha Whittlesey of Ohio, and Albert S. White, United States Senator and railroad president. Of the sixty-six signers, thirty-five were from the States north of Virginia, including two from the District of Columbia, and excluding Maryland; twenty-three were from the States, Kentucky, Tennessee, Ohio, and Indiana; and eight were from Virginia, North Carolina, and Louisiana.[170]

A fourth difficulty that the Society had to face was the condition of affairs in Liberia. Incompetence in the colony was not unconnected with incompetence in the Board. If the Board had provided sufficient supplies and sent them with the emigrants, much of the debt and much of the dissatisfaction in Liberia would never have existed. In June, 1830, Mechlin, colonial agent, was in the United States and reported on conditions in the colony. At that time, he urged the Board to make its own purchases of provisions and send them out with the colonists. He warned them that goods purchased of colonial merchants and paid for by drafts on the Society would be at an advance of from one hundred to two hundred per cent over the cost of the same goods in this country. Agricultural implements were needed; also building tools and nails.[171] Three years later he wrote from Liberia repeating his request. Each vessel of immigrants should bring also provisions for their subsistence for six months.

[170] Ibid., vol. xiv, pp. 130–135.
[171] Letters of American Colonization Society, MS., Mechlin to Gurley, Washington, June, 1830.

The means at the disposal of the Board will thus be economized, and the necessity of such heavy drafts from this quarter be obviated, and a fruitful source of murmuring and dissatisfaction be removed. . . . The emigrants pr. Brig Roanoke were landed without one ounce of provisions or other supplies, in consequence of which I have been obliged to purchase of Capt. Hatch.

The arrival of the large number of emigrants sent out in 1832, seven hundred and ninety, two hundred and forty-seven of whom were manumitted slaves,[172] caused the agent much embarrassment on account of inadequate provision for receiving them.[173] Some of the expeditions contained intelligent and industrious negroes, but these were, as a class, free negroes. Mechlin remarked:

Had we for twelve or eighteen months past received 300 or 400 people of this description instead of the shoals of emancipated slaves who have been landed on our shores, the colony would have presented a very different aspect, and instead of the miserably depressed state of agriculture we should have had flourishing plantations. . . .[174]

Here was a practical demonstration of the danger of a universal and immediate emancipation of all the slaves in the United States. Between the crossfire of the Northern Colonizationists, who demanded that more emigrants be sent out and that those who were sent out should be chiefly those emancipated for this express purpose, and the colonial governor, who insisted that more provisions should be purchased and sent with emigrants and that those who were sent out should be not too largely of the recent slave class, there is no doubt that the problems of the Board were serious and pressing, especially as the Southern slaveholders were supplying all the slaves the Society could attempt to transport. The perplexities of the situation will be understood when attention is called to the fact that, despite the advice of the colonial agent to the Board, Elliot Cresson, who, if he was ignored, would have stirred up a hornet's nest from Maine to Louisiana in order to gain his point, wrote to the Society: "I would beg that if only 227 are slaves, out of the 800 sent last year, you will from motives of sound pol-

---

[172] African Repository, vol. viii, p. 366.
[173] Letters of American Colonization Society, MS., Mechlin to Gurley, Liberia, Feb. 28, 1833.
[174] Ibid.

icy, keep it out of notice"; and again, "Can you from all sources send 2800 this year instead of 800, if funds are found?"[175]

Word began to come from Liberia in 1833 that the condition of the colonists was anything but desirable. Protests came to the Managers from Maryland Colonizationists,[176] and from other interested persons. J. B. Pinney, one of the most successful agents the Society ever had, was in Liberia in 1833 and wrote: "At present it is disheartening to go among the sick. The constant complaint is 'we have no sugar, nor molasses, nor rice,' etc. etc. 'We can get no fresh soup, nor chicken.'" Pinney urged the Board to send nine months' provisions with each vessel of emigrants. Many of the houses, too, were leaky, he said, and many houses were not ready for occupancy, though they were badly needed. A great deal of the distress, he thought, was due to the selection of an incompetent agent, and one who lacked religion, interest and energy.[177] Very unsatisfactory accounts came also from a number of the colonists.[178] Gurley himself admitted the distress in the colony, and thought it was due in considerable measure to the incompetency of the agent.[179] In a word, this was the darkest hour in the history of the colony. Its darkness was rendered all the more prominent by the fact that it followed a period of great promise in Liberia. Reports had been coming in of the prosperity of the colonists, and it was believed the time had come when the operations of the Society could with safety be greatly enlarged.[180]

---

[175] Ibid., Cresson to Gurley, Glasgow, Scotland, Mar. 15, 1833.
[176] Ibid., C. C. Harper to Gurley, Baltimore, Apr. 13, 1833; Wm. L. Stone to Gurley, New York, Mar. 19, 1833; C. C. Harper to Gurley, Baltimore, Apr. 24, 1833; Miss Christian Blackburn to Gurley, Clay Mont, Va., May 22, 1833.
[177] Ibid., J. B. Pinney to Gurley, Liberia, May 17, 1833.
[178] Ibid., Phillip Moore to Gurley, Liberia, May 10, 1833; July 27, 1833; Remus Harvey to Gurley, Liberia, July 30, 1833; H. Teage to Gurley, Liberia, July 30, 1833.
[179] Ibid., Gurley to Fendall, New York, Oct. 4, 1833; Gurley to Gales, New York, April 17, 1834.
[180] Minutes of Board of Managers of American Colonization So-

It would be unjust to accuse the Board of Managers of a wilful neglect of the Colony. The minutes of that Board bear convincing testimony to the sincerity and philanthropy of those who controlled the Society. There is no doubt that the distress of the colonists weighed heavily upon those Managers. If, then, it be asked what was the cause of it all, the answer must be that there were a number of contributing causes. The following are suggested as the most important: (1) the lack of experienced, practical, business men in the membership of the Board, (2) the incompetency, if not the sheer negligence, of the colonial agent, (3) the insistence of Northern Colonizationists upon a too vigorous colonizing policy, when viewed in connection with the preparations in Liberia for receiving immigrants, (4) the importation of too large a proportion of slaves among the colonists and (5) the financial embarrassments of the Society. Finally, among the problems of which it seems important to speak at this stage of our inquiry, is the movement toward and the accomplishment of the reorganization of the Society.

The American Colonization Society was reorganized undoubtedly through the initiative of the Philadelphia and New York Societies. Among those who urged such a change, Elliot Cresson was the leader. Of Cresson, Isaac Orr, an agent of the parent Society, wrote in 1830 he "has the patronage of Philadelphia under his thumb, to a greater extent that I dare tell *him*. . . . And woe to the day when that commanding influence shall in *any way* be broken or thrown aside."[181] From 1830 until the reorganization had been consummated, this belligerent Friend lost no opportunity to tell the Board, in the most direct terms, what he thought of them. He wrote Gurley in August, 1830: "must I believe that there is something in the atmosphere of your City militating against the performance of business

ciety, MS., Nov. 22, 1830; Feb. 28, 1831; Letters of American Colonization Society, MS., Wm. A. Weaver to Gurley, Washington, Dec. 28, 1831.

[181] Ibid., Orr to Gurley, Philadelphia, July 15, 1830.

according to universal usage elsewhere?" The uncertainty of the Board's plans for sending out a proposed expedition of emancipated slaves, which, at the Board's request, he had put himself to considerable inconvenience to arrange for, called forth from him the following remark: "Your Board give me leave to write to McPhail. What am I to write about? I can form no guess of their intentions. . . . You must select your own vessel and relieve me from further anxiety and chagrin. Another such would bring on a nervous fever judging from what I have already suffered." In the form of a confidential postscript, he adds: "By the way what a perverse set you are at Washington. . . ."[182] Again he wrote: "So little does your honorable and reverend Board seem to think it worth while to conciliate the confidence and kindly feelings of your patrons . . . that I almost despair of ever getting a satisfactory answer to any subject that I may trouble you with."[183] Again, he writes:

I now demand your *ultimatum*, promptly; or I forever wash my hands of the concern. You pledged yourselves to send 100 on the 11th October. Do you, I ask, intend to redeem that pledge? If so, there is no time to be lost. If not, I will take the advice of my physician, go in the country and leave you to get a vessel when it suits you. . . . Don't forget the sawmill. It is of first importance. The plantation ground ditto. *Schools* ditto.[184]

In 1833 Cresson was in England and Scotland for the purpose of arousing an interest in favor of Colonization and of undoing the influence of the Garrisonians, who were there painting in the very darkest colors the motives of American Colonizationists. Of this Abolition influence in the British Isles he writes: ". . . unless you mean to abandon England ingloriously to these modern Vandals you *must* turn over a new leaf. . . . It is only by laborious search, that I occasionally light upon a straw to keep me from sinking."[185] Upon his return, he refers to Gurley as "that paragon," for having as Cresson says, "denounced

---

[182] Ibid., Cresson to Gurley, Aug. 5, 1830.
[183] Ibid., Cresson to Gurley, Sept. 6, 1830.
[184] Ibid., Cresson to Gurley, Sept. 10, 1830.
[185] Ibid., Cresson to Gurley, Glasgow, Mar. 15, 1833.

me for making complaint, after I had in vain *implored* him to do the cause and myself justice before the British public year after year."[186] But Gurley was so accustomed to Cresson's hyperboles that, as he commented: "I have become somewhat hardened against them."

As Cresson was busy in the North Middle States working up sentiment in opposition to the existing organization, so Robert S. Finley was, in the Western country, exerting a similar, though markedly less powerful influence. Summing up the objections met with against the methods of the Board, he names them as follows: (1) a want of system and energy in the Board in the execution of its plans, (2) failure to send out expeditions at the time at which they were advertised to sail, (3) failure to establish, in Liberia, a settlement on the higher and more healthful territory, (4) failure, on the part of the officers of the Society, to reply to important communications from contributors, slaveholders offering slaves, persons asking for advice and information, and so on.[187]

The testimony of these two men contains an important element of truth, but both undoubtedly went much too far in their charges against the Managers. So far as they charged business incompetency, they did an important service in pointing out the need of reform; so far as they charged dishonesty and impure motives, their charges fall completely to the ground. Not many men realized the heavy burden that rested upon the secretary of the Society. A man, who, like Gurley, was admirably and primarily fitted to keep the sections together and inspire in men of every part of the Union an interest in the cause, was not likely to be possessed of those qualities which make an admirable office secretary, such a man, for instance, as Judge Samuel Wilkeson, who was soon to give new life to the affairs of the organization. Gurley was contemplative rather than

---

[186] Ibid., Cresson to Gales, Philadelphia, May 4, 1835.
[187] Ibid., Finley to Gurley, Ohio River, Sept. 11, 1831; W. Meade to Gurley, December 6, 1831.

energetic; a thinker rather than an actor. It was his duty to keep up, both through the press, through the agencies, and by his own personal visitations to various parts of the country, an active interest in the subject of Colonization; to superintend, from New Orleans to Maine, the collection of funds, the preparation of expeditions, their provisioning, and the collecting of emigrants; the general supervision over the administration of the colonial agent in Liberia, and the impartial and judicious treatment of so dependent a class as those received into the colony—all this, and a general supervision of the government of a colony four thousand miles from home, a colony from which much was hoped, both for America and for Africa.

All this had to be done, and the Society that attempted it was supported by no endowment, no financial aid from the government, except some very inadequate aid from several of the State legislatures. And the Society was not even incorporated until nearly the end of the period of which we here speak. In these days of duplicators, typewriters, stenographers, fast mail trains, and a highly developed postal system, we probably do not appreciate the burdens that a man of such position as that occupied by Gurley had to bear. The task of the Abolitionists was to agitate the subject of slavery in the States north of Mason and Dixon's line. The task of the Colonizationist was to conciliate the North and the South, to agitate the peaceable and gradual abolition of slavery and the transportation of the blacks to Africa, and to found on that continent a republic where freedom could be actually experienced and which would be a model for the rest of Africa.

Reorganization was being talked of as early as 1834. In that year Leonard Bacon of New Haven, Connecticut, suggested that the active management of the Society be placed in the hands of five or seven men and, to prevent the possibility of their using unwisely their power, that they be made subject to a supervisory body. Reports should be made at each annual meeting, and at these meetings representation of auxiliary societies should be in proportion to the amount of funds contributed to the parent treasury.[188] Dissatisfaction was further evidenced, at the annual meeting in 1835, when a delegate from the New York Society made an effort to secure the election on the Board of Managers of four additional men, two of them aggressive members of the Pennsylvania Society, and by an effort by the same member to secure the passage of resolutions calling on the Board of Managers to reduce their office expenditures. These efforts failed.[189]

Whatever accusations are made concerning the distribution of seats on the Board of Managers, the only body, prior to 1839, which had an active part in shaping the policies of the Society, there can be no complaint made on the score that the selection of those officers was in the hands of the South after 1836, and it appears there is no evidence that at any time since its organization in 1817 it pursued a pro-slavery policy. In 1836 the members of the committee which at the annual meeting nominated the Managers was composed of two delegates from New York, two from Virginia, and one from Ohio.[190] For 1837, all five members of the nominating committee were from the Middle and Western States, not a Southern State being represented on the committee,[191] although the appointments were made by the chairman, C. F. Mercer, of Virginia. The Managers elected for 1837 were reelected for 1838.[192]

From 1837 to the time when the reorganization of the parent Society was effected, the New York and Philadelphia Societies pursued a policy calculated either to kill the older organization or to force it to submit. It must not be forgotten that of all the societies in the United States, these two were able to command the largest financial resources. They were powerful enough to secede from the parent So-

---

[188] Ibid., Bacon to Gurley, New Haven, Conn., Jan. 3, 1834.
[189] African Repository, vol. ii, pp. 49–50.
[190] Ibid., vol. xii, p. 12.
[191] Ibid., vol. xiii, p. 35.
[192] Ibid., vol. xiv, p. 29.

ciety and, in cooperation with New England, establish an organization that would undoubtedly have alienated the South immediately from the whole scheme, and it must be repeated that the orthodox Colonizationist was never a sectionalist, never a disunionist. Between 1837 and 1839 these two societies jointly presented bills for the payment of which the parent Society was in no sense obligated to them, and failed to redeem pledges made by them to the parent Society for the payment of a percentage of their collections in New York and Pennsylvania.[193] After the reorganization was effected, a referee, himself a citizen of New York, decided every material point favorably to the parent Society.[194]

In 1837 an effort was made among the New York, Pennsylvania, and Maryland Societies to agree upon a "Constitution of General Government for the American Settlements on the Western Coast of Africa." The proposed plan was accepted by the New York and Pennsylvania Societies but rejected by that of Maryland. It was then proposed that the three organizations send delegates to Philadelphia for the purpose of effecting a union among themselves. This the Maryland Society refused to do. Instead, it was agreed to send to the Washington Society's office an "Outline of a new Constitution for the American Colonization Society," which should replace the constitution then in force. The parent Society was requested to send copies of the proposed changes to the several auxiliaries, to be considered by them and voted upon at the annual meeting at the end of 1838.[195] By the terms of this proposed constitution, the Board of Managers was to be replaced by (1) a Board of Directors, and (2) an Executive Committee. By the old constitution, the Managers had been chosen at

[193] Minutes of Board of Managers of American Colonization Society, MS., April 6, 1837; Sept. 28, 1837; June 15, 1838; October 16, 1838.
[194] Minutes of Board of Directors of American Colonization Society, MS., vol. iii, pp. 419–422; African Repository, vol. xv, p. 19 ff.
[195] African Repository, vol. xiv, pp. 287–289.

the annual meeting by a vote of all members who were in attendance. By the proposed constitution, the Society was to be composed, not of individuals as units, but of State societies as units. The Board of Directors was to be a body composed of delegates chosen by the State societies; each such society contributing not less than one thousand dollars to the parent treasury to be entitled to one delegate, or member of the Board of Directors. Each such society having under its care a colony was to be entitled to two members of the Board; any two or more such societies uniting in the support of a colony, comprising at least three hundred persons, were to be entitled to two members, each, on the Board.

By the proposed plan, the Board of Directors was to meet annually, when they were to appoint an executive committee, with such paid officers (ex-officio members of the executive committee) as was deemed wise. The executive committee was thus a sort of subcommittee of the Board and was subject to its supervision and authority. By the proposed plan, each auxiliary society was to be allowed to send as many as five delegates to each annual meeting of the Society.[196]

In the meantime there had been a correspondence among leading Colonizationists in reference to the wisdom of making so radical a change as it was proposed to make. Thomas Buchanan, later Colonial Governor of Liberia and already a leading member of the Pennsylvania Society, thought that the change should be entire, in so far as the relations between the several auxiliary societies to the parent organization was concerned. "I would have a general Board of Delegates from all the State Societies which were willing to unite for that purpose, with powers of legislation for the Colony, the appointment of officers, etc. But without the power of sending out emigrants which should be reserved to the State societies." He favored the establishment, in Philadelphia or New York, of an executive committee. He

---

[196] Ibid., vol. xiv, pp. 287-289.

thought the societies that had established independent colonies in Africa should surrender their jurisdiction to a common government organized by the parent organization.[197]

Elisha Whittlesey, of Ohio, thought that there were changes needed in the organization, "but," said he, "I think we should correct, and not annihilate." Of the proposed board, composed of representatives from the State societies, to have supervision over the colonies in Africa, he thought: "Such a Board would never form, or if at all, not more than once, or twice. You could not obtain delegates from Louisiana, Tennessee, and Kentucky who would meet here or at the East, to attend to the concerns of the Society." It had been proposed also to put the control of the finances of the Society in the hands of the New York and Pennsylvania societies. Whittlesey's comment was: "Such a step would cut you off from the South at once. We want to inspire more confidence in the South, instead of lessening that which we have." As to the location of the central office, for there was a movement to make Philadelphia or New York the central office, he thought it should be located "at the seat of the General Government, on common, neutral ground. Here the Managers are easily collected together, and they better understand how to harmonize the discordant elements at the North and at the South than those who reside elsewhere. The New York and the Pennsylvania Society must not leave us either. Whatever is wrong must be corrected, and then we must have more zeal and energy."[198]

The views of Gurley were very similar to those of Whittlesey. He called attention to the fact that the movement for reorganization was distinctly a movement of the Pennsylvania and New York Societies; that whatever criticism they made of the administration of affairs by the Board of Managers came with poor grace from the very societies

---

[197] Letters of American Colonization Society, MS., Thomas Buchanan to Samuel Wilkeson, Philadelphia, May 10, 1838.
[198] Ibid., Whittlesey to Wilkeson, Washington, June 3, 1838.

which had sanctioned those elections; that the energy of the parent organization had been impaired by the refusal of these two societies, the most able to contribute, to redeem their pledges; that the Managers, far from profiting by their connection with the Board, had often assumed voluntarily the responsibility for large amounts which, had they been called on to make good, would have weighed heavily upon them. He favored an early settlement of the relations between the auxiliary and the parent societies, but thought that the central office should, by all means, remain at the national capital. "To destroy the parent Board," said he, "is, in my judgment, to ruin the cause at the South."[199] Joseph Gales, a North Carolinian by birth, who since 1834 had been the treasurer of the parent Society, put the blame for a considerable part of the financial distress of the Society directly upon the New York and Pennsylvania societies, through their refusal to meet the pledges made by them at the time of the agreement by which they pursued an independent policy. And this, he thought, was the chief cause of the widespread criticism among the Society's friends.[200]

During this discussion of the changes desirable in the parent society, Judge Samuel Wilkeson of Buffalo, New York, and one who may, with considerable justice, be called the father of Buffalo, was invited by the Board of Managers to become general agent for the Society, with power to commission, instruct, or remove agents, as he thought necessary. To him was committed also the supervision of the finances. In short, he was made practically dictator of the Society's affairs in the United States.[201] Wilkeson accepted the task, magnanimously refusing compensation until the Society should be free from debt.[202] He threw himself into

---
[199] Ibid., Gurley to Wilkeson, Washington, June 4, 1838.
[200] Ibid., Gales to Wilkeson, Washington, Aug. 4, 1838.
[201] African Repository, vol. xv, pp. 6-7; Minutes of Board of Managers of American Colonization Society, MS., Dec., 1838.
[202] Letters of American Colonization Society, MS., Wilkeson to Gurley, New York, July 7, 1838.

the work with an energy uncommon among men but characteristic of himself. Possessed of none of the suavity with which Gurley made friends wherever he went, inclined to underestimate the inspirational side of a movement based upon public opinion, he lived in Western New York, made money, got things done, was a chief among pioneers, and suffered from the gout.

Hardly had Wilkeson begun his duties in the Colonization cause, when Cresson began to complain about the need for reform. "I hope," wrote he, "you will dismiss the idlers at Washington next month and give the friends of the cause new hopes thereby that the *mice* in the treasury will not eat up all the *meal*."[203] Here, as elsewhere, there was an element of value in Cresson's criticism, but it was far overstated. The Board might probably have done well to have dispensed with the services of one or two of its office force, after the cause came under such formidable discouragement, but Wilkeson himself found that the public had been misled in its belief that much further economy was practicable.[204] The new general agent went to work with a will, however, and reported to the Managers in December, 1838:

> I have found it very difficult to obtain such agents as are required. . . . In some sections of the country the hostility of abolitionists is dreaded. The cause of colonization has been so long neglected, that the societies heretofore organized have everywhere been suffered to die, and many men formerly warm colonizationists . . . are unwilling to encounter the difficulties now presented. Very many believe that the low state to which colonization [has come] is owing to the impracticability of carrying it on by private charity. . . . Very many others . . . believe that some radical change in the organization and management . . . is necessary to its success. Even in those sections . . . which have been abandoned to the abolitionists . . . I have found that a large proportion of the people are glad to hear once more of colonization and hail it as a great conservative principle that will save our country, and elevate the colored man.[205]

At the annual meeting in January, 1839, the interest was

---

[203] Ibid., Cresson to Wilkeson, Woodstock, Vermont, Nov. 28, 1838.
[204] Ibid., Wilkeson to Gales, New York, Nov. 16, 1838; Nov. 30, 1838; Gales to Wilkeson, Washington, Nov. 28, 1838.
[205] Letters of Board of Managers of American Colonization Society, MS., Dec. 10, 1838.

intense. The New York, New Jersey, and Pennsylvania Societies sent delegations that numerically reached the maximum allowed by the rules. Besides, Virginia had a full and able delegation, her representatives being C. F. Mercer, Wm. C. Rives, James Garland, Henry A. Wise, and Abel P. Upshur. Of the total number of delegates, thirty-one, New York, New Jersey, and Pennsylvania sent seventeen, Virginia six, and the West four, the District of Columbia sending four.[206] The reason for the full delegations is obvious. New York, New Jersey and Pennsylvania had come to bring about radical changes in the organization. These changes undoubtedly constitute the first official recognition, of consequence, of one section as opposed to another, in the constitution of the Society. They constitute the first step made by Colonizationists in the estrangement of the upper South and the Southwestern States. That some changes were needful for the very life of the Society is obvious. That those changes took the direction they did is altogether regrettable.

In the first discussion, at the annual meeting, there was no agreement between the delegates from the North Middle States and the Virginians. A committee, composed of two Southerners and four from New York and Pennsylvania, reported a compromise, in which the Virginians took what they could get, and it was adopted by the representatives and became, in name, the amended, but in fact, the new constitution. The changes adopted were not so radical as those recommended by the Maryland, Pennsylvania, and New York societies in 1837, but they were quite radical enough.[207] The name and the object of the Society were, in the revised instrument, stated to be the same as in the old; but that was about all. It may be well to compare it with the original constitution, on the one hand, and with the proposed one, on the other.

(1) The name and professed object of the Society remain the same in all three.

---

[206] African Repository, vol. xv, p. 19 ff.
[207] See above.

(2) By the old constitution, the parent Society was a society composed of individuals; by the proposed constitution it was to be a federation of auxiliary societies; by the instrument actually adopted it was to partake of the nature of both. Every citizen of the United States who paid annually as much as one dollar into the treasury was to be considered a member; but membership on its Board of Directors, the actual governing power of the Society, was confined to societies contributing certain fixed amounts. Every society contributing not less than $1000 was entitled to two directors of the Board; every society having under its care a colony was entitled to three delegates; every two or more societies jointly maintaining a colony of not fewer than three hundred settlers, was entitled to three delegates. Any individual contributing as much as $1000 to the parent treasury was entitled to membership for life on the Board of Directors.

(3) By the old constitution, the Society was to meet annually; by the proposed instrument, the Board of Directors was to meet annually; by that adopted, both the Society and the Board of Directors were to meet annually.

(4) By both the proposed and the new constitutions, any State Colonization Society maintaining a colony in Liberia was given the right to appropriate its funds to the maintenance of such colony.

(5) By the new instrument, all sums paid into the treasury of the parent Society were, after the payment of expenses for collecting and after paying a certain portion of the existing debt, to be applied to the benefit of the colony of Monrovia, where the Colonial Governor was to reside.[208]

To understand how radical was this change, and how completely it deprived the South of even a respectable voice in the management of an enterprise in which it was asked and urged to make continued and important contributions, it is sufficient to call attention to the fact that the very first Board of Directors, after the adoption of the new consti-

---

[208] African Repository, vol. xv, p. 19 ff.

tution, was composed of eight members from the States north of Maryland, two from those south of the District of Columbia, two from the District of Columbia, and two from Ohio.[209] A whole section, itself the very center of operations of the Society, deprived of any effective representation in its proceedings, could not be expected to continue to exhibit an active interest. Indeed, when one takes into consideration the sectional bitterness of the time, it is remarkable how long some of the Southern States did lend their support to the movement that was now in northern hands. For years Virginia, Mississippi and Louisiana did important service for the Society. But from 1839 there is evident a new spirit, a spirit that must not be attributed altogether to the rise of cotton production but also to the loss of a hearing in the councils of Colonization.

But it may be asked, why did not the Southern States pay into the treasury enough to entitle them to an equal representation with the Middle States? Simply because of the two facts: (1) the South was not able to make contributions equal to those of the more prosperous section, and (2) no matter how many slaves a Southern slaveholder gave away for emigration to Africa, the South was not thereby given credit for a single dollar in its representation among the directors. The reorganizers of the Society committed a capital blunder in ignoring this important fact. And then there was that other consideration, to which Whittlesey had already called attention. New York and Pennsylvania and, for that matter, all New England, were so much nearer the seat of the Society than were the Southern States that where members of the Board of Directors came from the States they represented the North would invariably outnumber the South in the number of those in attendance. It is sufficient here to say that the estrangement of the South was not due altogether to economic changes in that section. The South, at least a part of it, began to lose interest in the American Colonization Society before it be-

---

[209] Ibid., vol. xv, p. 27.

gan to lose interest in the cause of colonization. By 1840 both Louisiana and Mississippi were seriously contemplating action independent of the American Colonization Society, and the basis of their position was that good faith to the South required it.[210] By 1843 McLain, Secretary of the parent Society, wrote:

More than half the South look upon us as a co. of abolitionists only called by another name.[211] And by April, 1852, Alabama had organized a Colonization Society entirely independent of the American Colonization Society, and because there was in the minds of many an impression that the Am. Col. Society partook too much of the abolition spirit to receive their countenance and support.[212]

Since 1830 there had arisen a great need for the incorporation of the Society. Several bequests had been lost, and some had not been made, because of the fact that the Society was not a corporate body. After one or two efforts to secure a charter of incorporation from Congress, all of which ended in failure, General Walter Jones declaring that a debate in Congress over the charter of the Society would have divided and agitated that body more than would the proposal to recharter the United States Bank,[213] the Maryland legislature granted it a charter in 1831.[214] This was not altogether satisfactory. During 1837 Clay made two efforts to secure in Congress a more satisfactory charter, but again it was refused. Finally, the Maryland legislature, in 1837, granted the amended charter.[215]

A word more as to the finances of the Society. Of those who, in 1838, were contributors on the plan of Gerrit Smith, that is, who subscribed one hundred dollars per year for a period of ten years, two were from Maine, one from Vermont, two from Massachusetts, one from Connecticut, one from Rhode Island, five from New York, two from

---

[210] Letters of American Colonization Society, MS., F. Knight to Wilkeson, Aug. 1, 1840, No. 704.
[211] Ibid., McLain to Dodge, Feb. 27, 1843, No. 720.
[212] Journal of Executive Committee of American Colonization Society, MS., Apr. 16, 1852.
[213] The Liberator, Feb. 15, 1834.
[214] Minutes of Board of Managers of American Colonization Society, MS., Feb. 15, 1837.
[215] Ibid., Mar. 30, 1837.

New Jersey, four from Pennsylvania, one from Delaware; sixteen from Virginia, one from South Carolina, four from Mississippi, seven from Louisiana, three from Maryland, two from the District of Columbia, and one from Ohio.[216] The total expenditures of the Society to November 13, 1838, were $379,644.15.[217] By 1839 the total debt of the Society was estimated by Wilkeson at approximately $70,000.[218]

It was not a bright day for colonization, in December, 1838; with a heavy debt, hardly an agent actively engaged in the work, a difference of opinion between the northern and southern branches of the Society as to the best means of giving it efficiency, and a North and West that had been invaded and, if not conquered, at least dumfounded by the accusations of the Abolitionists. This was enough, but this was not all. When the New York delegates went back to report they found that Society unwilling to ratify their agreement to the amended constitution. Wilkeson, who labored earnestly for the cooperation of the Pennsylvania and New York Societies wrote, in May, 1839: "A negotiation between the Emperor of Russia and the States of Holland in the sixteenth century could not be more diplomatically ceremonious than that between your two societies."[219] Difficulties were real when a man of his indomitable will admitted, "I confess I feel discouraged. . . . Can there be any organization that will unite all friends of the cause in support of the Am. Col. Society? If not, the friends of the cause ought to know it."[220] But there were brighter days ahead.

---

[216] African Repository, vol. xiv, back cover.
[217] Letters of American Colonization Society, MS., Gales to Wilkeson, Washington, Nov. 14, 1838.
[218] Ibid., Wilkeson to Ker, Washington, July 25, 1840. No. 680.
[219] Ibid., Wilkeson to Rev. Hope, May 9, 1839.
[220] Ibid., Mar. 28, 1840, no. 119.

CHAPTER III

American Colonization and Garrisonian Abolition.

The bitterest opposition Colonization ever encountered came from the Abolitionists of William Lloyd Garrison's school. Next to these, its fiercest enemies were the slaveholders of the Southeastern States. One who turns the pages of Garrison's Liberator for the years 1831 to 1835, will be struck by the fact that in some issues more space was given to tearing down the influence of the Colonization Society than was used in direct opposition to the institution of slavery. Henry Clay told the truth when, in 1838, he said: "The roads of Colonization and Abolition lead in different directions, but they do not cross each other,"[1] but no more hostile denunciation was ever used in depicting the crimes of slaveholders than was used in characterizing the Colonizationist leaders. This is all the more surprising when the fact is known, and it is a fact, that those very Colonizationists with whom Garrison came in contact were as truly opposed to slavery as Garrison himself. Elijah Paine, one of the foremost citizens of Vermont and for years President of the State Colonization Society, was as earnest an advocate of emancipation as any Abolitionist in the North,[2] but The Liberator made no distinctions.

In the struggle for supremacy the Garrisonians took the offensive. The opposition began with them and continued until Colonization journals refused longer to take notice of Abolition speeches or articles.[3] Between 1831 and 1840 the opposition often took the form of direct meetings in

---
[1] African Repository, vol. xiv, pp. 17-18.
[2] Ibid., vol. xv, pp. 44-48.
[3] Letters of American Colonization Society, MS., W. McLain to Hon. Edw. Storrs, December 30, 1841, No. 494; McLain to Samuel Elliott, vol. iv, No. 1425.

debate.[4] Frequently after the debate a vote would be taken to ascertain the sentiments of the audience. When, in 1835, Gurley made a tour of New England, there was no dearth of challengers among the Garrisonians. At Boston he chanced into a session of one of their conventions and had hardly taken his seat when a Garrisonian leader arose and moved a resolution declaring the principles of the American Colonization Society to be "unrighteous, unnatural, proscriptive, and the attempt to give permanency to the institution [of slavery], a fraud on the credulity and an outrage on the intelligence of the public," and challenging any person present to defend the Society. Gurley arose, and the result was a two days' debate.[5] Proceeding to Concord, New Hampshire, he found another convention in session, and here also he was drawn into a discussion which ended quite favorably to Colonization, if we are to judge by the subscriptions received from prominent men of the State at a meeting held a day or two later in the same city and resulting from the debate. Among the subscribers were the governor, an ex-governor, Judge Upham, and many members of the legislature.[6] These are but illustrations of what was going on throughout the North and West between Colonization agents and radical Abolitionists.

It must not be forgotten that there were two distinct classes of Abolitionists: (1) moderates and, (2) Garrisonians. This classification was well known in the North, and the distinction is so important for our present purposes, for reference in this chapter is made almost wholly to the Garrisonians, that attention is here called to it. It will be profitable to consider briefly an important point in

---

[4] African Repository, vol. ix, p. 218; vol. x, pp. 125–126; Letters of American Colonization Society, MS., Gurley to Fendall, Boston, June 1, 1835.

[5] Letters of American Colonization Society, MS., Gurley to Fendall, Boston, June 1, 1835; Minutes of Board of Managers of American Colonization Society, MS., vol. iii, p. 190 ff.

[6] Minutes of Board of Managers of American Colonization Society, MS., vol. iii, p. 193. Letters of American Colonization Society, MS., Gurley to Fendall, Boston, June 11, 1835.

COLONIZATION AND ABOLITION 127

connection with the origin of the Garrisonian group and of the Colonizationists.

Garrison founded his group upon a sectional sentiment; Colonization was founded upon a national sentiment. Garrison's sowing was of the wind and, as we shall come to see hereafter, his reaping was of the whirlwind. Colonizationists have been accused of many unworthy motives, but never yet have they been accused of ever having sown a seed of disunion and civil strife. It was born out of a desire to unite the North and the South in the settlement of the negro problem. Garrison was determined to free the slaves at once, whether or not the result was the disruption of the Union; Colonizationists were determined to forego immediate emancipation, for the sake of accomplishing both ultimate emancipation and the preservation of the Union. This is the very heart of the distinction between the creeds of Garrisonians and Colonizationists. As to ulterior aims and motives, in the origins and progress of the two organizations, the paramount aim of Garrison has been universally admitted to be the immediate and unconditional emancipation of all the slaves in the United States. The sincerity of his aims has never been seriously questioned. Unfortunately, and thanks to the vituperation of the Garrisonians themselves, the motives of the Colonizationists have been widely misrepresented since 1831. It is the purpose of this study to set forth the true aims of orthodox Colonizationists, or, from another point of view, to demonstrate that their aims were as sincerely expressed as sound policy would admit, and that, where motives were concealed, they were concealed in order to retain the good will of the slaveholder in order to secure the freedom of his slaves.

However, it is desired here chiefly to set forth and compare the methods used by the Garrisonians and the members of the American Colonization Society in their relations with each other and with the Southern slaveholders, and to set forth also the results of the methods pursued by each.

A favorite method employed by Garrison to prejudice the

North against the Colonization movement was to take speeches made by Clay, or articles written by Gurley and others and, by a process of garbling, create in the minds of readers of the Abolitionist newspapers an entirely erroneous view of the attitude of Colonizationists toward the whole subject of slavery. The Colonizationists desired to appeal to all sections of the Union. They, therefore, were careful not to alienate the sympathies of slaveholders. An important fact which Garrison either failed to appreciate or consistently ignored was that the Colonization Society desired far more earnestly to abolish slavery than it expressed in its official journal. It would have been much more difficult for him to make a plausible garbled account of its attitude, as expressed in all its official records and private correspondence—and only here could be found expressed its true attitude on that question—than to compile such an account from the African Repository.[7] A striking example of the method employed is contained in Garrison's Thoughts on African Colonization, page 149. In an effort to prove Dr. Caldwell, one of the most active founders of the Colonization Society, a proponent of slavery, Garrison offers the following quotation:

> The more you improve the condition of these people, the more you cultivate their minds, the more miserable you make them in their present state. You give them a higher relish for those privileges which they can never attain, and turn what you intend for a blessing into a curse. No, if they must remain in their present situation, keep them in the lowest state of ignorance and degradation. The nearer you bring them to the condition of brutes, the better chance do you give them of possessing their apathy.

It is true that Dr. Caldwell made the remark as quoted; but he followed it immediately, and as the expression of his own view, with the following sentiment, which Garrison omitted from his quotation:

> Surely Americans ought to be the last people on earth to advocate such slavish doctrines,—to cry, peace and contentment to those

---

[7] For an example of Garrison's method, see both The Liberator for December 8, 1832, pp. 193-194, and African Repository, January, 1833, pp. 346-347. See also African Repository, first article, March, 1833.

COLONIZATION AND ABOLITION

who are deprived of the blessings of civil liberty. Those who have so largely partaken of its blessings—who know so well how to estimate its value, ought to be foremost to extend it to others.

When Garrison was called to account for this utter perversion of the views of Dr. Caldwell, he admitted he had not read Dr. Caldwell's remarks, but, at the same time, when he should have been content with doing Caldwell, already in his grave, the justice of a frank confession of his own serious blunder, he made an effort to prove by other extracts and quotations, that he had, after all, not done that leader injustice in an estimate of his views. In the latter attempt he ingloriously failed.[8] As a matter of fact, both Francis Scott Key and Caldwell had been active in securing the liberty of negroes in the District of Columbia taken illegally into slavery.[9]

A method similar to the above, employed by The Liberator, was that of publishing as evidence of the proslavery sentiment in the Colonization Society, divided votes at annual meetings, although these votes were expressions of policy alone, and were in no true sense an expression of the views of the organization upon the subject of slavery.[10] In a number of instances, accusations made had no foundation whatever in fact.[11] Garrison himself, while on a tour of England in advocacy of his cause, stated that the American Colonization Society

originated with those who held a large portion of their fellow-creatures in worse than Egyptian bondage; that it was generally supported by them; and that it was under their entire control—that not one of its officers and managers had emancipated his slaves, and sent them to Liberia . . . that it maintained that no slave ought to receive his liberty, except on condition of instant banishment from the country. . . .

It was "the apologist and friend of American slaveholders."[12] These accusations are so sweeping in their scope

---
[8] The Liberator, Nov. 2, 1833; Jesse Torrey, A Portraiture of Domestic Slavery in the United States, pp. 86-87, Philadelphia, 1817.
[9] Torrey, pp. 49-52.
[10] The Liberator, March 2, 1833; April 6, 1833; Sept. 21, 1833.
[11] African Repository, vol. ix, pp. 201-203; United States Telegraph, July 24, 1833.
[12] The Liberator, October 19, 1833.

that a refutation of them here would require needless repetition. But if the positions taken in this study have been successfully maintained, the motives of Colonizationists were utterly misstated by Garrison.

The columns of The Liberator were at times self-contradictory. For instance, the issue for September 21, 1833, contained a reprint which required for insertion the whole of the first and part of the second page; it was an account of the maltreatment of the Northerner, Rev. J. B. Pinney, whom the South Carolinians erroneously thought had come to Columbia in advocacy of Colonization. And on the next column was another reprint which contained an insinuation that the Colonizationists were in collusion with South Carolina slaveholders.

Again, there was circulated about 1839, by the Abolitionists, a so-called Authentic Narrative of James Williams, an American Slave, which set forth the cruel treatment received by southern slaves at the hands of their owners. Upon an examination into the authenticity of the Authentic Narrative, it was found that the pamphlet was a fabrication, and it was repudiated by the antislavery committee which made the investigation.[13]

During a session of the Methodist General Conference, in Baltimore, an ultra-Abolitionist delegate presented an Abolition petition containing eleven or twelve hundred signatures. When investigation was made it was found that "scores of names were signed twice, and many . . . were . . . forgeries, or declared to be so by the parties. Hundreds were ascertained to have been signed to a temperance memorial, and had been surreptitiously appended to this. Whole families . . . were subscribed, who declare they had never seen the memorial. . . ."[14] Negroes returning from Liberia and bringing accounts entirely untrustworthy were employed by Garrisonians to set forth the "true" condition of affairs in Africa.[15]

---

[13] African Repository, vol. xv, pp. 161–163.
[14] Ibid., vol. xvi, pp. 350–351.
[15] Letters of American Colonization Society, MS., B. M. Palmer to Gurley, Charleston, S. C., May 26, 1834.

In 1842 an Abolitionist lecturer of Vermont assured his auditors that the Colonizationists were throwing money away, having already made away with more than one hundred million dollars since 1817. Upon protest from a clergyman who was in the audience, the lecturer assured his hearers that his statement was drawn from the official records of the Society. As a matter of fact he had overstated his figures something over ninety-nine and a half million dollars.[16] An Indiana Colonization agent reported that in that State the Abolitionists were using as an argument against the Society the statement that "the men who are engaged in taking free blacks to Liberia bring back two or three slaves for every black taken out."[17] Judge Samuel Wilkeson, General Agent of the Society, wrote to a Vermont Colonizationist:

> The abolitionists in many parts of the country are becoming quiet. You observe that they have made some statements which you believe untrue but have not the means of correcting them. Those who control the abolition press generally are destitute or reckless of truth, making statements of which they have not the evidence of truth, or which they know to be false. For instance, Mr. Garrison published me last fall as a large slaveholder in Florida. I called on his agent and assured him that I never owned a slave, and requested him to contradict the charge, which instead of being done, the falsehood has gone the rounds of every abolition paper in the Union.[18]

Besides these direct misstatements of fact, the Garrisonians made sweeping assertions that are utterly incapable of proof, but which cannot be refuted except by a consideration of the whole history of the Society. Garrison charged, for instance, that the American Colonization Society " is pledged not to oppose the system of slavery "; " apologizes for slavery and slaveholders "; " is nourished by fear and selfishness "; " aims at the utter expulsion of the blacks "; " is the disparager of the free blacks "; " deceives and misleads the nation."[19]

When the debt of the Colonization Society was published

---

[16] Ibid., Dr. A. Proudfit to Whittlesey, New York, September, 1842.
[17] Ibid., B. T. Kavanaugh to McLain, Indianapolis, April 18, 1846.
[18] Ibid., Wilkeson to J. P. Fairbanks, June 21, 1839.
[19] African Repository, vol. ix, pp. 105-109.

in the February Liberator, 1835, that periodical was exultant, exclaiming: "MENE, MENE, TEKEL, UPHARSIN. Debt of the Handmaid of Slavery, $46,000." In the same issue, of eight and one-half feet in columns of printed matter on the first page, all but five inches is devoted to tirades against the Society, an important part of it being made up of garbled quotations from Colonization leaders.[20] Cresson writes from Glasgow of C. Stuart, confederate and warm co-worker with Garrison while Stuart was in America, that the latter denounced all those who used West India sugar as "doomed to hell, with damnation for their portion."[21] An Indiana agent reported that the Abolitionist candidate for governor of that State, who was also a member of the Indiana Supreme Court, in an attack upon Colonization spoke "in a most loose, vulgar, and abusive manner insomuch that the ladies were driven off."[22] Examples of the immoderate, misleading and untrue statements of Mr. Garrison's paper are the following: "We are becoming daily more versed in the corruption of the advocates of the American Colonization Society. With all their insolence, they are dastardly." "The records of the Colonization Society are obvious exhibitions of deceitfulness." "As it is at present organized, the American Colonization Society cannot justly make any pretension to justice or mercy, with more plausibility than they could who brought the natives of Congo from their own land."[23] Commenting on the debt of the Colonization Society, the same publication exclaimed:

We have not room for all the speeches that were delivered, but the following extracts [which, by the way, were very misleading summaries of those delivered at the annual meeting] show that the Genius of Contradiction presided on the occasion, assisted by Hypocrisy, Falsehood, Desperation and Folly. The days of the Society are numbered. Glory to God in the highest![24]

---

[20] Ibid., vol. xi, p. 57; vol. x, pp. 356–360; The Liberator, Feb. 22, 1834.
[21] Letters of American Colonization Society, MS., Cresson to Gurley, Glasgow, Mar. 15, 1833.
[22] Ibid., Kavanaugh to McLain, Indianapolis, April 30, 1846.
[23] The Liberator, May 18, 1833.
[24] Ibid., Feb. 8, 1834.

One would think that the editor would have hesitated in his sweeping characterizations, for in the same paper is contained the admission:

> Were numbers necessary to the success of the Colonization Society? It has enrolled upon its list, the high and the low, the rich and the poor, all classes of people, in multitudinous gatherings and multiform varieties. Did it need the sanctity of religion? What theological institution, what religious sect, what presbytery, synod, general assembly, conference, or church, what eminent divine or deacon, what religious periodical or newspaper, has it not until recently counted approvingly on its side? Did it need political favor? It has been appropriated by all parties. . . . In short, in its ranks have stood, hand in hand, the Presbyterian and the Quaker, the Episcopalian and Baptist, the Methodist and Unitarian, the Universalist and Infidel—the freeholder and slaveholder. . . .[25]

It seems not to have occurred to the editor that an organization which could boast of such a host of supporters was not to be condemned in terms of wanton ridicule and sarcastic vituperation.

A further method of the Garrisonians was to draw in lurid colors utterly untrustworthy pictures of slavery as a system, pictures which fired the minds of the New Englander and exasperated the Southerner, who was perfectly acquainted with the system.[26] On a par with these were the unqualified statements of Garrison that (1) slaveholding is in all cases sinful, (2) it should be immediately prohibited, (3) "If it were evident that only by a short delay, he could be better prepared to receive the boon of liberty, still the slave ought to be a free man *now*. . . ."[27]

The Colonization agent had to endure not only this wholesale condemnation of the cause in which he labored but also, in many cases, personal calumny. Elliot Cresson, on a mission to England for the promotion of the Colonization cause, wrote from Edinboro:

> In no place has the A[nti] S[lavery] party had recourse to more abject means of insult. . . . In these assaults, *for myself,* supported by the consciousness of my high mission, I care not; but if you do not vindicate yourselves thro' me and meet the libels of the A. S. Party, by *prompt* letters . . . the cause must suffer. Let them

---
[25] Ibid., Dec. 13, 1834.
[26] Ibid., May 3, 1834, p. 71.
[27] Ibid., March 7, 1835.

know that I enjoy your entire confidence, and that every penny received, is religiously devoted to legitimate purposes—for to check the current of benevolence, I found it whispered about that I was *without authority from you—disbursing your funds for my own purposes,* and any other means as miscreants deemed most likely to circumvent me.[28]

Indeed, he became restive under the continued vexations to which he was subjected. He could not hear from Colonization headquarters frequently enough to keep up such a defensive as desired and, in exasperation, he asked, "How can I fight (for fight I must) if I have neither weapons or ammunition? Must I like the spider spin them out of my own unaided self?"[29]

So reckless had the Garrisonians become in their determination to gain their ends that they resorted to the frank statement of sentiments which, but for the burning question of slavery, would have branded them for all time as traitors to their country. When the discussion between this country and Great Britain over the northeast boundary between the United States and Canada was at its height, an American negro, Redmond, who was a Garrisonian lecturer and was speaking in Scotland, openly advocated war between the United States and Great Britain, even at the risk of the defeat of his own country, and for the reason that it would bring about the emancipation of the slaves at the South.[30] The British Garrisonians were in accord with this view. One of their newspapers gave this exaggerated view of the slave system in America:

> The horrors of the slave system, as pursued in the Southern States, are unutterable; nothing that the wildest imagination can conceive surpasses the cruelties inflicted on the wretched negro victims; and if it were in our power to stir up the spirit of the slaves to rebel against the heartless planters . . . we would use that power, though all America was thrown into disorder, and presented one wide field of bankruptcy and ruin.[31]

A contributor to Fraser's Magazine, taking his data from

---

[28] Letters of American Colonization Society, MS., Cresson to Gurley, Edinboro, Mar. 19, 1833.
[29] Ibid., Cresson to Gurley, Adelphi, June 6, 1833; London, October 6, 1831.
[30] 27th Cong., 3d sess., H. Rept. No. 283, p. 1026.
[31] Ibid., pp. 1026–1027.

a recent publication of the American Abolitionists, urged upon the British the high moral duty to declare war against the United States, with the ultimate aim of freeing the slaves in the South. Taking the Abolitionist statements at their face value, the writer urged that America "holds nearly three millions of unoffending human creatures in the most cruel bondage; in a thraldom infinitely worse than Egyptian, Turkish, or Sclavonian. In fact, we doubt if the annals of the human race afford an example of any system of oppression at all approaching to that which is proved . . . to exist in America." The dissolution of the Union was, then, highly desirable, both for the security of Great Britain's possessions and for the abolition of slavery in the United States. Immediately upon the declaration of such a war, if it were made clear that it was to be prosecuted as a war for emancipation, the free blacks of Jamaica would lend their aid at once. "In one morning a force of ten thousand men might be raised in this quarter. . . . In three weeks . . . the entire south would be in one conflagration."[32]

The North Carolina Quaker, Jeremiah Hubbard, who was willing to go as far as any man in a rational program for the abolition of slavery, made these observations upon Garrisonian methods:

> I would give thee a little specimen of his style and manner of writing; in his opinion of the Colonization Society, he says:—"The superstructure of the Colonization Society rests upon the following pillars. 1. Persecution. 2. Falsehood. 3. Cowardice. 4. Infidelity. If I do not prove the Colonization Society to be a creature, *without heart, without brains, eyeless, unnatural, hypocritical, relentless, unjust, then nothing is capable of demonstration!!!*" His language to slaveholders, or of slaveholders is, "They are hypocrites, manstealers; and such as hold offices in the United States," he says, "are guilty of corrupt perjury, and unless they repent, will have their part in the lake that burns with fire and brimstone." This kind of language is not at all calculated to make good impressions on the minds of slaveholders, even of those of whom it may be true, and it is utterly false as respects many who hold slaves—they would be very glad to have it in their power to put their slaves in a better situation. . . .[33]

---

[32] *Fraser's Magazine*, London, April, 1841, pp. 494–502.
[33] *African Repository*, vol. x, p. 37 ff.

Hubbard was Clerk of the yearly meeting of Friends of North Carolina, a member of both the Colonization Society and an Abolition Society, though not of Garrison's school, a leader among a group of seven or eight thousand Quakers of North Carolina, who had contributed thousands of dollars toward the Colonization Society, had fought slavery for upwards of fifty years, had for forty years repeatedly memorialized the legislature for permission to conscientious slaveholders to manumit their slaves, had assisted about one thousand slaves to seek their liberty in a free State. And Hubbard's comment is: "After all this, by the above positive denunciation we are indirectly assailed by the colonization persecutors as liars, cowards, infidels, without heart, without brains, eyeless, unnatural, hypocritical, unjust. Such language, my brethren, is not calculated to conquer enemies, gain friends, soften hard hearts, or convince infidels, even if it were true."[34]

The fierceness and boldness of these Abolitionist attacks were not without tremendous effect. Some of the most consistent Colonizationists of New England were startled by their "revelations." Ezra S. Gannet was one of this class. He had read statements made in Boston by Thomas C. Brown, a former colonist who, having become disgruntled because of the failure, up to this time, of the Colonization Society to pay a claim held against them for lumber that Brown had shipped,[35] had been employed as a Garrisonian lecturer to "inform" the New Englanders of conditions in Liberia and of the attitude of Colonizationists toward slavery. Gannet was wise enough to write to Colonization headquarters for their statement of the facts about which Brown had spoken.[36] The reply was satisfactory and Gannet continued his relations with the Colonizationists.[37] In his reply, he refers to the "most unmerited and

---

[34] Ibid., vol. x, pp. 214–215.
[35] Letters of American Colonization Society, MS., Grimke to Gurley, 1854.
[36] Ibid., Gannet to Gurley, Boston, June 19, 1834.
[37] Ibid., Nov. 12, 1834.

shameful abuse from violent Anti-Slavery" writers, to which the Society and its agents had been subjected, and of the "extravagance and intemperance of Mr. Garrison." The anti-slavery agitator, Dr. Thomas Hodgkin, of London, wrote to the American delegates to the Anti-Slavery Convention held in that city in 1840: "I admit that you have completely succeeded in drawing a repulsive picture of the Society, but I do not admit that it gives a fair idea of the reality."[38]

A group of Colonizationist students from Western Reserve College wrote Gurley in 1832 of the effect The Liberator had already had in the College before Garrison had been publishing it two years. Before its appearance upon the reading tables of that institution the student body had expressed no doubt of the sincerity of the Colonization movement. By 1832 not only students but the faculty were enlisted in two opposing groups. One group wrote:

We had always supposed ... that the Colonization Society was friendly to human rights, was the avowed enemy of slavery, an uncompromising foe of the oppressor; and that its ultimate *design* and *tendency* was to free the captive. ... We had supposed these to be its claims, and that these were incontrovertible. But they are flatly denied in this same land of Ohio, and the institution denounced, as wanting even the common sanction of benevolent design![39]

It was thus throughout New England and the West. If Garrison caught the ear of some of the most prominent men of those sections of the Union, it is not difficult to picture the effect his clear cut, unmistakable charges had upon the minds of those who accepted without deep reflection the sentiments they heard or read upon a topic so absorbing as that of negro slavery. From Portland, Maine, the report from the Colonizationist agent came, that "a prodigious current turned after" Garrison.[40] The Secretary of the Society, after a

---

[38] African Repository, vol. xvi, pp. 311-313.
[39] Letters of American Colonization Society, MS., Students of Western Reserve College, Hudson, Ohio, to Gurley, October 29, 1832.
[40] Ibid., Cummings to J. N. Danforth, Portland, Maine, February 14, 1832.

tour of New England during the summer of 1834, reported evidences of a distinct change of sentiment in New England unfavorable to the Society. Coming as it does from him, the following statement is not without value, as showing the view taken by Gurley of the motives and hopes of Colonizationists. He says:

> Yet in the light of clearest evidence, that the American Colonization Society was designed and has been sustained with the view of affording means and motives for the voluntary, peaceful and entire abolition of slavery; that its moral influence favorable to emancipation, has been and is operating most extensively and powerfully at the South, the anti-slavery men of the North denounce it as the friend and ally of slavery, and attempt its overthrow with more zeal and effort, if possible, than even that of slavery itself. Because the friends of colonization are indisposed to pursue a course which must, in their opinion, put in imminent jeopardy the peace and safety of a large portion of the country, endanger the security and even the very existence of the Federal Government, because they believe that the consent of the South is indispensable to any plan for the abolition of slavery, they are denounced as enemies to the colored race and to the cause of Liberty.[41]

There is a good deal of the prophetic in this utterance.

If there was any distinctive feature of William Lloyd Garrison's efforts from 1831 to 1839, it was the alienation of New England and the West from the spirit of cooperation with the South, in the effort to get rid of slavery, to the spirit of antagonism against the South, in the effort to force that section to abolish slavery. If the methods of Garrison during those years had any inevitable result, it was that of replacing nationalism by sectionalism. A generation had not passed away before the surmises of Gurley had become regrettable fact. Eight years after the tour upon which comment has just been made, he was in New England again; and this time he found churches closed against him and all those who worked with him; he found the New England public apathetic toward the essentially national efforts of his Society; he found the clergy either cowed into silence by the pronounced views of their congregations or else themselves victims of the adroit, if unscrupulous, lecturers, editors, and agitators who visited every

---

[41] *African Repository*, vol. x, pp. 129–139.

New England and Western town.[42] By 1840 Garrison had accomplished very well one thing— the consolidation of New England and the then Northwest in an aggressive sectionalism. Those individuals from the North who had visited the South, or who had resided there, understood that the denunciations of Garrison were based upon a picture of a system of slavery that, as a system, had no existence save in the mind of that leader.[43] But, unfortunately, those were not the days of railroad and telegraph lines, and Garrison and the masses whom he influenced knew little of the real system of slavery that existed in the South.[44]

Public opinion unified and sectional passion excited, the next step in the program of the Garrisonians was to enter politics. Hereafter the fitness of a candidate was to be judged by his agreement or disagreement with their views on the subject of slavery. This step had been reached before the end of the thirties.[45] It was the most dangerous step Abolitionists ever took. It is always dangerous for any considerable section to test the fitness of those political leaders who sit as the nation's lawmakers by their position upon any issue that is essentially sectional. By 1840 the New Hampshire Garrisonians had so far developed their scheme of coercion as to determine to unsettle all clergymen in the State who would not subscribe to their views.[46] If we will remember that the mass of the people of New England knew little of the system of slavery as it actually existed at the South, and also that it was these same people who elected or refused to elect those candidates and those clergymen who offered their services to the State and to the Church, we shall better understand why the very leaders

---

[42] Journal of Executive Committee of American Colonization Society, MS., Nov. 25, 1842, pp. 294-307; Letters of American Colonization Society, MS., Danforth to Gurley, December 21, 1832; S. M. Worcester to Gurley, Amherst College, November 5, 1834.
[43] Ibid., G. D. Abbot to Gurley, New York, Jan. 15, 1833.
[44] Ibid., Amos A. Phelps, Andover Theological Seminary, Jan. 15, 1828.
[45] African Repository, vol. xv, p. 19 ff.
[46] Letters of American Colonization Society, MS., Prof. O. P. Hubbard to Wilkeson, Dartmouth College, May 5, 1840.

in New England thought were anti-Garrisonians in 1832, while, in 1840, many of them had gone over to that faith.

It must not be supposed that William Lloyd Garrison and The Liberator, alone, conquered the Colonization spirit of New England and the Northwest. There were other speakers and other papers, many of them. It seems that at the Granville, Ohio, postoffice in 1836, there were being taken, or were sent, more than three hundred Abolition publications and only one publication of the Colonizationists.[47] The President of the Granville Colonization Society wrote that of six hundred and ninety periodicals, religious, scientific, professional, and Abolition, emanating from one hundred and twenty presses, there was but one copy of the African Repository and no other Colonization paper taken; also, that "Anti-Slavery lecturers have for several years past visited us every few weeks or months; sometimes remaining a week or two and lecturing as often as they could collect a congregation."[48] Gurley in 1842 estimated the proportion of Colonization to Abolition lecturers to be about one to one hundred.[49] At any rate, there had come over some prominent Colonizationists a radical change of sentiment, and some Colonization leaders became such opponents of the Society as to out-Garrison Garrison.

One of these was Arthur Tappan who, by 1833, came to the opinion that "The Colonization Society is a device of Satan and owes its existence to the single motive to perpetuate slavery."[50] And Gerrit Smith, who had given thousands of dollars to the Society and had expressed his displeasure with the methods of Garrison, was a radical of the radicals by 1838. He had been asked to contribute to the erection of a Methodist Church in New Orleans. He refused to do so, and stated his reason as follows:

Suppose I were invited to contribute to the cost of erecting a heathen temple, could I innocently comply with the request? . . .

[47] Ibid., Seven Wright to Gales, Granville, Ohio, March 23, 1836.
[48] Ibid., W. S. Richards to Gurley, Granville, Ohio, March 28, 1838.
[49] Ibid., Gurley to R. S. Finley, Dec. 14, 1842, No. 489.
[50] Ibid., Tappan to Gurley, New York, June 26, 1833.

Now, I take it for granted, that the Religion which is to be preached in the "place of worship" which you invite me to assist in preparing is the Religion of the South; and I put it to your candor, whether it is not, therefore, fairly to be considered as an idolatrous "place of worship."[51]

Besides the direct attacks made by the Garrisonians upon the Colonization Society and those who were interested in it, that party worked indirectly but very effectively to the prejudice of Colonization by discouraging the blacks from offering to emigrate to the colony. The word "emigration" was replaced by the words "banishment," "expatriation," and so on. Although the records have been examined, not a single case of involuntary exportation has been revealed; but the use of those terms kept many a negro from offering to go to Liberia. The free blacks, who at one time hailed with delight the opportunity of returning to the land of their fathers, began to adopt resolutions in opposition to the Society, and after the thirties there was a marked indisposition among them to emigrate to the colony.[52]

In the South probably the most effective argument against the Colonization Society was that it was but a form of Abolitionism; in the North and Northwest, that its purpose was to "rivet the chains of the slave." The persistence of those who used these contradictory arguments ought to be well nigh conclusive of the motives of Colonizationists. But hitherto it has never been so.[53] Henry Clay expressed the position of the Society when he said: "Both objections cannot be founded in truth. Neither is."[54] The proslavery

[51] African Repository, vol. xiv, pp. 48-49.
[52] Carey, p. 2; Letters of American Colonization Society, MS., Burr to Gurley, Richmond, Va., January 27, 1834; African Repository, vol. xvi, p. 114; Speech of Edward Everett at Anniversary of American Colonization Society, January 18, 1853; Manuscript Division, Library of Congress, Massachusetts Broadsides, 24th Anti-Slavery Bazaar.
[53] African Repository, vol. i, pp. 341-343; vol. vi, p. 1 ff.; vol. ix, pp. 228-229; vol. xii, p. 298; vol. xiv, pp. 17-18; vol. xix, p. 152.
[54] No more complete refutation of the charges of the Abolitionists, who declared that the Colonization Society forged the chains of the slaves, can be given than the following references to private letters written by leading agents of the Society. They contain what ought to be a final answer to those who made, or continue to make, those charges. Letters of American Colonization Society, MS., Bir-

slaveholders, and it is a pity Garrison could not realize that there were actually antislavery slaveholders in the South, ought to have understood that an organization that was as persistently opposed by the Abolitionists as was the Colonization Society, could not be considered an advocate of a general and immediate abolition of slavery; and the Abolitionists ought to have understood that an organization that, in 1832, could not maintain an agency in either Georgia or South Carolina, was hardly to be convicted of collusion with slaveholders.[55]

Colonizationists believed that a general, immediate, and unconditional emancipation of all the slaves in the Union was impracticable and undesirable: impracticable (1) because there was no constitutional right of the federal government to enact a general emancipation provision, (2) because the States alone having the right to pass emancipation measures would do so only as the public sentiment of each slave State became favorable to emancipation, (3) because public sentiment in the slave States was not yet favorable; undesirable (1) because it was believed that three millions of negro slaves set free at one time would be unable to care

---

ney to Gurley, Huntsville, Alabama, July 12, 1832; Mechlin to Gurley, Liberia, February 28, 1833; Cresson to Gurley, Mar. 15, 1833; Danforth to Gurley, Boston, December 28, 1832; J. H. Cocke to Gurley, Norfolk, January 14. 1833; Gallaudet to Gurley, Hartford, March 24, 1833; Finley-Birney to Gurley, New Orleans, April 13, 1833; Gurley to Fendall, Boston, August 3, 1835; T. B. Balch to Wilkeson, Locust Hill, October 11, 1839; Balch to Wilkeson, New Baltimore, November 20, 1839; J. D. Mitchell to Cresson, Liberty, December 28, 1839; Henkle (see Cresson to Wilkeson), February 27, 1840; Ker (see Cresson to Wilkeson), Miss., March 12, 1840; W. McKenney to Wilkeson, Greensboro, N. C., November 6, 1840; Mrs. M. B. Blackford to Gurley, Va., January 28, 1843; C. W. Andrews to McLain, Virginia, Mar. 27, 1843; Tracy to Gurley, Boston, May 8, 1843; Pinney to McLain, April 5, 1845; D. L. Carroll to McLain, New York, July 5, 1845.

No effort has been made to continue these references beyond the year 1845, for it is believed that there is no doubt about the position of the Colonization Society after that time. Nor is the above a complete list. It is deemed, however, sufficient to set forth the true view of the Society on the subject of slavery.

[55] Minutes of Board of Managers of American Colonization Society, MS., March 7, 1832; March 12, 1832; March 26, 1832; April 9, 1832; July 11, 1832.

for themselves, and would be more wretched than under a system of slavery, (2) because the so-called free negro was not in any true sense free, and it was believed would not become really free until he was taken back to his native country and there, under the supervision of sympathetic governors, was taught self-sustenance and self-government, (3) because of the danger of a race war in the States of the lower South. They recognized slavery to be an evil. The remedy for it they believed to be gradual emancipation, made practicable through (1) cooperation between the different sections of the Union, (2) the education of slaveholders, (3) and the transportation of those manumitted or emancipated. They hoped and believed that such States as Maryland, Virginia, Kentucky, and Tennessee would enact general emancipation measures within a period of time not very remote, and that with these States free, the rest would follow, as the success of emancipation and transportation combined was demonstrated. They hoped to exert a powerful *moral* influence in favor of emancipation, but were opposed to the use of *illegal* means or means whose result might be to involve the sections in civil war, or bring about the dissolution of the Union. The gradual abolition of slavery was not to be an incidental object of the Society. It was to be one of the two direct, distinct, and primary objects: (1) to give real freedom to the nominally free American negro, by returning him to his native land and there encouraging his highest development, (2) to exert the most powerful *moral* pressure consistent with national peace and unity in favor of an emancipation as rapid as practicable, and both universal and absolute.[56]

From its origin, the Society used with eagerness every opportunity to secure the liberation of slaves by offering to transport them to the colony, unless the condition of its treasury was such that it could not afford the expenditure.

---

[56] African Repository, vol. vii, pp. 49, 176, 200-201, 314; vol. ix, pp. 228-229; vol. x, p. 148; vol. ix, pp. 188-189; vol. i, pp. 15-16; Letters of American Colonization Society, MS., Ker to Gurley, New Orleans, April 2, 1832; East Attleborough, December 24, 1831.

When slaveholders wrote for advice as to the disposition of their slaves, as they often did, the Society consistently advised the emancipation of those in bondage, unless the case involved some peculiar circumstance. There has been found on the records of the Society no instance in which the organization ever assisted a slaveholder to retain the possession of slaves whose right to liberty was called into question. There are a number of instances in which the Society intervened in suits to secure the liberty of slaves, the total number involved running up into the hundreds. After 1839 the organization became almost aggressively anti-slavery. Abandoning its former position—the use of moral suasion to bring about gradual emancipation—it became, in many respects, a moderate abolition society. During this latter period it would send throughout the land reports on the number of slaves offered to it, on condition that it would transport them, and would directly appeal for funds to secure the liberation of the negroes. It is believed that this is a fair statement of its position on the subject of slavery. If so, it will be seen that the Garrisonians did great injustice to the whole movement and the leaders engaged in it.

The fundamental difference between the Garrisonian and the Colonizationist was this: the Garrisonians approached their task from the point of view of the eradication of an evil; the Colonizationists, from the point of view of the solution of a problem. Of the three phases of the question, the practicability, the desirability, and the method of the immediate liberation of the slave, the Garrisonian assumed the first two and considered only the third a problem; the colonizationist recognized a problem in all three. To the Colonizationist, the difference between gradual emancipation and immediate emancipation was not equal to the calamity of the dissolution of the Union, or an American civil war, or both. To the Garrisonian, the difference was worth that much. The Colonizationist chose rather to delay the day of complete emancipation than to live to see the day of the division, probably a bloody division, of the Union. The Garrisonian chose the dissolution of the Union rather than the delay of a general emancipation.

Whatever difficulty present day writers on the Abolitionist movement have in explaining the denial of Lincoln that he was a member of that party, or, whatever difficulty they may have in explaining his preference for Colonization, they may see, from this point of view, that, taken for granted his paramount consideration of the Union and its preservation, the only logical position he could take was that taken by Colonizationists. Lincoln undoubtedly opposed negro slavery, but the evidence seems conclusive that he emancipated the slaves, not out of his hatred of slavery, but out of his love for the Union. He stated very clearly his position in the following words:

> I would save the Union. I would save it the shortest way under the Constitution. The sooner the National authority can be restored, the nearer the Union will be "the Union as it was." If there be those who would not save the Union unless they could at the same time save slavery, I do not agree with them. If there be those who would not save the Union unless they could at the same time destroy slavery, I do not agree with them. My paramount object in this struggle is to save the Union and is not either to save or to destroy slavery. If I could save the Union without freeing any slave, I would do it; and if I could save it by freeing all the slaves, I would do it; and if I could save it by freeing some and leaving others alone, I would also do that. What I do about slavery and the colored race, I do because I believe it helps to save the Union; and what I forbear, I forbear because I do not believe it would help to save the Union.[58]

The preservation of the Union was his paramount consideration; the emancipation of slaves was an important consideration, but nevertheless, it was a secondary consideration. He would have sacrificed immediate emancipation for the sake of preserving the Union. The Garrisonians would have sacrificed the Union for the sake of immediate emancipation. In short, Lincoln's position was precisely that of the Colonizationists and precisely the opposite of that of the Garrisonians. If Garrison's influence in bringing about the

---

[57] J. F. Rhodes, History of the United States from 1850–1877, vol. iv, p. 74.

Proclamation of Emancipation were not overestimated, and if his influence in bringing about the American Civil War were not underestimated, he would be given a more just, if not a more exalted, place in American history.

A well known historical writer assures us, in reference to anti-slavery leaders, that "it must not be supposed that . . . even the agitators realized that slavery had the latent power of dividing the Union and bringing about civil war."[58] This statement, it seems, is at variance with the facts. Between 1831 and 1845 they were so frequently and so earnestly warned of the logical consequences of their course, by patriots who represented every section of the Union, that those who neglected those warnings must be charged with either ignorance or indifference. If they did not see, it was because they had closed their eyes to the light. When Harrison Gray Otis of Boston spoke in Faneuil Hall, in 1835, he said:

> Now, sir, if it were the object of our meeting here to debate the expediency of taking measures for the abolition of slavery, I would regard it as identical with the question of the expediency of dissolving the Union. I am sure it would be so considered by the Southern States. My conviction results from forty years acquaintance with prominent individuals of those States, of all parties, and in all the vicissitudes of party. Be assured that whenever that question shall be agitated in our public assemblies, under circumstances which should indicate the prevalence or the probability of a general sentiment in the free States in favor of acting upon that subject, the Union will be at an end. They would regard all measures emanating from such a sentiment as war in disguise upon their lives, their property, their rights and institutions, an outrage upon their pride and honor, and the faith of contracts—menacing the purity of their women, the safety of their children, the comfort of their homes and their hearths, and, in a word, all that a man holds dear. In these opinions they might be mistaken, but in support of them they would exhibit a spectacle of unanimity unparallelled among so numerous a population upon any subject, at any time, in any part of the world.[59]

"Every effort," said he, "intended to propagate a general sentiment favorable to the immediate abolition of slavery, is of forbidding aspect and ruinous tendency." "I witnessed the adoption of the Constitution, and through a long

---

[58] Hart, Slavery and Abolition, p. 3.
[59] African Repository, vol. xi, pp. 311–318.

series of years, have been accustomed to rely upon an adherence to it as the foundation of all my hopes for posterity. It is threatened, I think, with the most portentous danger that has yet arisen."

Judge William Halsey of New Jersey expressed his view of the results of abolitionism:

> It is time for the friends of Colonization to come out and . . . shew the extremely dangerous tendency of their proceedings and oppose by every means *except force,* mobs, and lynch laws. The situation of things requires the serious consideration of the friends of the harmony and integrity of the Union. We appear to be asleep upon a volcano, insensible of our danger. It may soon burst forth and spread desolation throughout our land.[60]

The general agent of the Colonization Society for Massachusetts wrote of the doctrines of the ultra-Abolitionists:

> It was seen by some from the beginning that the leaders of that society were propagating a deep and refined metaphysical system, which must naturally end in the "no-human-government theory"; in the doctrine that not only slavery, but the state, the church, and even the legal relations of husbands and wives, parents and children, ought to be abolished.[61]

In a debate in the Senate in 1839 Henry Clay declared that the ultra-Abolitionists were resolved to persevere at all hazards and without regard to consequences, however calamitous. Continuing, he said:

> With them, the rights of property are nothing; the deficiency of the powers of the General Government is nothing; the acknowledged and incontestible powers of the States are nothing; civil war, a dissolution of the Union, and the overthrow of a government in which are concentrated the fondest hopes of the civilized world, are nothing. A single idea has taken possession of their minds, and onward they pursue it, overlooking all barriers, reckless and regardless of all consequences. . . . Utterly destitute of constitutional or other rightful power, living in totally distinct communities as alien to the communities in which the subject on which they would operate resides, so far as concerns political power over that subject, as if they lived in Africa or Asia, they nevertheless promulgate to the world their purpose to be to manumit forthwith, . . . and without moral preparation, three millions of negro slaves, under jurisdictions altogether separated from those under which they live. . . . Does any considerate man believe it to be possible to effect such an object without convulsion, revolution, and bloodshed? . . . The abolitionists, let me suppose, succeed in their present aim of uniting the

---

[60] Letters of American Colonization Society, MS., Halsey to Wilkeson, Newark, January 12, 1841.

[61] African Repository, vol. xviii, pp. 369-376.

148 THE AMERICAN COLONIZATION SOCIETY

inhabitants of the free States as one man, against the inhabitants of the slave States. Union on the one side will beget union on the other. And this process of reciprocal consolidation will be attended with all the violent prejudices, embittered passions, and implacable animosities which ever degraded or deformed human nature. A virtual dissolution of the Union will have taken place, whilst the forms of its existence remain. . . . One section will stand in menacing and hostile array against the other. The collision of opinion will be quickly followed by a clash of arms. I will not attempt to describe scenes which now happily lie concealed from our view.[62]

In Ohio, Elisha Whittlesey in 1839 openly charged the Abolitionists with views hostile to the Union, "as well from the tendency of their measures, as from a sermon preached last year at Braintree, Massachusetts, that went the rounds, as canonical; in which a separation of the Union is hailed as the most happy of all events."[63] In 1833 C. F. Mercer, of Virginia, gave this challenge to the Abolitionists:

Let those who oppose the colonization of Africa, by our colored population, because it is not a scheme for the immediate abolition of slavery in America, justify, if they can, to God and man, their hostility to a plan of enlarged policy, as well as of expanded benevolence and piety, because it does not propose to accomplish *all* that they desire, and because they desire to do that which if accomplished, *as they propose, would prostrate the fair fabric of our Union, and with it the hopes of freedom to man.*[64]

James Garland, of Virginia, said of the effects of Garrisonian abolitionism: "Week by week, day by day, and hour by hour, they are creating among your youth feelings of strong prejudice and hostility to the institutions of the South," and he stated in unmistakable terms that aggressive action from the North would be met with a definite, united opposition from the South.[65] John Tyler in 1838 said: "Philanthropy, when separated from policy, is the most dangerous agent in human affairs. It is no way distinguishable from fanaticism." Of that form of philanthropy called abolition, he says: "It would pull down the pillars of the constitution, and even now shakes them most terribly. . . ."[66]

---

[62] Ibid., vol. xv, p. 50 ff.
[63] Letters of American Colonization Society, MS., Whittlesey to Wilkeson, Canfield, Ohio, November 27, 1839.
[64] African Repository, vol. ix, pp. 265-267.
[65] Ibid., vol. xiv, pp. 43-47.
[66] 27th Cong., 3d sess., H. Rept. No. 283, p. 961.

The secretary of the Colonization Society saw clearly the tendency of Garrisonian Abolition, and he deplored the rashness which prompted it. Nowhere is the real unionist spirit of the Society better set forth than in his letters written to its Managers. He traveled and knew sentiment in every part of the Union; and he writes from New York, in 1834:

> For one, I feel that an awful crisis is fast coming upon the country and that the slave question is to shake the Union. . . . If the mild principles of our Society can [?] in the public mind, all will be safe. But if the pulpit and press of the North is to be enlisted in the cause of instant unconditional Abolition, the whole land will be filled with violence. The signs of the times are portentous.[67]

The next summer he wrote from Boston:

> That the centre of the nation is to be *deeply moved* and *speedily on the subject of slavery is certain*. At the next Congress, we should, . . . make a powerful and earnest appeal to the General Government. Nothing *can* be *lost* by such a measure—*everything may* be gained—the preservation of the Union, a gradual, cautious, plan of voluntary emancipation, and the regeneration of Africa. Should the doctrines and measures of the Abolitionists predominate in the non-slaveholding States, disunion, if not a general servile war will follow.[68]

The plain unvarnished fact is that William Lloyd Garrison was woefully deficient in his love for the American Union. To produce conclusive evidence of this, it is only necessary to quote three resolutions offered by him at a meeting of the Essex (Massachusetts) Anti-Slavery Society, in 1842:

> Resolved, That the American Union is and ever has been since the adoption of the Constitution, a rope of sand—a fanciful nonentity—a mere piece of parchment—" a rhetorical flourish and splendid absurdity "—and a concentration of the physical force of the nation to destroy liberty, and uphold slavery.
>
> Resolved, That the safety, prosperity, and perpetuity of the non-slaveholding States require that their connection be immediately dissolved with the slaveholding States in form, as it is now in fact.
>
> Resolved, That the petition presented to the U. S. House of Representatives, by John Q. Adams, from sundry inhabitants of Haverhill, in this county, praying Congress to take measures for a peaceful dissolution of the Union, meets our deliberate and cordial approval.[69]

---

[67] Letters of American Colonization Society, MS., Gurley to Gales, New York, April 17, 1834.

[68] Ibid., Gurley to Fendall, Boston, August 3, 1835; **Gurley to Gales**, Portland, September 18, 1835.

[69] African Repository, June, 1842, vol. xviii, p. 189.

150   THE AMERICAN COLONIZATION SOCIETY

If the antislavery agitators did not realize "that slavery had the latent power of dividing the Union and bringing about civil war," it was not for lack of warning from the sanest statesmen of the time.

If the spirit of Garrisonianism was the spirit of disunion, the spirit of Colonization was the spirit of national unity.[70] Garrison's attempt to "prick the consciences" of slaveholders ended by hardening, rather than "pricking" them, and the result was sectional bitterness. Garrison broke the bonds of Union; Colonizationists attempted to heal them. The tendency of Abolition was to pull to pieces; the tendency of Colonization was to bind together. The Garrisonians believed in antagonism; the Colonizationists believed in cooperation. The Abolitionist slandered; the Colonizationist sympathized. When the slaveholder passed by, the Abolitionist pointed the finger of scorn at him; the Colonizationist called him brother, and sought to help him solve his problem—the negro problem. The Abolitionist exclaimed, "You must"; the Colonizationist said, "Let's see if we can." The most important unofficial organization in making the Civil War irrepressible, if it was irrepressible, was ultra-Abolitionism; the most important unofficial organization in trying to bring about a peaceable settlement of the negro problem was the Colonization Society.

It must not be forgotten that Garrisonians were attempting—or, what was the same, so far as the alienation of the South was concerned, forced the South to the belief that they were attempting—to do a thing that was in plain violation of the federal Constitution. The most eminent constitutional lawyers in the United States agreed that the federal government had no power to interfere with the institution of slavery in those States in which it existed. Daniel Webster's view was as follows:

---

[70] Ibid., vol. i, p. 225; Nov., 1832, p. 275; Minutes of Board of Managers of American Colonization Society, MS., November 20, 1835, p. 197; Letters of American Colonization Society, MS., Wilkeson to Rev. A. Yates, March 31, 1840, No. 141.

COLONIZATION AND ABOLITION 151

In my opinion, the domestic slavery of the Southern States is a subject within the exclusive control of the States themselves; and this, I am sure, is the opinion of the whole North. Congress has no right to interfere in the emancipation of slaves, or in the treatment of them in any of the States.[71]

We have already seen that Clay's views coincided with that of Webster. Harrison Gray Otis was convinced that the Garrisonians were attempting to ignore the limitations of that instrument.[72] Even the constitution of the American Anti-Slavery Society contained the admission "that each State in which slavery exists has by the Constitution of the United States the exclusive right to legislate in regard to its abolition in said State."[73] And when it was proposed in the New York Anti-Slavery Convention in 1838 to eliminate a clause of its constitution similar to that just quoted, both Judge William Jay and Wendall Phillips opposed the elimination. Jay asked: "Is there a sane person in this assembly, who does not in his heart believe that . . . a law [a general abolition law] passed by Congress, instead of breaking the fetters of the slave, would instantly dissolve the bands of this Union? The South would not and ought not to submit to a usurpation so flagrant and profligate."[74] And yet, it was just such attempts as this that led Southerners to distrust the movements of their opponents.

To Colonizationists it seemed worse than useless, it seemed the height of folly, to make constant and consistent use of slander and abuse in the attempt to bring about emancipation in the South, which could constitutionally be brought about only with the consent and by the action of the slave States themselves. The Colonizationists were right. The difference between the policy pursued by the Abolitionists and that pursued by the Colonizationists was the difference between the inevitableness of a civil war, before a general emancipation, and the improbability of such a war, before a general emancipation.

---

[71] African Repository, vol. ix, pp. 188–189.
[72] Ibid., vol. xi, pp. 311–318.
[73] Ibid., vol. xiv, p. 173.
[74] Ibid., vol. xiv, p. 182 ff.

The essential mistake the Garrisonians made was in assuming that every slaveholder was a slaveholder from choice, and therefore, might be justly called a "manstealer," "liar," etc. ad infinitum. For instance, the Garrisonian denunciation was applicable to Mrs. Dabney Minor, of Virginia, who bought two negro slaves for the express purpose of freeing them and sending them to Liberia.[75] Mrs. Mary B. Blackford, also of Virginia, in her private letters to the Society frequently lamented the existence of the institution in her State. "From childhood I have bewailed the unnumbered ills of slavery. This (the Colonization Society) is the only plan at all practicable, of lessening, or removing them, and fervent is the love and gratitude I feel, to those who like you do much for this great cause."[76] She was pained to read in the Garrisonian periodicals wholesale denunciation, for she knew that many persons at the South "make the most noble sacrifices for the benefit of the negro."[17]

The Liberator's blanket invective was applicable also to Mrs. Ann R. Page, of Virginia—than whom not a purer or a nobler spirit lived in the whole of New England—and yet, a slaveholder! This combination was incomprehensible to the Garrisonian. Ergo, Mrs. Page was a "hypocrite," a "manstealer," a "liar,"—in short, was doomed to everlasting punishment. And yet, Mrs. Page almost wore her life away in anxiety over the welfare of her negroes. Day after day, for years, she gathered them together each morning and prayers were offered, scripture read, and they were urged to lead such lives as their mistress hoped for them. The expense involved in keeping them as she thought they should be kept brought on the estate a large debt. In the midst of her perplexities her husband died and, by the laws

---

[75] Letters of American Colonization Society, MS., W. S. White to Gurley, Charlottesville, Va., April 7, 1839.
[76] Ibid., M. B. Blackford to Gurley, Fredericksburg, Va., September 18, 1840.
[77] Ibid., M. B. Blackford, Fredericksburg, Va., September 18, 1840.

of the State, the slaves had to be sold—one of the greatest trials of her life was to see the law take its course in this instance. Of her slaves she said:

> My purpose respecting these people I hold to be so sacred that I desire not, and even fear to counsel with my dearest and wisest friends, because they would all advise me to relieve myself from this bondage in which I outwardly live, and which, in their kindness for me, they have thought would ere now have ended my days. ... I come to *Thee*, and look up through the blood of the Covenant for direction in all the affairs of this estate. And with regard to the frequent failures of some of these people in duty, let me not be put off by these things, from my settled purpose of doing them good.

When the day for the forced sale came, she retired to her room, dreading the probability that a number of the slaves would be purchased by the slavedealers present and sent to the States at the Southwest. Against this she prayed; and when the sale was over, it was found that although more than one hundred had been sold (many still remained unsold) not one had fallen into those dreaded hands. The negroes were all to remain near their former home. If this were the place, it would be a pleasant task to go further into the story of the life of this exalted character, whose treatment of her "people" was known throughout the entire State, and whose life would have been a benediction to any community in which she lived—even a community composed entirely of Garrisonians![78]

Taken baldly, as stated by Garrison, his unmeasured words were applicable also to General John H. Cocke, of Bremo, Virginia, whose hesitation about sending his negroes, those who were willing to go, to Liberia arose, not from his unwillingness to be rid of slaves but from his conviction that they were not able to care for themselves. At last he found among them a valuable man, a stone mason, a man of good moral character and who gave promise of doing well for his family and for the colony. For six months before the slave expressed his willingness to leave Bremo, his liberty had been at his option. With him were

---

[78] Ibid., Mrs. A. R. Page to Gurley, Milwood, Va., March 26, 1831; African Repository, vol. xx, pp. 298-305.

to go his wife and six children.[79] While the head of the house was interested in the colonization of his blacks, the mistress, no matter how many visitors had come to enjoy her hospitality, every day gathered the children of her "people" for instruction, while a pastor was employed to give religious instruction to their parents.[80] Finally, the all-inclusive character of Garrison's criticism covered the case of Miss Mary C. Moore, of North Carolina, who was not only willing but anxious to liberate her eight or ten negroes and pay the expense of their transportation to Liberia, although her needle was her only means of support when the slaves were gone. A citizen of her community, who was unwilling to see her bear this expense, asked a pointed and significant question: "Do you know of any abolitionist who will take these slaves and send them to Liberia, or place them in a state of freedom, in any of the States in which it is permitted to emancipate, or in which free colored persons may reside? Miss M. will cheerfully yield her right to such individuals. But she prefers Africa."[81]

In so far as the Abolitionists opposed the system of slavery, there can be no doubt that they did a great service to the cause of human freedom; but when this opposition took, as it continually did among the Garrisonians, the form of intemperate and untrue pictures of the system, and when it was distinctly applied in terms of personal abuse and slander to every man or woman in the South who owned a single slave, it tended more and more not only to make a general and peaceable emancipation an utter impossibility, but also to result in the enactment of measures more stringent than ever by State legislatures against the privilege of emancipating; and it was probably the means of preventing many a negro from securing his emancipation at the hands

---

[79] Letters of American Colonization Society, MS., Cooke to Gurley, Bremo, March 31, 1833.
[80] Ibid., S. B. S. Bissel to McLain, Greenwich, Conn., February 15, 1845.
[81] Ibid., T. P. Hunt to Gurley, Wilmington, N. C., June 17, 1834; African Repository, vol. xvi, pp. 263-264.

of his owner. It thus resulted in precisely that which the Garrisonians professed to oppose: "If it were evident that only by a short delay, he could be better prepared to receive the boon of liberty, still the slave ought to be a free man now."[82]

It must not be supposed that the writer is unmindful of the fact that, during that important decade beginning with 1830, there was going on in the lower South a most important change of sentiment on the whole question of slavery, and that this change must not be too largely attributed to resentment that resulted from Garrison's methods. That change of sentiment was due, in great measure, to the rapid development of the Southwest and the increase in cotton production. Laborers were needed; the soil was, much of it, virgin and fertile; negro labor seemed admirably suited to the cultivation of cotton. The economic wastefulness of the slave system was not yet duly appreciated. The result was the internal slave trade between the upper and the lower South. Professor Thomas Dew's contribution to the Pro-Slavery Argument is indicative of this profound revolution in the attitude of the South toward both negro slavery and the Colonization Society. The Society made an effort to counteract the influence that Professor Dew's essay was undoubtedly beginning to have.

Jesse Burton Harrison wrote his Review of the Slave Question after correspondence with and with the cooperation of the most important officials of the Colonization Society, who gave him every encouragement. Harrison states the burden of his essay to be as follows:

> To show the necessity of her [Virginia, in particular, and the South, in general] promptly doing something to check the palpable mischiefs her prosperity is suffering from slavery. We design to show that all her sources of economical prosperity are poisoned by slavery, and we shall hint at its moral evils only as they occasion or imply destruction to the real prosperity of a nation.[83]

He undertook to show that "an improving system of agri-

---
[82] See above.
[83] J. B. Harrison, Review of the Slave Question, pp. 9-15.

culture cannot be carried on by slaves"; that no soil, except the richest can be profitably cultivated by slaves, and even then only if its fertility is inexhaustible; that slaves are unfit to develop manufactures, one of the needs of the South; that "slave labour is, without controversy, dearer than free"; and that slavery discourages immigration. He further declared that "Virginia possesses scarcely a single requisite to make a prosperous slave labour State." "We state as the result of extensive inquiry, embracing the last fifteen years, that a very great proportion of the larger plantations, with from fifty to one hundred slaves, actually bring their proprietors in debt at the end of a short term of years. . . ."

Undoubtedly Dew's Essay had far more influence than did that of Harrison. The effort, in this study, is not to minimize the importance of the change that came over the South as a result of economic conditions, or to exaggerate the influence of the Garrisonians, but rather to compare the methods used by Colonizationists and Garrisonians and to set forth that, while both were positively opposed to the slave system, the methods of the latter were pregnant with serious mischief, while those of the former were indicative of a farsighted statesmanship. Dr. S. M. E. Goheen, the Missionary of the Methodist Episcopal Church to Liberia, said in 1838:

Having been educated in a non-slaveholding State, I was daily taught to look upon the man who held slaves as a monster scarcely human, and at all times to regard those engaged in or holding slaves as participating in crimes of the deepest dye; and notwithstanding I have resided in one, and traveled in several slave States, and *never* beheld the shade of a shadow of an attempt at the cruelties said to be practiced (daily) upon the slaves, yet it was impossible for me to overcome early prejudices, or to believe anything else than that slavery as there practiced, was the greatest evil in the States, or in the world, which I *now* very much doubt.[84]

Instead of the methods used by the Garrisonians, the employment of statements untrue, in point of fact, and foolish, in point of policy, the Colonizationists came much nearer the true statement of conditions in the slaveholding States

---

[84] *African Repository*, vol. xiv, pp. 364–365.

and nearer securing the cooperation of the South in a gradual emancipation, by the employment of more accurate statements. This is well exemplified in a letter written by Gurley while in England in 1841:

> I will not question the Honesty and benevolence of the great body of English and American Abolitionists, yet I regard many of their writings and proceedings as unjust to the public of the United States, particularly to the slaveholders and pernicious in all their tendencies. No one can more desire than the writer to see modification and amendment of the legal codes of the slaveholding States, in favor of the slaves. Atrocious crimes and cruelties are doubtless occasionally committed, in those States, on the persons of slaves. . . . Generally (and I speak from personal observation and inquiry in nearly all the Southern States of the American republic,) the citizens of those States are kind, humane, generous, and, in proportion to the whole population, equal to that found in most parts of Christendom, devout and exemplary Christians. No better friends have the slaves in any part of the world than are to be found in those States. Cases of harsh treatment, of severe punishment, of wanton disregard of their feelings, of the voluntary and cruel rupture of their domestic ties, of withholding . . . the necessaries of life, or denying to them opportunities to hear Christian instruction and worship God, are not common; they are exceptions, not the rule. Liabilities to evil in the system of slavery are great; trying separations and wrongs among the slaves frequent, yet many laws which darken the statute books of the slaveholding States are in practice nearly, if not quite, obsolete; and humanity and religion are exerting a mighty and increasing influence for the protection and good of this dependent people.
>
> Many, very many, masters and slaves are bound together by the ties of mutual confidence and affection. A large proportion of the slaves exhibit an aspect of comfort, contentment, and cheerfulness. There is much to regret, much to condemn, fearful evils which are perhaps never brought to light, in the system of slavery; yet all things (the very heavens themselves, as some would represent) are not wrapt in gloom. It is not to diminish the general sense of injustice as well as impolicy of slavery, viewed as a permanent system, that I thus write, nor that I would lessen the moral powers that are working for its abolition, but in reference to truth, and because he is blind who sees not that injustice to the master is injury and a crime against the slave. He who bears false witness against me, and seeks to destroy my reputation, must not expect to be my counsellor. If the abolitionists of New England and Old England have no influence among American slaveholders, and little with the citizens generally of the United States, to their errors in principle, and more to their faults and offences in practice, must they trace the cause.[85]

Let us compare the effects on public opinion of these two methods, the Abolition method of antagonism and abuse and

---

[85] 27th Cong., 3d sess., H. Rept. No. 283, pp. 1024-1025.

the Colonization method of cooperation and sympathy, the one designed to bring about the immediate, and the other the gradual abolition of slavery.

Dr. John Ker, one of the most prominent Colonizationists in the South, who almost single-handed succeeded in defending the right of individuals of Louisiana to emancipate their slaves when they were willing to send them to the colony, when the State legislature was about to enact a very radical measure denying that right to a slaveholder who offered upwards of three hundred slaves to the Society,[86] wrote, in 1831:

> The greatest difficulty we have to encounter is the *jealousy* of *Northern interference,* and of what the world thinks proper to call, "religious fanaticism." What, with you and me and all Christians would constitute the *highest* motive to exertion in this course, would only tend in Louisiana, (if urged at all), to paralyze and destroy the force of *other motives,* which fortunately are sufficient. I have myself received permission to use the names of some of the most influential men in the State; but it is difficult for you to conceive how essential it will be to present and great success, to avoid most scrupulously, anything which could excite the morbid sensibility of slaveholders and Southern men by jealousy of our Northern Brethren.[87]

Let those who still believe that there existed between the Colonization Society and the slaveholders of Virginia a collusion whose object was the perpetuation of slavery, read the following comment upon the result of Garrisonian methods. A careful perusal of the quoted extracts from this private letter of a prominent Virginian ought to carry some weight in our views relative to (1) the supposed tendency of the Society to "rivet the chains of the slaves," (2) the views of active Southern Colonizationists on the subject of emancipation, (3) the methods advised by these men to bring about emancipation, (4) characteristics of the Southern temper on the whole subject of slavery, (5) the effects of Garrisonian abuse. The writer says:

> It is a great mistake to suppose that the people of our State generally will shrink from ... discussion, or are too sensitive to per-

---

[86] African Repository, vol. xviii, p. 99 ff.
[87] Letters of American Colonization Society, MS., Ker to Gurley, Natchez, Miss., November 24, 1831.

mit it. On the contrary, I believe a very large proportion of the people, are willing to enquire into the merits of the slave system, and that many have their minds open to conviction upon the subject. Such violent tirades, however, as those issuing from the Anti-slavery presses of the North are calculated to do infinite mischief to the cause, and to rivet with a double bolt, the bonds they are intended to lose. You know that no man is more opposed to slavery than I am and have been for years. It is not, therefore, that any of their declamations about cruelty, manstealing, etc., has any effect on me, that I deplore their course, but I confess I am vexed to think that we, who entertain opinions averse to slavery here, who are ready and willing upon all proper occasions to assert and act upon them, who are perfectly acquainted with the subject, and with the temper of the people in this matter, should see all our hopes of finally eradicating this evil, spoiled and marred by the intemperance and folly, not to say wickedness, of those who are perfectly ignorant of the subject, its difficulties and dangers, but who ruin our chance of influence, by professing a common object with us. The object of all discussion on this subject, to do good here, should be, not to render the slaves discontented but to shew to the whites, of all classes, the baneful effects of the system upon them. It is perfectly obvious that slavery is a subject placed beyond the control of the General Government. It would therefore avail but little, so long as this Government lasts, if every man north of Mason and Dixon's line were deeply impressed with the impolicy, cruelty, injustice, or barbarity of slavery. That could not emancipate one wretch from bondage. "Emancipation" can never be effected without the consent of the slaveholders, and this can never be obtained by either abuse or threats. What we want is temperate argument, going to shew, the evils of slavery to ourselves, our posterity, and our country; the superiority in cheapness, convenience, and efficacy of free labor; then that the condition of the slave as well as the master would be improved by emancipation, and pointing out a mode in which this can be done safely without upturning at once all the foundations of society. Satisfy our people on these points and you will have thousands of converts to emancipation. The fact is . . . [abolition fanaticism] . . . paralizes our efforts. No friend of emancipation amongst us, cares to open his mouth on the subject, for fear of being branded as an ally of Garrison, and of doing evil instead of good to the cause he would advocate.[88]

Another Virginian, who would certainly not be included among her pro-slavery citizens, said of the Garrisonians:

Upon no other point connected with slavery have I ever known such unanimity in Virginia. The feeling of all of every age, that think about it, is this. It is a subject with which you *shall* not interfere; except indeed by scolding and calling names at the distance of three hundred miles; and that if, through the just judgment of Providence on our land, you shall ever get Congress to act on this subject, that moment the Union is dissolved.[89]

---

[88] Ibid., Edward Colston to Gurley, Martinsburg, Va., July 9, 1833.
[89] Letter to Washington Colonization Society, MS., W. M. Atkinson to Polk, Washington, D. C., January 27, 1834.

Colonel Addison Hall thought in September, 1835, that the reaction against abolition excitement had become so strong in Virginia that "it paralizes all effort. It would not only be unsuccessful, but attended with personal danger."[90] James Garland, a congressmen from the same State, who had in former years been an interested Colonizationist, was driven, by the exaggerations of Garrisonians, to become an opponent of even Colonization. In later years he resumed his interest in the Society, but against every Garrisonion effort he stood distinctly pledged.[91] And his position on the subject of slavery became violently anti-Garrisonian. A Methodist minister of New Orleans in 1838 wrote that the reaction against ultra-Abolitionism had had a distinctly harmful effect upon the comfort of the slave, and had been destructive of sentiment favorable to emancipation. The results of the efforts of Colonizationists had been favorable to emancipation.[92]

Francis Scott Key thought that both the free negro and the slave, in all the Middle States, had been subjected to additional restraints directly as a result of the efforts of the Abolitionists. The efforts of these agitators he characterized as "most unfortunate."[93] Elliot Cresson wrote from New Orleans: ". . . so morbid is the South from the recollection of abolitionism, that it is scarcely credible how little will excite a storm."[94] There was a widespread complaint among the Colonization agents of the South, and among active Colonizationists of that section, that this anti-Garrison feeling had become so strong and so dangerous that the South had not only become less considerate of its slaves, but it had also begun to confuse abolition and colonization, looking upon the latter as "the A. B. C. of Abolition." Thousands of Southerners were undoubtedly driven

---

[90] Letters of American Colonization Society, MS., Col. A. Hall to Gurley, Richmond, Va., September 3, 1835.
[91] African Repository, vol. xiv, pp. 43–47.
[92] Ibid., vol. xiv, pp. 48–49.
[93] Ibid., vol. xv, p. 113 ff.
[94] Letters of American Colonization Society, MS., Cresson to Wilkeson, New Orleans, April 25, 1840.

to an extreme proslavery position as a result of Garrison's efforts.[95]

Mathew Carey, of Philadelphia, and Roger M. Sherman, of Connecticut, may be taken as men of standing and influence in the sections from which they came. Both admitted the sincerity of the Garrisonians and at the same time both deplored the impolitic and injurious efforts that those abolitionists were making. Sherman was invited to attend the Anti-Slavery Convention in Albany, in 1839. In his refusal to be present Sherman expressed very clearly his views:

> Had the Rev. Dr. Edwards, and others, who publicly espoused measures of emancipation adopted in Connecticut soon after the Revolutionary War, called slaveholders Man-Stealers, in staring capitals . . . would it not have excited, in the Northern Yankees, more of resentment than conviction, and less of compliance than opposition? The Southern people have felt, and to a great degree, justly, that the Abolitionists of the North were addressing their fears; and not merely their understandings or consciences. They have been addressed in terms of opprobrious criminations rarely softened by the language of respect. This has made them inaccessible, . . . and has, I fear, put off emancipation for at least half a century. . . . Could a missionary, thus addressing civilized heathen, hope for a favourable audience?[96]

As representatives of the West, both Henry Clay and Elisha Whittlesey thought that the Garrisonians had done incalculable injury to both the white man and the slave, and even to the free negro.[97] A Colonization agent, Rev. M. M. Henkle, working in Ohio, summed up the results of Abolitionism as follows: ". . . contributing say $50,000 pr. annum to inflame the passions of the North, wake the resentments of the South, fetter more firmly the bonds of

---

[95] Ibid., Wilkeson to Rev. T. B. Barto, March 27, 1840, No. 100; W. McKinney to McLain, New Bern, N. C., April 15, 1840; J. B. O'Neall to Wilkeson, Springfield, S. C., March 6, 1841; Wm. Crabtree to Wilkeson, Savannah, Ga., March 10, 1841; Gurley to R. S. Marvin, February 7, 1842, No. 582.

[96] African Repository, vol. xv, pp. 242-244; Letters of American Colonization Society, MS., Carey to Gurley, Philadelphia, December 22, 1829.

[97] African Repository, vol. xii, pp. 10-12; Letters of American Colonization Society, MS., Whittlesey to Wilkeson, Canfield, Ohio, March 16, 1840.

the slave, and strain the tender ligaments of the political Union, to the last stretch of endurance. . . ."[98]

The most conclusive and interesting proof that Colonization had an influence beneficial and pronounced upon public sentiment at the South, and particularly upon slaveholders, is contained in a study of emancipations that were brought about by the influence of the Society.[99] But—and on this point present day writers have failed to do justice to the Society in their estimates of its importance—the effect upon public opinion is not to be measured alone in the number of emancipations effected or the size of the colony established. By far the most important influence the organization exerted prior to 1845 was its influence upon public opinion on the question of slavery. That influence was positive, though in large measure intangible and immaterial.

That between 1830 and 1840 the Colonizationists were drawing public sentiment, from New Orleans to Vermont, to a common view of the best solution of the whole negro problem, there is abundant evidence. In 1832 Dr. John Ker reported a large part of the most prominent political figures of Louisiana favorable to the colonization mode of dealing with slavery and the free negro.[100] In the same year, the Colonizationists were making their way into the confidence and were gaining the support of important officials in Virginia.[101] In 1834 there were still citizens of Vermont who were willing and anxious to meet their brethren from New Orleans, and settle the slavery question on the terms proposed by the Colonizationists.[102] In 1837, a joint committee of the Illinois legislature unanimously approved the colonization method, as had the officials of Louisiana and the citizens of Vermont. The Colonization societies, in their opinion, "were silently, but surely winning

---

[98] Letters of American Colonization Society, MS., Henkle to Gurley, Cincinnati, Ohio, June 18, 1838.
[99] See chapter below on Colonization and Emancipation, passim.
[100] Letters of American Colonization Society, MS., Ker to Gurley, New Orleans, April 4, 1832.
[101] Ibid., Atkinson to Gurley, Petersburg, Va., July 27, 1832.
[102] African Repository, vol. x, p. 148.

their way upon public opinion, and entwining powerfully around the affections of the people." As to the Abolitionists, they "have forged new irons for the black man, and added an hundred fold to the rigor of slavery. They have scattered the firebrands of discord and disunion among the different states of the confederacy." The Colonization scheme was their choice.[103] In 1838 the Southern Literary Messenger was satisfied with the Colonization scheme as being the "juste milieu," "the bread platform upon which the friends of this unhappy race may meet in soberness and safety."[104] And in 1840 the committee of the Pennsylvania Legislature, to which the matter had been referred, reported colonization to be, in their opinion, "the only mode by which an equality of rights can be secured to that unfortunate race [the negro]."[105]

Next, as to the results of Abolition and Colonization upon those religious bodies whose influence and organization extended throughout the Union. It has already been seen that before the rise of Garrisonism, there was great unanimity of sentiment in favor of Colonization among nearly all religious denominations. Again and again the Methodist church passed resolutions in its national gatherings warmly recommending the cause to the attention of its ministry. The same was true of the Presbyterian and of the Baptist churches. But as has also been seen, one of the most significant changes of sentiment brought about by Garrison's efforts was the change in the position New England churches took between 1831 and 1845. In 1831 public opinion was being led by sentiment in the churches; in 1845 public opinion was leading sentiment in the churches.

A study of the division of the Methodist church, 1844–1845, is of peculiar interest as exhibiting this change of sentiment that had been going on at the North. In 1834 a Methodist Conference, sitting at New Haven, Connecticut,

---

[103] Ibid., vol. xiii, pp. 109–111.
[104] Ibid., vol. xiv, p. 308.
[105] Ibid., vol. xvi, pp. 136–137.

recommended the Colonization movement, and deplored the opposition of the Abolitionists, as "directly calculated to injure the best interest of colored men, whether bond or free," and also calculated to have the "most unfavorable results" upon the progress of Christian principles.[106] And yet, just ten years later, the organization of the Methodist church was rent in twain, and the territory from Maryland to the Gulf of Mexico came under the jurisdiction of the Southern Methodist Church. There has been much discussion upon the causes of that division; but the leading cause seems to the writer to be almost obvious, when viewed in the light of the attitude each section of that church took toward the Abolition and Colonization societies. It is universally admitted that the question of slavery was almost the sole cause of the disruption of that church. But was it the attitude of the Northern Methodists or of the Southern Methodists that brought about the division? In 1834 united Methodism was very favorable to the Colonization scheme. In 1845 the Southern Methodists were still favorable to it; but the Northern Methodists had come so far under the influence of Garrison, or they had been so far carried away from their position of ten years before by the tide of public sentiment, that, either because the majority of Northern Methodists had become Garrisonian or at least aggressively Abolitionist, or else because so strong a minority of them had gone over to that party, they forced the Northern majority by a threat of secession from them and secured the passage of a resolution whose effect was practically to suspend a Southern Bishop who had inherited two slaves.

The fact is that the Southern Methodist Church in 1845 retained the same good feeling for Colonization that it had in 1835; but the Northern section of Methodism had been borne away on the tide of Abolitionism. Whatever may be said about the legal forms the separation took, and whether by the acts of separation the Southerners seceded from the

---

[106] Ibid., vol. x, p. 127.

general body or the general body seceded from the Southerners, or whether the separation was completely by agreement—neither church seceding, but both agreeing peaceably to separate—it is nevertheless a matter of fact that in terms of ultimate and real causes, the Northern Methodists changed radically their views while those of the Southern Methodists remained practically what they had been in 1834. In 1835 both Northern and Southern Methodists were, as a body, opposed to radical Abolitionism. In 1845 the Southern Methodists were still opposed to it; while the majority, or a commanding minority of the Methodists of the North had become favorable to it. In 1835 Northern and Southern Methodists warmly recommended the Colonization Society. In 1845 it was the Southern church that warmly recommended it. That year the Mississippi Conference of the Southern Methodist Church unanimously adopted a resolution commending the cause of Colonization.[107]

Northern Methodists had been drawn away from their former ground by the tide of public sentiment; Southern Methodists remained where they had stood ten years before. And George F. Pierce, later Bishop Pierce, was right in declaring at the General Conference of 1844: "The difficulties are with the New Englanders. They are making all this difficulty. . . ."[108] Indeed, the Northern section of the church had gone so rapidly to the position of the Abolitionists that they were ahead of the regulations of their book of discipline. There had been no disciplinary rule adopted by which a slaveholding bishop could be suspended from the exercise of his functions; and the resolution of suspension was adopted largely, it seems, as a matter of expediency, to prevent the secession of the whole of New England Methodism.[109] Either because of its own convictions, or to save to itself New England Methodism, the

---

[107] Letters of American Colonization Society, MS., Pinney to McLain, New Orleans, December 13, 1845; December 14, 1845.
[108] G. G. Smith, Life and Times of George F. Pierce, chap. vi.
[109] Ibid.

Methodist Episcopal Church changed its attitude and thus abandoned the ground it had held in common with Southern Methodism.[110] Few Virginians in 1846 were more ardent Colonizationists than Bishop John Early, president of the Petersburg Colonization Society. And that year both bishops of the Southern Church were Colonizationists,[111] as were leading Southern Methodist ministers, like William Winans of Mississippi, or John E. Edwards of Richmond.

One can without difficulty recognize the meat upon which the New Hampshire minister fed who, in advocating the resolution which brought about the division of the Methodist Church, declared: "Men-buyers are exactly on a level with men-stealers."[112] That was not the spirit of Colonization; it was the spirit of Garrisonian Abolition. It rent in twain other religious bodies. And it was because Garrisonian Abolition was fundamentally and essentially destructive of economic, social, political, and religious national unity. The influence of Colonization was exactly the reverse. We have seen its unifying influence in our study of its effect upon the public opinion of the United States. It was so in society. It was distinctly so in the church.

Finally, in comparing the methods and results of Garrisonian Abolition and the Colonization Society, it may be interesting to look for a while at the interchange of views that was taking place among Colonization leaders, and see how far those views will aid us in refuting the oft-repeated charges of the Garrisonians that, after all, Colonization was an enormous obstacle in the way of emancipation, and that its ally was the slaveholder.

As early as 1828 Elliot Cresson was urging upon the Secretary of the Colonization Society the importance of hearty cooperation between the Abolitionists and Colonization-

---

[110] African Repository, vol. xix, p. 252.
[111] Letters of American Colonization Society, MS., T. C. Benning to McLain, Petersburg, Va., May 5, 1846; Rev. J. E. Edwards, Richmond, Va., May 25, 1846.
[112] Smith, p. 123.

ists.[113] In 1831 one of the largest contributors to the Society in Kentucky was a man who had liberated his slaves and for five years refused to eat with a slaveholder, especially if he were a Methodist.[114] Robert J. Breckenridge, of Kentucky, had made great sacrifice of reputation in order to aid the Colonization Society to hasten the day of general emancipation in his State.[115] William M. Blackford, a leader among Colonizationists of Eastern Virginia, expressed himself as follows on the subject of slavery:

> We have had reason to curse slavery within the last day or two, from a painful exemplification of it's evils occurring under our own eyes. A year ago I bought [and therefore, by the reasoning of the Abolitionists, he was a man-stealer] a negro woman from a trader, to prevent her separation from her husband. She was truly gratified and has made us a faithful servant ever since. Her husband belonged to an estate. In dividing it, a sale became necessary, and without letting me know of it, he was sold to a trader. He was seized on the streets, handcuffed, and then permitted to take leave of his wife. He entered our yard, crying, and presented himself in that situation to his wife, who had not the remotest idea of such an event. I leave you to imagine the feelings of his wife— and also of Mrs. B[lackford]. It has prayed upon the latter's mind very much, and will, I fear, make her sick. The man was addicted to drink, but was civil and industrious, and made an affectionate husband. But I needn't pain you by reflections on this subject.[116]

J. Burton Harrison expressed the hope of Colonizationists generally when he wrote: "I am firmly persuaded that Kentucky is the most hopeful of all the slaveholding States (let me call them 'transition' States which seem not devoted to slavery in perpetuity, as Maryland, Virginia, Kentucky, and perhaps others) except Maryland."[117] A letter which is typical of scores of letters that were sent out to the Society's friends from the central office, contains the following: "We must if possible start a ship *next month.* About 40 liberated slaves are now waiting and must be *sent*

---

[113] Letters of American Colonization Society, MS., Cresson to Gurley, Philadelphia, August 23, 1828.
[114] Ibid., Finley to Gurley, Winchester, Ky., June 8, 1831.
[115] Ibid., R. J. Breckenridge to Gurley, Lexington, Ky., August 16, 1831.
[116] Ibid., W. M. Blackford to Gurley, Fredericksburg, Va., October 4, 1832.
[117] Ibid., Harrison to Gurley, New Orleans, May 16, 1833.

168   THE AMERICAN COLONIZATION SOCIETY

or *sold* for the *South!*"[118] John McDonogh, one of the foremost Colonizationists of Louisiana, sought from the legislature of that State permission to educate his slaves—for it was against the law for him to do so without obtaining permission from the legislature. He owned slaves valued at $150,000.00, and it was his purpose to colonize them all in Liberia, as they gave evidence of the ability to care for themselves.[119] Gerrit Smith, who would hardly be, by any student of Abolition, accused of pro-slavery leaning, wrote, in 1828, concerning the alarm among slaveholders suspicious of the Colonization Society: "I must think that our slaveholders are causelessly alarmed at the American Colonization Society."[120] He realized perfectly well that the sympathetic attitude the Society assumed in its official journal towards the slaveholder was assumed, not out of a love for slavery, but out of a belief that the only way to persuade the slaveholder to emancipate his slaves was to secure first his friendship and respect and, as a result, the liberation of his slaves.[121]

Of course it was no difficult matter for the Abolitionists to take these very sympathetic utterances and build up a conclusive argument setting forth the base motives of Colonizationists. And they did so, although the motive that they "proved" was exactly the opposite of that which the Colonizationists actually had. What was used as a bait to to secure the liberation of slaves was pictured by the Garrisonians to be the outcropping of the evil spirit back of the scheme. And yet a fair statement of its position was frequently made to the public in the African Repository. For instance, in 1830 it was there stated: "That the system of slavery must exist *temporarily* in this country, we as firmly

---

[118] Ibid., McLain to Mrs. Ann Richardson, November 14, 1840.
[119] African Repository, vol. x, p. 24.
[120] Letters of American Colonization Society, MS., Smith to Gurley, November 17, 1828.
[121] Ibid., Smith to Gurley, Peterboro, N. Y., Feb. 6, 1831.

believe, as that for its existence a single moment, there can be offered justly no plea but necessity."[122]

It was reasonably conclusive proof both of the sincerity of the Society and of the effectiveness of its methods that Francis Scott Key, appealing to Philadelphia for funds, reported that more than six hundred slaves were at that time offered by slaveholders on the condition of their removal to Liberia, and that only the funds were needed to secure their immediate liberation.[123]

While the appointment of Dr. Ezekiel Skinner as colonial agent was under consideration, he thought wise to make clear his position on the subject of slavery. It was this:

> I have ever held slavery in abomination as the blackest of the black catalogue of human crimes, the criminality of which is not in the least lessened by the authority of human laws and which will carry the souls of those who are guilty of this crime before the bar of God blacker with moral pollution than the skins of those whom they unjustly held in bondage.
> I am friendly to the Colonization Society as presenting the only means now with[in] our power to emancipate many whom we have reason to believe would otherwise die in slavery.[124]

This statement caused neither a withdrawal of his appointment nor criticism of his position.

At the annual meeting of the Society in 1834, Breckenridge thus stated the position of Colonizationists in their relation to the slaveholder: "We stand in the breach for him, to keep off the Abolitionists. We are his friends, but only to give him time. . . . And if he attempts to maintain slavery as perpetual, every one of us will be upon him too." At the same meeting Gerrit Smith reviewed several of the charges made against the Society, among which was the charge that there were at that time 265,000 persons "now in slavery, who would have been free if it had not been for the influence of this Society." A second charge was that all colonies whatever on the Coast of Africa went to sup-

---

[122] African Repository, vol. v, pp. 328–330; Letters of American Colonization Society, MS., Gurley to Fendall, New York, November 4, 1833.
[123] African Repository, vol. vi, pp. 138–139.
[124] Letters of American Colonization Society, MS., E. Skinner to Gurley, Ashford, Conn., January 23, 1834.

port, rather than suppress the slave trade. In its review of the speech, The Liberator maintained that both these charges were true.[125] It is an interesting fact that at that meeting it was a resident of Connecticut who urged the Society to confine its efforts chiefly to the transportation of free blacks, touching the question of slavery and emancipation as lightly as possible; and it was a resident of Maryland who urged that it concentrate its efforts upon transporting to the colony slaves emancipated for that express purpose—in short, that it become more pronouncedly a society whose purpose was the liberation of slaves.

Dr. Reese, one of the most prominent members of the New York City Colonization Society, thus expressed himself on his attitude towards slavery: "Sir, I abhor slavery, and therefore am I a friend of Colonization. . . . If slavery should not eventually, under the influence of kindness and confidence, be abolished, it would be because the visionaries of the North would prevent it."[126]

If there was ever a time when the Colonizationists were unscrupulously assailed from both the press and the platform of the Garrisonians, that time was from 1831 to 1840. R. R. Gurley, Secretary of the Society, saw more and knew more of that storm than did any other individual. During that period the Society's purposes were continually misrepresented, and Gurley knew, for he directed, the movements and efforts of the organization. In a number of personal letters written to members of the Board of Managers during this period, Gurley sets forth clearly both his own views and the views of those Colonizationists with whom he talked as he traveled for the Society from Massachusetts to Georgia.

Of the influence of colonization in Maryland he writes: "In Maryland, the spirit of Colonization is increasing among the slaveholders and no difficulty is experienced in

---

[125] The Liberator, Feb. 8, 1834. Here will be found an account of the speeches made at this important meeting of the Society.
[126] Ibid., May 24, 1834.

procuring emigrants of the best character, out of the city of Balto."[127] Of his hopes for Virginia he writes: "I trust Virginia will receive the special attention of the Board. Let her voice be with us; let her consent that Congress shall *appropriate money to colonization* and we have triumphed —slavery will go down with the consent of the South, and the Union will be preserved."[128] And again: "The people of the South must look to the Colonization policy as to the sheet anchor of their safety. Can they be so blind as not to see or so destitute of wisdom as not to prepare for the gathering storm? Can the South be induced to propose and support Colonization as a National measure looking to the final abolition of slavery? Will Virginia lead in the scheme? If so, all is safe."[129] Or again: "Let it be ours to bind together all the moderate and sober friends of Liberty and Africa in the Union."[130] After a journey into Louisiana and Mississippi, where several large bequests had recently been made for the Society, he commented: "Each successive year, hereafter, will bequests to our Institution be multiplying and increasing, thousands of slaves will be placed under the protection of the Society, and all motives concur to urge us to adopt all proper methods ... to enable us to secure such bequests and the freedom and colonization of such slaves, as may be entrusted to our care."[131] Kentucky, he thought, had proved a profitable field for Colonization effort, and he believed that the result was a rapidly growing disposition among her slaveholders to liberate their slaves, on condition of their emigration to the colony.[132]

Whether or not the very advocacy of gradual emancipation was of itself a hindrance to immediate emancipation there might be, and doubtless was wide difference of opin-

---

[127] Letters of American Colonization Society, MS., Gurley to Fendall, Boston, August 3, 1835.
[128] Ibid., Gurley to Gales, Boston, Oct. 3, 1835.
[129] Ibid., confidential, Gurley to Fendall, Boston, October 7, 1835.
[130] Ibid., Gurley to Gales, Philadelphia, December 12, 1835.
[131] Ibid., Gurley to Gales, Louisville, Ky., July 25, 1836.
[132] Ibid., Gurley to Fendall, Athens, Ga., June 7, 1837.

ion. If Abolitionists had urged this as the inevitable result of any scheme of gradual emancipation, the Colonizationists could have had no just quarrel. Such a question might have been threshed out on the battleground of reason. The great blunder the Garrisonians made was not in arguing that the tendency of Colonization was necessarily to put off the hoped-for day, but that it was the deliberate purpose of Colonizationists to put off that day. There have been found, among the records of the Colonization Society, prior to 1846, two letters which go to show that the members of one auxiliary Colonization Society, in Tennessee, and a number of lukewarm friends of the cause in Alabama based their support of Colonization upon the ground, either of its usefulness as an ally of the slaveholder, in removing the distracting free blacks from the possibility of their influence over the slaves, or of its usefulness in relieving a section undoubtedly burdened with free blacks.[133] And the writer of the letter from Alabama understood well enough the true objects of Colonizationists, to accuse his neighbors of "Machiavelism." Voluminous evidence, forsooth, upon which to make out a case for the Garrisonians!

It would not be difficult to show that there were cases in which the Garrisonians themselves prevented emancipations. In 1839, for instance, a Colonization agent was approached by a Kentucky slaveholder, who desired to emancipate his twenty slaves, giving them five hundred dollars, on condition of their willingness to go to Liberia. Upon invitation, the agent addressed the slaves and secured their consent to go. But the next morning they had all, save one, changed their minds. The cause of this change the master attributed (1) to the influence of the Garrisonians, who continually reminded the slaves that the Colonizationists desired to "banish" them, or to "expatriate" them, and (2) to the rumors that had come to them of violent cases of seasickness and deaths, which, with the rest, the Garri-

---

[133] Ibid., H. A. Wise to Gurley, Nashville, Tenn., January 9, 1830; W. C. Dennis to Gurley, Blakeley, Ala., December 21, 1838.

sonians did not hesitate to publish.[134] In 1840 the executor of Thomas Hall of Virginia who, by his will liberated some twenty-five of his slaves—each to be given twenty-five dollars if he agreed to go to the colony, and those refusing to go to revert to slavery—in reporting those who desired to emigrate, expressed his desire to go about through the community and solicit from his neighbors subscriptions to increase the allowance of the negroes who were about to leave; but he was prevented from doing so "by the wretched policy of the abolitionists," who had "created a prejudice against even colonization here, that threatens all hope of carrying on its operations south of Mason and Dixon's line. A man is in danger of being charged with a leaning to abolition if he advances Colonization."[135]

Such examples could be multiplied many times, and yet, it would be manifestly unfair to argue that the Garrisonians were opponents of emancipation. The charges of the Garrisonians were every whit as unfair. There were those in Kentucky who believed that, but for the extreme and radical opposition of the Abolitionists to Colonization, Kentucky would by 1840 have been practically ready to pass a general emancipation law. And of a large number of slaves owned by Mr. Black of Tennessee, and offered to the Society upon certain conditions, but who had fallen into the hands of ill-disposed heirs and sold to the Southwest, Secretary McLain wrote: "We begged hard for them but the country did not respond and now they are beyond our reach —and involved in perpetual slavery."[136] May it not be asked whether some of the money used in spreading baseless slanders against the Colonization Society might not profitably have been used in contributions to that Society, to secure the liberation of proffered slaves?

A leading minister of Mississippi declared, in New York, that the Colonization Society had had a tremendous influ-

---
[134] Ibid., G. W. Fagg to Wilkeson, Elizabethtown, Ky., September 19, 1839.
[135] Ibid., E. Broadus to Wilkeson, Culpeper, Va., August 11, 1840.
[136] Ibid., Cresson, Washington, June 3, 1844.

ence in preparing the way for the opening of the door of a gradual, but complete emancipation in that State, but that the rise of rabid Garrisonism had been one of the foremost agents in closing "every door that had been opened for the escape of the slave. . . ."[137] A plain miller of eastern Virginia, not troubled with the "too liberal construction" fears of his more learned fellow citizens, wrote to the Society, requesting the transportation of his family of six slaves, and expressed the opinion that, if the federal government and the Abolitionists would cooperate with Colonizationists, they could "heal a disease that, if not arrested, is likely to dissolve the Union."[138] From these evidences it seems clear that among the results of Garrisonian Abolition in the South are to be mentioned not only a change very unfavorable to voluntary emancipation, but also a large number of instances of actual prevention of immediate emancipation. And yet it would obviously do violence to the true interpretation of the Garrisonian faith to accuse its representatives of hostility to the immediate emancipation of slaves.

J. G. Birney, at this time an agent of the Colonization Society and soon to become Abolitionist, gives an interesting summary of his view on prospects in the South. These views are entitled to considerable weight, in the light of Birney's later prominence in political abolition and his place in the Liberal Party. In 1833, he wrote, of the prospects of getting rid of slavery in the slaveholding States:

The only effectual way that seems open to my view, is the withdrawing of Virginia from the Slave States, by her adoption of some scheme of emancipation. Should this be done, the whole system of slavery in the U. S. would, upon the very pressure of public opinion, be brought, and that in a few years, in shivers to the ground. In proportion as the slaveholding territory is weakened in political influence, it will be weakened in the power of withstanding the force of public sentiment; and the last State in which slavery shall exist . . . will . . . be perfectly odious. (The proceedings of the Abolitionists of the North have a very injurious effect here—they seem to furnish a kind of justification of slavery itself to the Southern slaveholders. I assure you, sir, I have nothing left but *hope* for

[137] African Repository, vol. xx, p. 183.
[138] Letters of American Colonization Society, MS., John Gray to McLain, Fredericksburg, Va., January 27, 1845.

the South. By the word *South*, I mean South—Ala., Missi., Loua. In 20 years they must be overrun by the blacks. There is no escape but in doing that, which, I am almost certain, will not be done.) What I would now suggest, would be to press with every energy upon Maryland, Virga. and Ky. for emancipation and colonization. If Virga. be not detached from the number of slaveholding States, the slavery question must inevitably dissolve the Union, and that before very long. Should she leave them, the *Union will be safe,* tho' the suffering of the South will be almost unto death. . . . I greatly approve of your opinion, that "for some years, at least, the North should *forbear*," that everything that looks like relief for the South may be attempted.[139]

Two and a half months later he wrote again:

I do not believe, that anything effectual can be done *South* of Tennessee. In the spirit of emancipation which the colonization cause has produced, the planters of the South see that it does *affect* the subject of slavery. This they are determined not to have touched *in any way*. It is my sincere belief that the South—at least that part of it in which I have been operating has, within the last year, become very manifestly, more and more indurated upon the subject of slavery.[140]

It was precisely this hope of winning the Middle States, that continued to permit slavery, and thus to win its way further and further down into the lower South, all the while making whatever efforts it could in the newer Southwestern States, that actuated the Colonization Society. With Virginia, Maryland, Kentucky, and Tennessee among the free States, the pressure of public opinion and the futility of physical opposition would make the entire Union some day, without a national upheaval, free from the blight of slavery. In the language of Francis Scott Key: "No slave State adjacent to a free State can continue so."[141] It was always in these "adjacent" States that the condition of the slaves was least undesirable, and hence, in which the accusations of the Garrisonians were most unfounded in fact. It was here also that the influence of the Garrisonians reached most directly, and where the reaction against both Abolition and Colonization, on account of the Abolitionists, was, if not more defiant, nevertheless most destructive.

If the sincerity of the Colonization cause, which the Gar-

---

[139] Ibid., Birney to Gurley, Huntsville, Ala., September 14, 1833.
[140] Ibid., Birney to Gurley, Danville, Ky., December 3, 1833.
[141] See above.

risonians charged with hypocrisy, has not yet been conclusively set forth, no more convincing documents could be recommended to the consideration of the investigator than the lengthy and comprehensive letter of Birney, on his severing his connection with the Colonization movement to become an Anti-Slavery leader, or a similarly lengthy and comprehensive letter of Gerrit Smith, just a short while before he also went over to the Anti-Slavery party. Birney's objection was not founded upon the discovery of any deviation from the straight line of an altogether laudable policy to place the free negro in a position where he would not be held down by the shackles of prejudice and, by peaceable means, to bring about the ultimate and entire abolition of slavery, but upon the belief that: "There is not in colonization any principle, or quality, or constituent substance fitted so to tell upon the hearts and minds of men as to ensure continued and persevering action."[142] And the letter of Gerrit Smith contains one of the most exhaustive, eloquent, and comprehensive defences of the motives of the leaders of the Society that has been presented to the public. His objection was not based upon any discovery of the slightest proslavery designs or feelings among those leaders, but upon the objection, in many respects the very opposite of that given by Garrisonians, that the Society had been neglectful of the American negro who was already free.[143]

It was a great struggle, that between the Garrisonians and the Colonizationists. Verily, it was the first American civil war on the subject of slavery. For ten years it raged. The outbreak of it was due to Garrison and his confederates and, from first to last, it was a defensive contest from the point of view of the Colonization Society. When it began, the States were divided into three comparatively distinct sections, the New England, the Middle, and the Southern. The Middle States extended from New York on the North to North Carolina on the South. There were three pre-

---

[142] The Liberator, August 16, 1834.
[143] Ibid., January 24, 1835.

vailing opinions. In the New England section, it was the Abolition sentiment, in the Middle section, it was the Colonization sentiment; in the Southern section, it was the positive pro-slavery sentiment. The outcome of that struggle is of deep significance; for when the end of it had come, the middle section had disappeared, so far as its importance as a "buffer state" of public sentiment is concerned. Henceforth there was to be a North and a South.

Striking evidence of this is seen on the one hand in the fact that as early as an annual meeting of the Society in 1834, the delegates from Pennsylvania and New York had thrown many of their former moderate views to the winds and were definitely antislavery; and on the other hand, the fact that the North Carolina Manumission Society founded in 1816 and, by 1825, boasting of fifty-eight auxiliaries and 1600 members, and the sympathy of probably a majority of the citizens of that State, founded with the avowed and definite purpose of freeing North Carolina slaves, held its last meeting in 1834, and failed in no small measure because of the revolt of North Carolinians from any thing that in the least savored of a Garrisonian program.[144]

Under able business management and an efficient corps of agents and advertisers, Colonization was to continue to do an important work; but the character of that work had changed. The struggle waged by the Abolitionists had made quite improbable, in the minds of the mass of Americans, the solution of the negro problem by the colonization plan. Many thousands of dollars were still to be contributed; but the contribution was made rather as an aid to the establishment of a model negro republic in Africa, whose effect would be to discourage the slave-trade, and encourage energy and thrift among those free negroes from the United States who chose to emigrate, and to give native Africans a demonstration of the advantages of civilization. In short, the eyes of Colonizationists were in great measure turned from a Southern slave system to a Republic of Liberia.

---

[144] University of North Carolina Magazine, vol. xiv, No. 4, p. 221.

Colonization continued to have a wide influence in almost every part of the country. But it ceased to have a controlling influence in any part of the country. The Abolitionists had enlisted those who were to be henceforth pro-Northern advocates; and it had definitely alienated the rest of those who had once been moderate. In a word, the Garrisonians had done much dangerously to divide the Union into two opposing sections whose sentiments were in the days to come little tempered by so moderate and unifying and healing a sentiment as that held by Colonizationists. From the point of view of its influence upon the subject of slavery Garrison undoubtedly won his fight, and in doing so, he was the forerunner and one of the leading "irrepressible" causes of the "irrepressible" conflict. Many bequests were yet to be made to the Society, many slaves were yet offered their freedom on condition of emigration, many efforts were yet made by those patriots, proponents of Colonization, to hold the Union together, and the Colonization Society lived on, doing a commendable work; but the character of its work was fundamentally changed by the conflict which began in 1831, and whose influence was actively alive as late as 1845, though the struggle for supremacy may be said to have come to an end.

By 1842 Garrison was calling the roll of his ultra-Abolitionist co-workers, and he noted the absence of most of them. "The time was," said he, "when Arthur Tappan stood deservedly conspicuous before the nation as an abolitionist, . . .; but where is he now?" "Where is James G. Birney? In Western retiracy, waiting to be elected President of the United States, that he may have an opportunity to do something for the abolition of slavery." "Where is Henry B. Stanton? Studying law, (which crushes humanity, and is hostile to the gospel of Christ,) and indulging the hope of one day or other, by the aid of the Liberty party, occupying a seat in Congress. . . ." "Where are Theodore D. Weld and his wife, and Sarah M. Grimke?" "Where is Amos G. Phelps? . . . He is a petty priest, of

a petty parish, located in East Boston. What a fall!"
"Where is Elizur Wright, Jr., once a flame of fire . . .?
Absorbed in selling some French fables which he has translated into English! 'Et tu, Brute!'" "Where is John G. Whittier?" "Where is Daniel Wise?" "Where is Orange Scott . . .? Morally defunct." And so on, through a list of seventeen names, on all which the African Repository commented: "He could not name ten others, who, in the days of his greatest success, were equally efficient in his service."[145] What was the trouble? Why had these flames gone out? Perhaps, New Englanders, the wisest of them, were coming to see the futility of blatant Garrisonism.

---

[145] African Repository, vol. xviii, pp. 327-329.

CHAPTER IV

Colonization and Emancipation, 1817–1850

A study of the operations of the American Colonization Society, if it is to set forth fairly and completely the Colonization movement, must present the efforts of that organization from two distinct points of view: (1) its effects and results in relation to the question of slavery, and (2) the degree of its success in establishing upon the west coast of Africa an asylum for the American free negro, or the American slave manumitted or emancipated with a view to emigration to the Society's settlements, and for Africans recaptured from slave vessels and restored to their native land. In a consideration of its bearings upon the solution of the problem of slavery, no more important topic can be discussed than the influence of the Society in encouraging a spirit in the South favorable to emancipation. An accurate estimate of that influence is as difficult as it is important. Records of emancipations or manumissions are so incomplete and unsatisfactory that no summary can be made which will be at once exhaustive and analytical. If every slaveholder who emancipated his blacks told us whether he did so as the result of a distinct influence exerted by the Society, the problem would be much simplified. But frequently the emancipator discussed but briefly the influences that led to the freeing of his slaves. In many cases he, himself, was probably unable to analyze those influences. Perhaps he had been led to give his negroes their freedom because he lived in a community where emancipation was "in the air." And perhaps that was the influence of the Colonization Society at work. Influence cannot be measured with a yard stick; and it is exceedingly difficult to measure it at all.

COLONIZATION AND EMANCIPATION 181

A further difficulty is found in the fact that several notices might appear in either the official minutes or the official journal, the investigator being unable to tell whether the notices referred to are notices of the same or of different cases of emancipation. The result is likely to be a confusion of estimates.

It has already been pointed out[1] that, from the hour of its organization, indeed, before that hour, it was hoped that one of the important influences colonization might exert would be that in favor of the gradual and entire abolition of slavery, through its influence in favor of voluntary emancipation. At an early date William Thornton had already expressed the desire and the hope that it might "afford the best hope yet presented of putting an end to the slavery in which not less than 600,000 unhappy negroes are now involved." He foresaw the day when conditions in the South would bring about the enactment of laws prohibiting emancipations, unless accompanied with a provision for removal from the state.[2] Before the Colonization Society was a year old, the Manumission Society of North Carolina had become interested in cooperating with it, and after ten years' observation of its influence in favor of the emancipation of slaves, warmly recommended it and pledged its own support.[3] In a memorial presented to Congress in 1819, a committee, composed of two Virginians, John Mason and General Walter Jones, one Marylander, Francis Scott Key, and one member from the District of Columbia, Dr. E. B. Caldwell, expressed the view that if Colonization resulted in the complete abolition of slavery, "Who can doubt that of all the blessings we may be permitted to bequeath to our descendants, this will receive the richest tribute of their thanks and veneration."[4]

---

[1] See above.
[2] Thornton Papers, MS., vol. xiv, MSS. Div., Library of Cong.
[3] Journal of Board of Managers of American Colonization Society, MS., September 19, 1817; Manumission Society of North Carolina to American Colonization Society, MS., September 17, 1827.
[4] Minutes of Board of Managers of American Colonization Society, MS., December 10, 1819.

The Managers, in their annual report in 1820, declared, "the hope of the gradual and utter abolition of slavery, in a manner consistent with the rights, interests, and happiness of society, ought never to be abandoned."[5] In their annual report in 1822, the same body expressed, not only the hope, but the satisfaction, of seeing distinct evidences of the willingness of slaveholders to liberate their slaves for the purpose of sending them to Africa.[6] The delight of those Managers was expressed in still stronger terms in 1823.[7] Lafayette, for whom the leaders of the Society had great respect, and who was one of its vice-presidents, looked to the day when its influence in bringing about emancipation would be of great importance.[8] From the time of its organization to about 1825, the leading motive of those who controlled the organization was the elevation of the American free negro; but the most important secondary result that they hoped the Society might have was the widespread cultivation of a sentiment favorable to emancipation. After 1825 the desire for the uplift of the free negro and the liberation of the slave came to be equally important, it seems, in the policy of the Society. And gradually, and for years thereafter, its efforts were directed more to securing the emancipation of slaves than to the elevation of the free negro. It has already been seen that Gerrit Smith, in leaving the Society, made this very criticism of it.

Although at no time was the influence of the Colonizationists exerted in opposition to emancipation, it is true that during its early years, the Society was careful to violate neither its own constitution nor local, municipal law on the subject of slavery. For instance, there were cases in which runaway slaves came to the Society's agents, requesting to be sent to Liberia.[9] Such requests were refused. Re-

---

[5] Origin, Constitution, and Proceedings of American Colonization Society, MS., vol. i, p. 107.
[6] Ibid., vol. i, p. 190.
[7] Ibid., vol. i, p. 209.
[8] African Repository, vol. i, p. 285.
[9] Letters of American Colonization Society, MS., C. Wright to Gurley, Montpelier, December 29, 1826; Minutes of Board of Mana-

quests were made to the Society to apply its funds directly to the purchase of slaves for transportation to the colony. These also were refused, though agents of the Society were willing and glad to furnish lists of slaves who might be purchased in order for transportation; and Gurley even went so far as to suggest that if funds were placed in the hands of the Colonization Society for the express purpose of being applied to the benefit of those who, if such funds were not available, would revert to slavery, the Society would gladly make use of such funds for the purpose designated.[10] And there is on record a case in which twelve or fifteen slaves in Virginia were held in slavery for want of funds to secure their being placed in the hands of the Society. Gerrit Smith, already turned Abolitionist, refused, it seems, to furnish the financial assistance, and John McDonogh, of New Orleans, a leader among Colonizationists, directed the treasurer of the Society to draw on him for the required amount.[11] When in 1843 McLain, Treasurer of the Society, was working for the cause in Louisiana, he reported to the Washington office that he hesitated to appeal for funds because the Louisiana Society wished the first three hundred dollars raised to be applied to the purchase of "the learned Blacksmith of Alabama," a remarkable negro slave. This he felt to be a violation of the constitution of the Society.[12]

The tendency, however, never was to construe too strictly, but too liberally, the terms of the constitution in this respect. The inclination of Colonizationists was so favorable to emancipation that now and then resolutions were submitted and adopted, whose object was to remind the Society that its purpose was, historically, to secure the elevation of the free negro rather than the liberation of the slave. Hon.

gers of American Colonization Society, MS., Sept. 26, 1827; December 12, 1827; May 19, 1828.
[10] Letters of American Colonization Society, MS., Gurley to Rev. H. J. Ripley, December 9, 1842.
[11] Ibid., Gurley to Ripley, December 9, 1842, No. 499.
[12] Ibid., McLain to Gurley, New Orleans, May 6, 1843; Finley to Gurley, Natchez, May 4, 1843.

Robert M. McLane of Maryland secured in 1849 the passage of such resolutions, which set forth well the attitude the Society took:

> Resolved, That in all action affecting this institution [slavery] in its social or political aspect, the American citizen and statesman who reveres the Federal Union has imposed upon him the most solemn obligations to respect in spirit and letter the authority of local and municipal sovereignties, and to resist all aggressive influences which tend to disturb the peace and tranquility of the States, that may have created or sanctioned this institution.
> Resolved, further, That the efforts of the American Colonization Society to facilitate the ultimate emancipation and restoration of the black race to social and national independence are highly honorable and judicious and consistent with a strict respect for the rights and privileges of the citizens of the several States wherein the institution of slavery is sanctioned by municipal law.[13]

Such reminders were needed especially for the auxiliary societies which, in many instances, were with the greatest difficulty prevented from going farther than was consistent with the constitution in the effort to liberate slaves. Notable among these was the Philadelphia Society. Elliot Cresson, for instance, wrote in 1830 that Philadelphians wished their funds used " for the special purpose of sending manumitted slaves," and suggested that free negroes be required to pay their own transportation expenses.[14] Thomas Buchanan, while agent for the New York and Philadelphia Societies, and a short while before his appointment as colonial governor of Liberia, secured not only the liberty of forty slaves but also a contribution of fifteen hundred dollars from their owner to be applied for their benefit.[15] In 1843 Treasurer McLain, of the parent Society, was writing to Virginians inquiring for the names of slaves whose liberation could be secured on condition of their removal to Africa. He thought he could raise the money with which to secure the liberty of some of them, though here he was undoubtedly going beyond the constitution of the Society. He wrote: "We have many friends who are beginning to

---

[13] Minutes of Board of Directors of American Colonization Society, MS., January 16, 1849.
[14] Letters of American Colonization Society, MS., Cresson to Gurley, Philadelphia, September 23, 1830.
[15] African Repository, vol. xiv, p. 54.

feel a strong desire to aid in sending slaves to Liberia who cannot be set at liberty unless they are sent and who cannot be sent unless somebody gives the means."[16] In 1843 the Massachusetts Society was placing on certain of its donations the proviso that they should be used in defraying the expenses of emancipated slaves.[17] In 1845 the Massachusetts agent wrote: "I think we can get the money for those seven slaves; and *some* of it will be money that we should not otherwise receive."[18]

A peculiarly interesting case is that of the Kentucky slave, Reuben. Rev. J. B. Pinney, agent for the Colonization Society, had gone to Kentucky to collect a group of liberated slaves, twenty-one of them, and conduct them to the port of embarkation for Liberia. Among the number was a family of children whose father was still a slave. A meeting was held in the church, of which the prominent Colonizationist, Dr. Breckenridge, was pastor. Reuben was asked if he would like to accompany his children. He expressed great desire to go. The audience was asked whether they desired at once to purchase Reuben and send him and his children. Hardly had the invitation to contribute been given when the President's table was surrounded by those who within a few minutes had contributed a fund sufficient to secure Reuben's release.[19] This is interesting not alone as an incident, but because it throws a light upon the attitude that a group of Colonizationists in a border slaveholding State took toward the emancipation of a slave for the purpose of transportation to the colony. Examples will hereafter be given to show that these efforts to secure the emancipation of slaves were not confined to the New England or the Middle States. Hundreds of slaves in Louisiana, Mississippi and Tennessee, as well as in Kentucky and

---

[16] Letters of American Colonization Society, MS., McLain to Tracy, March 7, 1843, No. 743; McLain to C. W. Andrews, March 7, 1843, No. 744.
[17] Ibid., Gurley to Whittlesey, Boston, June 9, 1843.
[18] Ibid., Tracy to McLain, Boston, April 21, 1845.
[19] African Repository, vol. xxi, pp. 11–12.

Virginia, were liberated because of the efforts of Colonizationists. Of the effect of Colonization upon the spirit of emancipation, considering the South in general, President Thomas of the Baltimore and Ohio Railroad wrote, in 1829: "... the exertions of the Society have already effected a moral influence which is obviously perceptible," although he realized that Colonization was only one of the various causes of the change in sentiment.[20] In 1830 Key announced that there were at that time more than six hundred slaves willing to go to Liberia and offered by their owners to the Society, as soon as its means were sufficient to care for so many.[21] Benjamin F. Butler, soon to be attorney-general in Andrew Jackson's cabinet, believed that the Colonization Society had already "done more to promote in the Southern States the Emancipation of slaves, than had been accomplished by all the efforts made with direct reference to such a result, since the revolution." He stated that the report of every auxiliary society in the South had testified to the willingness of many slaveholders to emancipate their negroes as soon as they could be transported and cared for by the Society.[22] William Maxwell, a leading Colonizationist of Virginia, bore witness to its power as an encouragement to slaveholders to manumit their slaves.[23] Elijah Paine, of Vermont, expressed a similar view.[24] In the African Repository for 1842, there are notices of between five and six hundred slaves emancipated for the purpose of transportation to Liberia, and it must not be forgotten that many slaveholders who were willing to send their negroes to the colony refused to allow their names to appear in the public press.[25] In 1845 the official journal of the Society announced: "Hundreds of slaves have already been set free

---

[20] Letters of American Colonization Society, MS., P. E. Thomas to Gurley, Baltimore, September 30, 1829.
[21] African Repository, vol. vi, pp. 138–139.
[22] Ibid., vol. vi, p. 162.
[23] Ibid., vol. xiii, p. 55.
[24] Ibid., vol. xv, pp. 44–48.
[25] Ibid., vol. xviii, passim.

in order that they might be removed to Liberia. Hundreds more are now offered to the Society, if it will assume the expense of sending them out."[26]

Of the effect of the Society's influence in Kentucky, the general agent for the West reported

> a growing disposition for gratuitous manumission and ... an avowed determination on the part of some of our most influential men to press with all their might the subject of gradual abolition in case a convention shall be called to settle the disturbances of our State, a resolution for which has been already introduced in the House of Representatives. I mention this for your *private* satisfaction; I mean to say its publication would be premature. Twenty-two slaves with the means of transportation were the other day willed to the Society by a gentleman in Bourbon County and eighty-odd have been very recently liberated by one man in Clarksville, Tennessee. I would mention several other cases of which I have been particularly informed.[27]

Again, in 1829, he wrote that many slaveholders were ready to liberate their slaves when they could be received by the Society.[28] A member of the Kentucky State Society called attention to the very widespread sentiment in favor of emancipation, and attributed it, in considerable measure, to the influence of the Colonizationists, though he admitted that an effort had been made to drag it into politics, the Jackson men saying "it is a party thing."[29] R. J. Breckenridge, while yet a resident of Kentucky, declared in 1831:

> It is now generally admitted, that a very large number of those owning slaves, perhaps as many as one-third of them, would decidedly favor the gradual emancipation of the slaves of this State; provided the great accumulation of free negroes supposed to be consequent on such a step could be avoided. Among the non-slaveholders, I never saw a person of ordinary intelligence, who was not decidedly favorable to some efficient project of that sort.

One of the secrets of the Society's influence throughout the upper South was that it proposed not only to emancipate, but also to remove; and it must never be forgotten that one of the most powerful objections to the abolition of

---

[26] Ibid., vol. xxi, pp. 145–149; vol. xix, p. 189; vol. xx, p. 229; Letters of American Colonization Society, MS., Mary B. Blackford to Gurley, Fredericksburg, Va., January 28, 1843.
[27] Letters of American Colonization Society, MS., B. O. Peers to Gurley, Maysville, Ky., December 11, 1826.
[28] Ibid., Peers to Gurley, Feb. 7, 1829.
[29] Ibid., Gurley, Lexington, Ky., September 5, 1828.

slavery, from the point of view of the South, was that the free negro would become a black peril to the South.[30]

Robert S. Finley, a son of the venerable Robert Finley, assured the parent Society that it could secure without difficulty all the emigrants it could accommodate. "I have heard," he wrote, "within the last ten days without making particular inquiries on the subject of hundreds of slaves who are only held in bondage until the Colonization Society will undertake to colonize them. And I have no hesitation in saying that there are *thousands* of slaves in this State who are merely held by their masters *in trust* for the same praiseworthy object."[31] In 1839, an assistant secretary of the Society wrote as hopefully as had Finley.[32] Elliot Cresson, traveling in the interest of the Society, wrote from Mississippi in 1840 that the whole South, and particularly Kentucky, seemed to be ready to cooperate in the colonization of its slaves.[33]

In Virginia there were not wanting signs of the Society's influence. The State Colonization Society and the Lynchburg Society reported large numbers of slaves, as well as free negroes, desiring to go to the colony, many of the slaves being offered their liberty on condition of removal by the Society.[34] Monroe once told Elliot Cresson that if the Society could raise funds sufficient to care for the settlers, he could procure ten thousand slaves by emancipation in Virginia alone.[35]

In North Carolina as late as 1840, the Society's agent reported continued growth of sentiment favorable to emancipation if accompanied by removal. One slaveholder, the

---

[30] African Repository, vol. vii, pp. 48–49.
[31] Letters of American Colonization Society, MS., R. S. Finley to Gurley, Lexington, Ky., April 12, 1831.
[32] Ibid., Knight to Wilkeson, Frankfort, Ky., November 30, 1839.
[33] Ibid., Cresson to Wilkeson, Natchez, Miss., April 13, 1840.
[34] African Repository, vol. iv, pp. 307–311; vol. v, p. 203; vol. vi, pp. 214–215; Letters of American Colonization Society, MS., Atkinson to Gurley, Petersburg, Va., December 17, 1831.
[35] African Repository, vol. xv, p. 84; Letters of American Colonization Society, MS., Gurley to Rev. Stephen Taylor, July 13, 1842, No. 148.

owner of upwards of one thousand negroes, was reported as determined to emancipate them all if the colony continued to improve and if the Society could make provision for them.[86] So efficient were the North Carolina Quakers in their cooperation with the Society, that they alone seemed able to supply all the emigrants that could be accommodated with the limited means of the Colonizationists. From 1825 to 1830, slaveholders in that State placed in the hands of these Quakers hundreds of slaves, on condition of their removal to Liberia.[87]

It must not be supposed that there were no counter influences. In comparing the Abolition and Colonization movements it has already been set forth that one of the strongest of these counter forces was the Abolitionists themselves. Whether by picturing in dark colors the motives of Colonizationists, or by assuring the negroes that emigration was not their privilege, but rather their banishment, or by picturing the terrors of the sea or the ferocity of the native Africans or the fatal consequences of the period of acclimation in the colony, or the fact that the negro had a right to enjoy the same privileges in America that his white brother had, or by speaking of slaveholders, and to slaveholders, in terms calculated to exasperate not only an enemy but a friend—in all these ways, and more, the Garrisonians were working up a sentiment which made it impossible for the Northern States and the Southern to meet on common ground in the solution of a great problem.

It is a fact, and a fact altogether neglected by proponents of Garrison, that no considerable section of American citizenship would have borne Garrisonian insult without uniting in opposition. His own New England would have risen in as radical opposition, as it did rise in radical support, if he had spoken of its citizenship in the same unmeasured terms

---

[86] Letters of American Colonization Society, MS., W. McKenney to Wilkeson, Greensboro, N. C., Nov. 6, 1840.
[87] Ibid., J. C. Ehringhaus to Gurley, Elizabeth City, N. C., September 30, 1826; Cresson to Gurley, Aug. 23, 1828; African Repository, vol. v, p. 94.

that he used in describing Southerners. This is true because a man's a man, and not a superman. Too much has been made of the peculiarities of Southern temperament and not enough made of the peculiarities of Garrisonian abuse. Garrison thought of the South in terms of Ephraim and his Idol, and that was true in 1831 of a part of the lower South. But a truer picture of the upper South in 1831 would have been that represented by Prometheus Bound.

Garrison's abuse furnished the South with the best justification it ever had for plunging into civil war. Ultra-Abolition made a patriot of many a man who could not have fought with great earnestness to preserve the institution of slavery. Garrisonian methods made patriots of Southern opponents of slavery, for they enabled the South to stand, not only as the defender of a bad thing but also as the defender of a good thing; not only as a defender of slavery, but also of the Constitution of the United States. Colonizationists took away the strongest ground the South had to stand on in her defense of slavery, for Colonizationists admitted that the Constitution stood between them and the positively proslavery advocates. Garrisonians, by refusing fully to admit that, had a large part in the very making of their arch-enemy Calhoun. They gave him the opportunity of defending the South in the same breath with which he defended the Constitution. They assisted him powerfully in making his reputation as a great political theorist, as well as a great proslavery advocate. It may now appear that radical abolitionism was pregnant not only with influences opposed to Colonization, but also with influences opposed to emancipation.

Other counter influences should be mentioned, such as the injudicious publication of articles advocating emancipation, the belief of some slaveholders that their "people" would not be safe in the colony from the dangers of hostile tribes and that proper provision was not made for receiving them, the fear that their slaves after being liberated might escape from the vessel before it left port, the unwillingness of many negroes to go to Liberia, the refusal of some slaveholders to encounter public criticism, the extreme sensitiveness of portions of the South, and particularly of Virginia, to any efforts made to secure aid from the Federal Government, and the widespread realization that already the Colonizationists had more applicants than their funds would permit of sending to Africa.[88]

Indeed, there was probably not a time during the whole period herein considered when, notwithstanding the counter influences of which mention has just been made, the Society could not have enlarged greatly its operations and secured the liberation of a much larger number of slaves than were given over to it, if it had had funds sufficient to settle them. As early as 1827 the Managers were compelled to refuse passage to recently emancipated slaves in parts of Virginia, and of slaves who would be emancipated to go to the colony.[39] The public journal of the Society contains many evidences that Abolitionists could have secured at once the liberation of hundreds and thousands of slaves if they had been willing to contribute to the support of the Society which could get slaves for the asking when Garrison could not have bought them at any price.

The panic of 1837 was very disastrous to the enlarging opportunities of the Society. John McDonogh of Louisiana thought that in 1840 there were hardly fifty solvent men in New Orleans,[40] and that same year the treasurer of the Society was appealing to friends in the North to furnish the means without which the liberty of certain slaves could

---

[88] Letters of American Colonization Society, MS., Hunt to Gurley, Brunswick, Va., October 5, 1826; Brand to Gurley, Richmond, Va., August 20, 1827; Brand to Gurley, Richmond, Va., November 3, 1827; M. B. Blackford to Gurley, Fredericksburg, Va., August 18, 1845; McLain to Rev. N. S. Dodge, February 20, 1843, No. 677; W. M. Blackford to Gurley, Fredericksburg, Va., October 21, 1829; C. S. Carter to Gurley, Richmond, Va., December 22, 1831; African Repository, vol. xii, p. 89; vol. xiv, pp. 43-47.
[39] Minutes of Board of Managers of American Colonization Society, MS., March 26, 1827.
[40] Letters of American Colonization Society, MS., Cresson to Wilkeson, New Orleans, April 2, 1840.

not be secured. "We are trying hard," wrote McLain, "to raise the means of sending to Liberia about 40 liberated slaves, who must be sold again into slavery if not sent soon. In these circumstances we should be unfaithful to the important trusts committed to us, if we did not appeal to every friend of the colored man for help."[41] Letters were sent to leading Colonizationists throughout the United States for aid in securing the liberty and transportation of slaves offered for the Colony.

In 1841 the general agent, Judge Wilkeson, thus instructed McLain who was working for the cause in the South: "Study economy and take the negro only who will go to slavery unless sent to Liberia, unless his expenses are paid."[42] Appeals were made during this year to save from slavery and the cupidity of heirs eleven slaves in Kentucky, and at another time, eighteen slaves from the same State.[43] The appeal of the Colonizationists was: "We must save them"; "What shall we do? We have now no means of defraying their expenses. Let them be sold? We never could justify this to the American people." "More emigrants offer than we can raise the means of sending." In 1842 a slaveholder of Nashville, Tennessee, desired to place in the hands of the Society for emigration sixty slaves; a slaveholder living near New Orleans made an offer of eighty slaves; a lady in Virginia desired to make the same disposition of some sixty of her "people," but the Society had not the funds to fit out an expedition.[44]

During that year the treasurer sent to a slaveholder the following refusal: "I wish it was in my power to inform you that the Soc. could pay the expenses of sending the family you wish to liberate. But the applications are so numerous and the Soc. so in debt, the Ex. Committee have

[41] Ibid., McLain to Hubbard, December 30, 1840, No. 487; President Humphrey of Amherst, December 30, 1840, No. 490.
[42] Ibid., Wilkeson to McLain, April 6, 1841, No. 114.
[43] Ibid., McLain to D. Baldwin, vol. iv, No. 1542; Theodore Frelinghuysen, August 26, 1841, No. 70.
[44] Ibid., Gurley to Jacob Gibson, February 14, 1842, No. 629; Gurley to George Barker, February 17, 1842, No. 641.

been obliged to resolve that for the present they can send out none but such as can pay their own expenses."[45] And within about three months he was appealing for $7500.00 with which to fit out an expedition, on which one hundred and sixty-seven slaves were to go to Liberia "if we can send them," otherwise a part of them were to revert to slavery. "Oh, that our Northern friends but understood the magnitude and importance of the great work in which we are engaged."[46] But appeals to New England failed of the desired results. Mr. Garrison had declared that it was the purpose of the Colonizationists to "rivet more firmly the fetters of the slave."

To those who suppose that the only reason slaveholders could offer for continuing to hold their slaves was that they preferred to do so, it may be of value to point out some of the problems involved in the liberation by a master of his negroes; and to show that there were slaveowners in the South who despised the institution and who were glad of an opportunity to be rid of the responsibility and burden when they found an opportunity to do so with safety, as they thought, to their country. In 1827 a Mississippi slaveholder, preparing his twenty-three negroes for emigration to Liberia, wrote the Society, telling of the farming tools and carpenter's outfit he hoped to give them on their departure, and thus expressed his gratification at finding a way out of the burden of slaveholding:

> I hope that it will be in the power of the Society to give them a passage early in June, that I may be enabled to wipe from my character the foulest stain with which it was ever tarnished and pluck from my bleeding conscience the most pungent sting. I had fully determined several years past to emancipate them about this time but had been much perplexed in my mind in relation to their future place of residence, until I learned that Heaven had provided an asylum in the land of their ancestors, where I had long been of opinion it was right that they should be transported and with them the seeds of civilization and Christianity to make some amends ... for the many wrongs and outrages committed ... by a people who styled themselves Christians for so many centuries.[47]

---

[45] Ibid., McLain to Dr. W. S. Holcombe, August 17, 1842, No. 236.
[46] Ibid., McLain to G. W. Campbell, November 29, 1842, No. 445; Gurley to Dr. A. Proudfit, No. 448; Gurley, No. 336.
[47] Ibid., Silas Hamilton to Gurley, Adams County, Miss., December 28, 1827.

Sometimes the difficulty was in the expense involved in the preparation of the slaves for liberty, and one would be surprised to read the many evidences of real desire on the part of those masters who offered their slaves to the Society to send their negroes well prepared, well equipped, and well provisioned.[48] William Johnson, of Western Virginia, who was the owner of nine slaves, one of whom he had bought with the express purpose of freeing him with his sister, was an uneducated, poor, but sincere slaveholder for conscience sake. After making two attempts "to try to git money to send them to liberia," he appeals to the Society to relieve him of the burden.[49]

In many cases the difficulty was simply one of deciding what to do with the slaves if they were to be freed. It has been seen that in most of the Southern States the laws against emancipations within the State were made more stringent and were more strictly enforced after the Garrisonian onset and the development of the cotton industry. The result was that slaveholders, no matter what they thought of the evils of slavery, could not lawfully manumit, except by transporting the manumitted to some part of the Union, or to some other place where such prohibitory laws were not in operation. Sometimes, it seems, the very consideration of the advantages of the Colonization movement led directly and immediately to the determination to emancipate, on condition of removal.[50] Sometimes the difficulty arose from the unwillingness to divide families, separating husband and wife, parents and children, one of the most repulsive aspects of the whole repulsive system of slavery.

It would not be practicable in a study of this nature to attempt a complete summary of even the most interesting instances of emancipation and transportation to the colony; but it is important to mention a number of such cases. A

---

[48] Ibid., A. M. Marbury to Gurley, Alexandria, Va., May 26, 1835.
[49] Ibid., Wm. Johnson to Fendall, Tyler County, Va., November 26, 1836.
[50] Ibid., McKenney, Norfolk, Va., December 27, 1832; C. W. Andrews to Gurley, Richmond, Va., February 1, 1836; C. C. Harper, Baltimore, Md., April 24, 1828.

flood of light is thereby thrown upon the inquiries: What portion of the South furnished the largest number of emancipations to the Society? What portion furnished the largest number of large single emancipations? What provisions were made for the emancipated slaves? What conditions were attached to the acts of emancipation? Did those who sent portions of their slaves to the colony express, after hearing from them, a willingness to send others? Were those emancipated chiefly the old and infirm, or were the emigrants able-bodied, valuable negroes? Up to and including 1832, among the emancipations with provision for emigration to Liberia, are the following:

A lady from near Charles Town, Virginia, liberated ten slaves; also two slaves whom she purchased because of their relation to her own. For these two she gave $800. They were manumitted for the purpose of emigration to Africa.[51] William H. Fitzhugh, a Vice-President and active member of the Colonization Society, by will liberated all his slaves, numbering about three hundred. Their liberation was to date from 1850. Upon their consent to go to Liberia, and they were to have their freedom whether or not they agreed to go to the Colony, their passage was to be paid and they were to be given fifty dollars each.[52]

David Shriver, of Maryland, by will emancipated his thirty slaves; Colonel Smith, of Sussex County, Virginia, by will emancipated seventy or eighty, leaving about $5000 for their transportation and settlement.[53] Miss Patsy Morris, of Virginia, by will emancipated her sixteen slaves, leaving $500 for their passage to the colony. Sampson David, of Tennessee, emancipated, by will, his twenty-two slaves, and Herbert B. Elder, of Petersburg, Virginia, twenty. A Georgian liberated forty-nine, the greater part of his fortune, on condition that they should go to the colony. In

---

[51] Carey, pp. 8–9.
[52] Minutes of Board of Directors of American Colonization Society, MS., January 18, 1849, p. 74.
[53] Carey, pp. 8–9; African Repository, vol. ii, pp. 29–30.

North Carolina alone there had been offered to the Society six hundred and fifty-two slaves.[54]

Mrs. Elizabeth Moore, of Kentucky, provided, by will, for the emancipation of all her slaves, about forty. Charles Henshaw, of Virginia, manumitted sixty to send them to Liberia.[55] A Mr. Funston, of Frederick County, Virginia, emancipated ten slaves, and by will provided $1000 to cover their transportation expenses.[56] Another Virginia slaveholder emancipated one hundred and ten slaves. Another, a Methodist minister of Suffolk, Virginia, emancipated upwards of thirty, leaving several hundred dollars to be applied to their transportation.[57] A Virginia lady emancipated twenty-five, and a slaveholder of Kentucky, sixty.[58] David Bullock, of Virginia, emancipated twenty-three, the oldest not over forty years. This slaveholder inquires for the negroes as to "their expectations when they arrive, as to their immediate support, and their future chance for living, whether they will have land allotted to them, etc."[59] Among those emancipated after 1832, are the following:

The New Orleans Picayune contains this announcement: "We understand that six hundred negroes, belonging to a gentleman of this city, lately deceased, are to be liberated according to his will, provided they are willing to go to Africa, in which case ample provision is to be made for their transportation."[60] Another slaveholder was willing to emancipate sixty, if funds could be secured with which to transport them to the colony.[61] John McDonogh, of New Orleans, was ready in 1842 to send eighty or eighty-five slaves, valued at $150,000.00, well trained and an unusual acquisition. Of McDonogh's negroes, about fifty-five

---

[54] Carey, pp. 8-9; African Repository, vol. ii, p. 163; vol. iv, p. 185.
[55] African Repository, vol. i, pp. 191-192.
[56] Ibid., vol. ii, pp. 352-353.
[57] Ibid., vol. iii, p. 27.
[58] African Repository, vol. iv, p. 251.
[59] Letters of American Colonization Society, MS., D. Bullock to Gurley, Louisa, Va., September 13, 1827.
[60] African Repository, vol. xiv, p. 63, copied from New Orleans Picayune, February 13, 1838.
[61] African Repository, vol. xviii, p. 80.

were adult and the rest children from six to twelve years of age. So far was the colonization mode of securing the emancipation of slaves favorably looked upon, even in Louisiana, that a New Orleans paper commented in the most favorable terms upon both the Society, Mr. McDonogh, and his philanthropic scheme of emancipating all his negroes, and upon the condition of the colony as revealed in the letters sent back to persons in the State from the negroes he had sent out. These letters abounded in expressions of thankfulness and gratitude to their former master for his generosity and liberal treatment of them.

McDonogh had worked out a plan by which the negroes were allowed to earn their own freedom, by using advantageously certain hours and days given them for that purpose by their master. It was one of the most interesting plans ever proposed for the liberation of slaves without actual expense to the owner. McDonogh found that, if the slave used well the time given to him, he could secure his own freedom within fifteen or seventeen years. This freedom he gave to those who were his own property. And although The Liberator and other Abolitionist papers severely criticised the plan, McDonogh was trying to recommend to the southern slaveholder a plan by which he could rid his country of slavery and at the same time do so without great loss to himself.[62]

In 1832 Major Bibb, of Kentucky, sent thirty-two of his slaves to the colony, and the following year he tendered freedom to the remaining forty, on condition that they would emigrate.[63] This year also, Dr. James Bradley, of Georgia, manumitted about sixty negroes, who emigrated to the Colony.[64] The following year Dr. T. M. Ambler, of Virginia, emancipated about thirty, who went to the Col-

---

[62] Letters of American Colonization Society, MS., McLain, New Orleans, La., July 2, 1844; Gurley to Proudfit, March 7, 1842, No. 677; African Repository, vol. xix, p. 48 ff.; pp. 141-142.

[63] Letters of American Colonization Society, MS., G. C. Light to Gurley, Cynthiana, Ky., June 6, 1833.

[64] Lugenbeel.

ony.[65] In 1834 Dr. John Ker, one of the most prominent Colonizationists in the Southwest, wrote asking that sixteen of a considerable number of slaves left free, on condition of their emigration, by James Green of Mississippi, be allowed passage:

> I am authorized to say that they [the executors] will pay the whole expense of their emigration, and, agreeably to the will of the Testator, will furnish them with a very handsome outfit, amounting, for those over twelve years old, to from three to five hundred dollars, and somewhat less for the younger ones. . . . You will allow me to bespeak for them . . . all the attention and favor which may be necessary to their comfortable and eligible establishment in the Colony.[66]

In 1836 Gurley visited Mississippi in the interest of the Society, and his report to the Managers throws an interesting light upon the attitude of that State toward emancipation, and also upon the estate of the deceased James Green, and the purpose of the principal executor in relation to the remaining slaves. Gurley was forcibly impressed with the liberality and cordiality of the Colonizationists of that State. They had contributed two thousand dollars "without my personal application to a single individual, and with my detention hardly for a day."

> On Monday, I visited James Railey, Esq. (principal executor of the estate of the late James Green) at his beautiful country seat. . . . Its generous proprietor opened to me fully his mind in regard to the estate . . . with written and verbal requests that it should be applied to the *emancipation and colonization of slaves from Mississippi in Liberia*. It will be recollected, that certain slaves emancipated by Mr. Green have been sent to the colony, and Mr. Railey informs me, that their outfit and supplies and passage cost about $7000. The trust might, in the opinion of some, be fulfilled, were $20000 in addition, applied to the benevolent purposes of the testator, but Mr. Railey states that *it has been determined to devote $25000* more to the objects of testator's charitable desires.[67]

Alexander Donelson of Tennessee died in 1834, emancipating his slaves by will. By the laws of the State, negroes freed within its bounds were compelled to leave or revert to slavery, unless they were by the county court permitted

---

[65] Ibid.
[66] Letters of American Colonization Society, MS., Ker to Gurley, Natchez, Miss., January 10, 1834.
[67] Ibid., Gurley to Fendall, June 30, 1836.

to remain. By decree of that court, Donelson's slaves were allowed to remain in the State until the time of embarkation, if they agreed to start for Liberia by January 20, 1836. The slaves were twenty in number. All were grown, and none over forty years of age. Donelson had left them all his personal property, amounting to a considerable sum. They had ample means to provide themselves with clothes, tools, and provisions. They could pay their own passage and still have money left after arriving in the colony. The son of the deceased had, by careful management, increased considerably the fund left by Donelson. He had left them together on the farm, had allowed them to continue their work, and had given them the proceeds of the crop.[68] In 1834 one hundred and nine slaves owned by Dr. Hawes, of Virginia, were liberated and transported to the Colony.[69]

A Colonizationist from Hanover County, Virginia, wrote the Society in 1836 that a family of thirty slaves had been liberated in that county, on condition of their emigrating to the colony. Their passage was to be paid, and a sum sufficient for their comfortable settlement was to be given them. Another family, twenty-seven in number, had been liberated in the adjoining county. To each of the twenty-seven a legacy of one hundred and fifty dollars was left for the purpose of enabling them to settle either in some free State or in some country where they might enjoy their liberty. They had apparently decided to go to Liberia.[70] During this year also, forty-two slaves, liberated by William Foster, of Mississippi, arrived in the colony.[71] In 1837 Thomas Potts, of Virginia, emancipated and sent to the colony fifty-nine negroes, paying the expense of their passage, amounting to four thousand and fifty dollars.[72]

[68] Ibid., T. H. Fletcher to Gurley, Nashville, Tenn., August 12, 1835.
[69] Lugenbeel.
[70] Letters of American Colonization Society, MS., N. C. Crenshaw to Fendall, Hanover County, Va., July 15, 1836.
[71] Sketch of the History of Liberia, MS.
[72] Letters of American Colonization Society, MS., Potts to Fendall, Sussex Court House, Va., October 13, 1837; November 18, 1837.

In 1840 an agent of the Society for Kentucky wrote: "A gentleman in this vicinity tendered me twenty slaves lately for emigration, upon condition that they were willing to go, and we would provide them means."[73] The year preceding this, John Rix, of North Carolina, sent twenty slaves liberated by him to Liberia. John McPhail, whose efforts for the Society in preparing for the sailing from Norfolk of a number of expeditions were of the greatest value, reported in 1839 that:

> I expect a family of fifteen probably the forerunner of a large number belonging to [a certain gentleman], if he should agree to the terms you may propose to take them out and provide for them six months after their arrival in Africa. . . . This is an affair I believe of much importance to the interest of the Society. I do not exactly know how many the gentleman owns but I am certain they amount to some hundreds; if he makes his mind up upon the subject he will send by every expedition some families. He writes to me in perfect confidence and says, "I wish nothing said of it either privately or publicly and no notice of it in the newspapers. . . ."[74]

In 1842 Wm. B. Lynch, of Virginia, emancipated nineteen slaves on condition of their willingness to go to Africa. For their passage he appropriated five hundred dollars.[75]

In 1844 Lieut. C. W. Tomkins offered for his sister to liberate about forty slaves if they would go to Liberia. The same year Mrs. Jane Meaux, of Kentucky, left, by will, liberty to fourteen slaves on condition that they would go to the colony. Each was to be given one hundred dollars upon agreement to go, besides being furnished with household and kitchen furniture. Of these slaves, the oldest was about thirty-five.[76]

Colonel Montgomery Bell of Tennessee sent companies of manumitted slaves to the colony at various times. By 1854, he had already sent eighty-eight, and it was his purpose to continue until the whole number, some two hundred

---

[73] Ibid., Henkle to Wilkeson, Louisville, Ky., May 5, 1840.
[74] Ibid., volume of omitted letters, 1839-1842, John McPhail to Wilkeson, Norfolk, Va., November 16, 1839.
[75] Ibid., W. B. Lynch to McLain, Lynchburg, Va., November 7, 1842.
[76] Ibid., Tomkins to McLain, Beaufort, N. C., September 1, 1844; T. E. West to McLain, Nicholasville, Ky., December 7, 1844.

and fifty had been transported.[77] Colonel Bell's slaves were very valuable. For a single one of them he had refused five thousand dollars, which was offered a short while before the negro embarked for the colony. Bell was merely waiting until the funds of the Society were sufficient to send the rest of the people.[78]

It will already have been observed that many acts of emancipation were incorporated in the wills of slaveholders. This was a favorite method of offering liberty to the slaves. The act of emancipation, no matter when effected, involved a radical readjustment of the affairs of an estate, and must have had much to do with the choice of this method. It may be well to consider some notable cases of slaves left free by will, in addition to those already noted. It will here appear that on a number of occasions the Society sued for the liberty of slaves. In many cases where suits were not instituted the liberty of the slaves was secured, or the possibility of their being set free investigated, by agents of the Society.[79] Sometimes they forestalled threatened or actual attempts to violate the provisions of emancipations contained in wills.[80]

By the will of Dr. Bradley of Virginia in 1831, all his negroes, numbering about fifty, were to be allowed to emigrate to the colony. Their expenses were to be paid out of the proceeds of the estate. Those who were unwilling to go were to revert to slavery.[81] They were of all ages, from infants to sixty years. In 1835 application was made for passage to Liberia for forty-four slaves left free by the will of Thomas Hickenbotham, of Virginia. Most of them were in the prime of life.[82] The same year, General Black-

---

[77] Journal of Executive Committee of American Colonization Society, MS., June 23, 1854.
[78] Ibid., January 16, 1854; December 30, 1854.
[79] Minutes of Board of Managers of American Colonization Society, MS., August 30, 1825; April 24, 1826.
[80] Ibid., October 22, 1827.
[81] Letters of American Colonization Society, MS., R. Jordan to Gurley, Monticello, Va., February 26, 1831.
[82] Ibid., C. H. Page to Gurley, New Glasgow, Va., June 4, 1835.

burn, also of Virginia, emancipated by will his forty-six slaves on condition of their willingness to go to the colony; the expense of their transportation to be paid out of the proceeds of the estate.[83]

One of the most interesting bequests of slaves to the Society was that of Captain Ross, of Mississippi. In 1834, Ross made a will bequeathing to his granddaughter a woman servant, Grace, with all her children, unless Grace should elect to go to Liberia, in which case she and her children were to be conveyed thither. The granddaughter was desired to maintain comfortably the testator's man servant, Hannibal and his sisters, Daphne, Dinah, and Rebecca. Hannibal was to receive an annuity of one hundred dollars, and each of his sisters an annuity of fifty dollars. In case they should elect to go to Liberia, there was to be given, in place of the annuities, to Hannibal five hundred dollars. Enoch, his wife Merilla, and their children were to be sent to some free State where they could be legally manumitted. To Enoch was to be given also five hundred dollars, unless he and his family should elect to go to Africa, in which case they should be conveyed thither, five hundred dollars being paid him upon his departure.

The rest of his slaves and property were to be left to Ross' daughter, Mrs. Margaret Reed, for the rest of her natural life, or until she was disposed to carry out the remaining provisions of his will, in relation to slaves and property. Upon Mrs. Reed's death, or her decision to carry out her father's design, all of the slaves of the age of twenty-one years and upwards, save those above referred to, and five others whose names were given, were to be assembled by the executors, who were to explain to them the provisions of the will and invite them to determine whether or not they desired to go to Liberia. Those who desired to go were to be conveyed thither, and those refusing to go were to be sold at auction, with the restriction that families were not to be separated. The proceeds from the

---

[83] Ibid., J. H. Peyton to Laurie, Staunton, Va., August 8, 1835.

sale and any other funds belonging to the testator's estate were, after the payment of expenses, to be paid into the treasury of the Colonization Society, to be applied to the transportation and maintenance of the slaves who elected to go. The total number of the slaves, when the will was made, was about one hundred and seventy.

Ross was a planter of excellent judgment. The returns from the estate were large. But the Captain, it seems, applied its great revenues to the comfort of his "people." It was estimated that the estate brought in a revenue of some $20,000 a year. Of the slaves, Gurley wrote: "His slaves were kept disconnected from those on other plantations, and therefore constituted one great family of one hundred and seventy in number, who have been treated more like children than slaves. For industry, intelligence, and good order, none are their superiors. To render them happy appears to have been the great object of their master." Dr. John Ker, whose name appears so often in any study of the Colonization movement in Mississippi, said of Ross: "His slaves . . . felt, in a high degree, the mutual attachment which is not uncommon in the South between master and slave, and which ought to put to shame the slanders of ignorant or wicked Northern fanatics. He ardently desired to provide for their welfare and happiness after his death."

Ross died in 1836, and his daughter made a will which was intended to carry out exactly the wishes of her deceased father. By 1840, however, the provisions of the will were being earnestly contested by certain of the heirs. The latter were able to arouse sentiment in their favor throughout the State, and the fight was carried into the State Legislature in 1841 or 1842, where the result was the passage of a bill in the lower house, by which it would have been made unlawful for the slaves to be emancipated even on condition of their removal to the colony. The High Court of Errors and Appeals had already decided favorably to the validity of the will, and the attempt of the legislature was in reality an attempt to annul an already announced decision of that court.

Dr. Ker just at this time rendered the Colonization Society the valuable service of opposing with great energy the passage of the bill when it came up for consideration in the Senate, of which he was a member. By a campaign of publicity and by great exertion he blocked this move to hold the slaves in slavery. The value of the estate in 1840, was estimated to be about $200,000, and it was to be used for provisioning the Ross and Reed slaves in Liberia and in providing educational institutions in the colony. In 1842 the total number of slaves who were intended to be benefited by the will was upwards of three hundred. It appears that, after years of effort and vigilance, the Society won its point and secured the liberty of the slaves. Let those who doubt the sincerity of Gurley, John Ker, Captain Ross, or Rev. Zebulun Butler, during the days when the Colonization scheme was assailed by Garrisonians as a hypocritical collusion with the friends of perpetual slavery, consule references here given bearing upon the efforts both in and out of the courts to establish the Ross and Reed wills.[84]

Another interesting example is that of Richard Tubman of Georgia. The law of Georgia did not permit the emancipation of slaves within the State; but Tubman tried to secure a special act of permission by making provision for a liberal legacy to several of the literary institutions of the State, if the permission to emancipate were granted. The legislature refused the request. Application was made to the Society to transport the slaves, except four old men whose mistress had consented at their request to keep them. Of the remaining forty-four none was over forty years of age. The widow of the deceased paid the negroes, the year after her husband's death, $1000 for the crop they had

---

[84] African Repository, vol xii, pp. 233–235; vol. xv, pp. 3–4; vol. xvi, p. 50; vol. xviii, p. 99 ff. Letters of American Colonization Society, MS., Gurley to Fendall, Rodney, Miss., July 22, 1836; Z. Butler to McLain, Port Gibson, January 10, 1844; Gurley to McLain, New York, July 22, 1845; Gurley to Butler, September 29, 1843, No. 228.

raised. The value of the slaves was estimated at not less than $40,000.[85]

In 1837 application was made for the transportation of thirty-five slaves belonging to William Hunton who, by will, had offered them their freedom on condition that they would go to the colony. Otherwise they were to revent to slavery.[86] In 1840 William Smart, of Virginia, left, by will, between twenty and thirty, all of his negroes, on condition that they should go to the colony.[87] During this same year, there were two other cases of emancipations in Virginia that should here be noted: James Fox liberated about fifty negroes on condition that they should go to Liberia, otherwise they were to revert to slavery;[88] and Mrs. Carter offered freedom to twenty-six on condition that they should go to the colony.[89] In Kentucky John Graham by will provided that after 1850 his slaves, fifteen in number, were to have their liberty on condition of their willingness to emigrate to the colony.[90] In 1842 Thomas Wallace, deceased, left by will fourteen slaves free on the condition of their going to the colony.[91]

Secretary McLain of the Society wrote to one of the Colonization agents in December, 1842: "Keep in mind the old gentleman near Nashville, Tennessee, who wants to liberate his 68 slaves before he dies to keep them out of the hands of his only heir who is opposed to their liberation. The Old man is in feeble health—he is poor and cannot defray their expenses. About $3000 will carry them to the colony and support them six months."[92] In 1843 Thomas Lindsay, of Missouri, emancipated by will twenty-one slaves

---

[85] Letters of American Colonization Society, MS., Wm. Y. Allen to Gurley, Augusta, Ga., December 29, 1836.
[86] Ibid., John Marr to Mercer, Warrenton, Va., October 23, 1837.
[88] Ibid., Brand to Wilkeson, Richmond, Va., August 18, 1840.
[89] Ibid., M. B. Blackford to Wilkeson, Fredericksburg, Va., September 16, 1840.
[90] Ibid., F. M. Bristow to Wilkeson, Elkton, Ky., November 24, 1840.
[91] Ibid., L. W. Andey, Flemingsburg, Ky., September, 1842.
[92] Ibid., McLain to Dodge, December 27, 1842, No. 516; McLain to Dodge, October 27, 1842, No. 342.

on condition of their emigration to Liberia; and in Virginia, Hardenia M. Burnley emancipated by will the same number, their transportation, outfit, clothing and maintenance in the colony for six months being provided for out of the estate.[93]

One of the most interesting cases of emancipation by will was that of Mr. Hooe of Virginia in 1845. Hooe provided for the emancipation of his two hundred slaves in Virginia and one hundred and fifty-eight in Mississippi and Alabama. Property sufficient to provide for their transportation was left to the Society, and the supervision of the execution of the will was placed directly in Gurley's hands as an executor. Gurley's comment was: ". . . so much depends on examples like that of Mr. Hooe as to the prospect of future emancipations, that special efforts should be made that the humane purpose contemplated may be fully realized." There was considerable probability that that portion of the will directing the emancipation of those slaves who were in Mississippi and Alabama would be contested. Gurley advised as to these, "to ascertain, as fully as possible, whether it is possible to institute any process, by which their case can be brought before the courts of the United States. . . . The executors are solemnly bound to neglect no possible legal means of securing the freedom of those slaves, and for one, I wish any measure, even if unpromising, adopted."[94]

By will of Stephen Henderson of Louisiana, his slaves, five or six hundred in number, were to be emancipated for the purpose of emigration to the colony. The first ten, chosen by lot, were to go within five years after Henderson's death; after ten years, twenty more were to go; and after twenty-five years the remainder. The will was contested but was upheld by the Supreme Court of Louisiana.[95]

---

[93] Ibid., G. C. Sibley to Gurley, Linden-Wood, Missouri, July 15, 1843; J. O. Steger to McLain, Richmond, Va., December 11, 1843.

[94] Ibid., Wm. Coppinger to McLain, Philadelphia, Pa., July 22, 1845; Gurley to McLain, New York, August 12, 1845, October 28, 1845.

[95] New Orleans Commercial Bulletin, August 15, 1845.

Besides these acts of emancipation of slaves for the colony and these bequests of money and of slaves, the records of the Society contain many interesting letters of inquiry. Many slaveholders offered the Society their slaves when it would be ready to take them. Many others wrote for advice as to the disposition of the slaves, advice which Garrisonians were denied the privilege of giving. The real sacrifice some slaveholders were willing to make for the sake of emancipating their slaves it set forth in these letters. The care with which they prepare the slave for the time when he must depend upon his own efforts is also evident. In short, the Society was a sort of clearing house where the views of moderate Southerners and moderate Northerners were exchanged, and where the spirit of emancipation worked silently but mightily. Several examples of letters of this character will suffice.

Rev. Thomas P. Hunt of Richmond, Virginia, desired to emancipate his twenty slaves, but was unable to provide funds sufficient for their transportation. He proposed that he be accredited as an agent in order to secure the funds necessary for their transportation to the colony.[96] Mrs. Barbie of Kentucky was perplexed as to the disposition of five or six slaves which she had not yet inherited, but which were to fall to her. She hoped they might be transported to the colony as soon after they came into her possession as possible.[97] A South Carolinian wrote for advice as to the disposition of his negroes, twenty-five in number. The act of emancipation would leave him a bare competency the rest of his life and he was consequently unable to bear the expense of transportation.[98]

A typical inquiry was that sent from Fincastle, Virginia, in 1832: "I have from fifteen to twenty negroes I wish to emancipate. Will your Society receive and transport them

---

[96] Minutes of Board of Managers of American Colonization Society, MS., August 14, 1826.
[97] Letters of American Colonization Society, MS., J. C. Crane to Gurley, Richmond, Va., October 26, 1826.
[98] Ibid., W. H. Robbins, Cheraw, S. C., October 12, 1827.

to Liberia?" or: "I have for a considerable time past determined to emancipate my slaves if such facilities would be afforded them (by the Society of which you are Agent) in getting off to the colony of Liberia, as are necessary and proper for their accommodation."[99] The slaves are valued at $3500.00. A Colonizationist from Lynchburg, Virginia, reported four groups of slaves held ready for manumission whenever the first opportunity offered to send them to Liberia.[100]

A citizen of Missouri desired to emancipate four slaves, three of whom he bought for the express purpose of emancipating them as soon as they had refunded to him, in labor, the amount expended in their purchase. Already he had executed to them deeds of emancipation on condition of their willingness to go to the colony.[101] A South Carolinian offered his thirteen negroes to the Society to be taken to Liberia. "He has long had it in his heart to do this; but he has not known in what way to effect it, and has requested me to open a correspondence with the Society. . . . Neither the old man nor his wife can die in peace without doing all they can to place their servants in a condition where they may enjoy liberty." The Society was to be given three hundred dollars toward the cost of transportation, and each negro man was to have one hundred dollars and each woman fifty dollars.[102]

In 1843 William B. Lynch, of Virginia, sent off his eighteen slaves for Liberia. Lynch had proposed to take them to the Northwestern States to enjoy their liberty; but after a visit of inquiry, he concluded that to enjoy an equal opportunity and real freedom, they must be removed to the colony. Upon their leaving for Liberia he paid five hundred

---

[99] Ibid., G. Terrill to Gurley, Fincastle, Va., September 10, 1832; T. L. Leftwich, Liberty, Va., Sept. 14, 1832.
[100] Ibid., W. M. Rives, Lynchburg Va., October 16, 1832.
[101] Ibid., John Conway to Gurley, Bonhomme, Mo., November 25, 1837.
[102] Ibid., B. Gildersleeve to Gurley, Charleston, S. C., April 7, 1841.

dollars towards the cost of transportation.[108] One of those choice Colonization spirits among the women of Virginia was Mrs. Mary B. Blackford. She had prepared Abram to be sent to the colony, and her care for him is of interest:

> Giving him his freedom and outfit is as much as I can do being limited in my funds. My brother writes me he is very apt in learning any trade he is put to and suggests his being put to learn the carpenter's trade before he goes, but, I fear if I kept him here for the purpose, something would occur to prevent his having his freedom. . . . my heart is greatly set on this plan. . . . Pray ask that he may be cared for during the fever; if he were to die I should feel a heavy responsibility on me.[104]

Joseph H. Wilson of Kentucky was anxious that his twenty-seven slaves should have a passage to Liberia. They were valued at $12,000; and besides emancipating them, he proposed to give them $1000 or $1200. The Society's agent thus commented upon Wilson's treatment of his negroes: "He has no children and makes his slaves the object of his kindness. . . . the only evil I can see is that when they set up for themselves, as free people, . . . they will feel the loss of the care of their present owners," for he here referred also to two other families of slaves whose masters desired to emancipate them.[105] Mrs. Mary B. Blackford, writing in behalf of a friend who desired to emancipate and send to the colony her six slaves, commented on the particular case:

> She will do her utmost in sending these people away, or rather in giving them their freedom, and I know it is entirely out of her power to furnish them with necessary funds. If some who judge slaveholders so hardly, knew all that I do of the conscientiousness, generous self-denial, insurmountable obstacles, which they would so gladly do away with, how differently they would regard them. In Virginia the owner is almost as much to be pitied as the slave.[106]

[108] African Repository, vol. xix, p. 201.
[104] Letters of American Colonization Society, MS., M. B. Blackford to Gurley, Fredericksburg, Va., September 2, 1843.
[105] Ibid., Pinney to McLain, Bardsville, June 10, 1844.
[106] Ibid., M. B. Blackford to McLain, Mt. Airy, Va., February 2, 1845; J. W. Norwood to Gurley, Hillsborough, N. C., 1826; Miss Judith Blackburn to Gurley, Mount-Vernon, March 29, 1831; J. L. Crawford to Gurley, Danville, Ky., February 27, 1842; G. W. McPhail to McLain, Fredericksburg, Va., November 11, 1845; African Repository, vol. vii, pp. 271-272.

It will be noted that no references have been made to slaves offered from Maryland, although that State was one of the first in the number offered for settlement in Africa. It will be remembered that very early in the thirties the Maryland Society assumed an independent attitude toward the parent Society. Thereafter the slaves offered were offered directly to the State organization, and no record therefore appears on the official documents of the Society.[107]

When an expedition was preparing to leave New Orleans the latter part of the year 1848, there were four hundred and seventy-nine negroes who had applied for passage to the colony. Of these, two hundred were those from the Ross estate, to revert to slavery if they were not removed by the end of January.[108]

The problem was not the difficulty in securing the emancipation of slaves or the want of inclination to encourage emancipation, but the want of funds to carry out their benevolent designs. If the Society had had the means it could have secured thousands more of the slaves of the South and could have made them freemen; and those who measure the work and influence of that organization by the actual number of slaves transported have gotten a very inadequate conception of its influence or its usefulness. The need of funds in the sending out of the expedition just spoken of is but one of many examples that might be presented to show the inability, for want of funds, to meet its opportunities. If the States north of Mason and Dixon's line had offered as much money in cash as the States south of that line offered in slaves, leaving out of account the many thousands of dollars contributed in cash to the treasury of the Society from the slaveholding States themselves,

---

[107] For reports of expeditions sent out to the colony, see Minutes of Board of Managers of American Colonization Society, MS., February 9, 1829; Journal of Executive Committee of American Colonization Society, MS., November 28, 1848; March 15, 1851; April 19, 1851; November 7, 1851; December 16, 1852; November 18, 1853; January 16, 1854; December 20, 1854; etc.

[108] Journal of Executive Committee of American Colonization Society, MS., November 28, 1848.

the statistics of emancipations would be written in quite different figures. Or if the influence of the Society were even measured by the number of slaves offered to it, rather than by the limited number it was able to transport, those figures would still require a radical revision.

But taking the figures as they are: by 1830 over two hundred of the slaves freed and sent out to Liberia had been emancipated by their masters for the express purpose of emigration to the colony.[109] In 1841 Gurley wrote that the Society "has secured the voluntary manumission of slaves, (about 2000) in value (viewed as property) nearly, if not quite, equal to the whole amount of funds given for the establishment of Liberia; while its influence to prepare for future emancipations it were difficult to estimate."[110] Judge Wilkeson estimated the proportion of emancipated slaves to free negroes taken to the colony as more than one for one.[111] By the beginning of 1855, about 3600 slaves had been actually emancipated with a view to their settlement in Liberia.[112] By the time the Society was fifty years old (1867) the number of slaves actually emancipated and sent to the colony was about 6000.[113]

---

[109] A Few Facts, published by American Colonization Society, MS., 1830.
[110] 27th Cong., 3d sess., H. Rept. No. 283, p. 1023.
[111] Minutes of Board of Directors of American Colonization Society, MS., July 20, 1841.
[112] Ibid., January 16, 1855.
[113] Half-Century Memorial, American Colonization Society, 1867.

A List of Slaves Emancipated or Offered for Emancipation for Emigration to Liberian Colony, 1825–1835, Inclusive.

The list given below must not be taken as official. It is a compilation collected from various sources. Doubtless it is very incomplete. It will be of value, however, as showing the distribution of offered emancipations and the number of slaves offered by individual slaveholders.

Year.	State.	Slaves Offered by	Number Offered.
1825	Va.	Name not given	100
"	"	David Minge	80 (approximately)
"	"	Charles Henshaw	60
"	"	N. C. Crenshaw	65
"	"	Rev. Cave Jones	2
"	"	Rev. John Paxton	11
"	Ky.	Miss Elizabeth Moore	40 (approximately)
"	N. C.	David Patterson	11
"	Md.	—— Dickinson	1
"	"	Name not given	20
"	?	Rev. Fletcher Andrew	30
1826	Va.	Colonel Smith	70 or 80
"	"	H. B. Elder	20
"	"	Henry Robertson	7
"	"	Miss Patsy Morris	16
"	"	A clergyman	30 (approximately)
"	"	A lady	12 (approximately)
"	Md.	David Shriver	30
"	Tenn.	Sampson David	23
"	O.	Rev. S. D. Hoge	1
1827	Va.	—— Funston	10
"	"	—— Ward	110
"	"	Rev. Robert Cox	30 (approximately)
"	"	Col. David Bullock	23
"	Md.	Daniel Murray	1
"	"	J. J. Merrick	3
"	"	Name not given	2
"	N. C.	William Fletcher	12
"	S. C.	—— M'Dearmid	26
"	?	Capt. J. D. Henley	1
1828	Va.	Name not given	17
"	"	Name not given	8
"	"	Name not given	5
"	"	Name not given	20 (approximately)
"	Ky.	Name not given	60 (approximately)
"	Ga.	Name not given	43
1829	Va.	Rev. T. P. Hunt	18
"	"	Edward Colston	6
"	Md.	Miss Margaret Mercer	15
"	"	J. L. Smith	12
"	"	Governor Ridgeley	400 (this case not certain)
1830	Va.	Dr. Tilden	6
"	"	—— Pretlow	3
"	"	G. W. Holcomb	5
"	"	Name not given	? (one family)

COLONIZATION AND EMANCIPATION

Year.	State.	Slaves Offered by	Number Offered.
1830	Va.	A lady	50
"	"	A lady	12
"	"	Name not given	? (all his slaves)
"	"	W. H. Fitzhugh	300 (approximately)
"	"	Miss Blackburn	12
"	"	Miss Van Meter	7
"	"	Name not given	7
"	"	John Morton	2
"	"	Noah Maund	9
"	"	John Matthews	6
"	"	?	2
"	"	John B. Carr	10
"	"	Name not given	6
"	"	A lady	50
"	"	A lady	1
"	"	Mrs. Merry	4
"	"	Mrs Ann Tinsley	2
"	Md.	F. S. Anderson	6
"	"	Name not given	20
"	"	Mr. Bell	2
"	"	J. Hughes	1
"	Ga.	Joel Early	30
"	"	Name not given	1
"	"	C. Bolton	9
"	Tenn.	Judge Wm. Brown	15
"	"	Rev. Williamson	23
"	Ky.	Richard Bibb	60
"	"	J. A. Jacobs	1
"	"	W. L. Breckenridge	14
"	Miss.	Dr. Silas Hamilton	22
"	?	Francis Kinlock	1
"	?	Richard Holmes	30
"	?	J. B. Blackburn	12
1831	Va.	H. Robinson	1
"	"	Dr. Matthews	1
"	"	Rev. John Stockdell	31
"	"	William Johnson	12
"	"	Name not given	6
"	"	Name not given	3
"	Md.	Thomas Davis	4
"	N. C.	—— Williams	8
"	"	Gen. Jacobs	7
"	Ky.	L. W. Green	1
"	"	Lee White	?
"	Tenn.	Name not given	4
"	Miss.	Mrs. E. Greenfield	18
1832	Va.	Dr. Wilson	3
"	"	George Reynolds	7
"	"	T. O. Taylor	9
"	"	Mrs. A. R. Page	15
"	"	Mrs. A. R. Page	14
"	"	Rev. M. B. Cox	1
"	"	Name not given	13
"	"	Two gentlemen	11

Year.	State.	Slaves Offered by	Number Offered.
1832	Va.	Name not given	17 (approximately)
"	"	Name not given	14
"	"	A lady	1
"	N. C.	J. A. Gray	14
"	"	Name not given	7
"	"	A lady	4
"	S. C.	Mr. Stewart	14
"	Ga.	Dr. Bradley	46
"	Tenn.	Name not given	8
1833	Va.	Dr. Aylett Hawes	109
"	"	Theophilus Gamble	2
"	"	Robert Coiner	2
"	"	Silas Henton	2
"	"	Rev. Hanks	9
"	Md.	Col. Wm. Jones	13
"	Ky.	Wm. O. Dudley	12
"	"	Cyrus Walker	6
"	"	Mrs. Mary Wycliffe	7
"	"	Rev. J. D. Paxton	5
"	"	A. M. and D. Caldwell	4
"	"	Mrs. Powell	3
"	"	Rev. J. C. Young	2
"	"	Heirs of Dr. A. Todd	4
"	"	Jonathan Becroft	3
"	"	Rev. D. Blackburn	2
"	"	James Hood	3
"	"	Dr. B. Roberts	1
"	"	John Holson	1
"	"	A. J. Alexander	1
"	Tenn.	George Ewing	10
"	"	Dr. McGehee	1
"	"	Robert Caldwell	1
"	Ga,	Rev. Ripley	14
"	O.	Benj. Johnson	6
"	Ill.	Cyrus Edwards	1
1834	Va.	Johnson Cleveland	?
"	N. C.	Name not given	4
"	Miss.	Name not given	19
"	Ga.	Name not given	1
1835	Va.	Isaac Noves	25
"	"	Thos. Higginbotham	50
"	"	Name not given	23
"	"	Name not given	7
"	"	Rev. J. M. Brown	1
"	"	—— Dawson	50
"	"	Gen. Blackburn	50
"	"	James Ogden	5
"	"	Name not given	? (several)
"	"	Miss Martha Walker	16
"	"	Mrs. A. R. Page	4
"	"	J. T. Atkinson	? (several)
"	"	—— Wever	25
"	D. C.	Name not given	1
"	Tenn.	Rev. F. A. Ross	21

Year.	State.	Slaves Offered by	Numbered.
1835	Tenn.	Name not given	20
"	"	Alexander Donelson	20
"	"	Name not given	20
"	Ga.	Name not given	1
"	"	Name not given	8
"	La.	H. M. Childers	30
"	Miss.	Name not given	20
"	"	William Foster	21
"	"	—— Brazile	? (four families)
"	"	Mr. Randolph	21
"	"	Name not given	150
"	?	Name not given	4
Total approximately................			3,300

CHAPTER V

COLONIZATION AND THE AFRICAN SLAVE TRADE

The American Colonization Society was organized in 1817. Its active opposition to the African Slave Trade began that same year, and did not end until the last slaver had been driven from the African Coast. Indeed, within two weeks of the first election of officers of the Society, a memorial was presented to Congress, praying that body to bestir itself to put an end to the traffic.[1] The following year a similar memorial was presented. It was the Colonizationist leader, Charles Fenton Mercer, who secured the passage of the Anti-Slave Trade Act of March 3rd, 1819, and the passage of that act is in large measure due to the efforts of the Colonization Society.[2] By the terms of the act, Africans illegally taken from their native land and recaptured by the authorities of the United States Government were to be returned to the coast of Africa. It provided, further, for the appointment of agents of the United States to look after such recaptured slaves upon their return.

President Monroe, who construed very liberally the terms of the Act, cooperated with the Society, sending agents and ships, and selecting as the location for the point of resettlement of returned natives the same portion of the African coast as that occupied by the Society. In short, he so construed the act as to make the government a partner in the efforts of the Colonizationists, though the government confined its cooperation to the purposes set forth in the Act, the selection of territory as an asylum for recaptured Africans. It was under this unofficial understanding between

---

[1] African Repository, vol. xviii, p. 129 ff.
[2] Ibid., vol. xv, p. 300.

the government and the Society that Mills and Burgess were sent out to explore the coast and recommend a point for the settlement. In his report Burgess—for Mills had died before reaching America—called attention to the destruction caused by the slave trade, and recommended as the most important objects the Society could keep in mind, from the point of view of its influence upon Africa: (1) the suppression of the slave trade, and (2) the elevation of the natives.[3]

In 1820 the Society, in a memorial, urged upon Congress the need of an agreement among the maritime powers "which shall leave no shelter to those who deserve to be considered as the common enemies of mankind."[4] The committee to which the memorial was referred reported a bill which contained a provision declaring the slave trade to be piracy. Again, in 1822, the same body was memorialized to take further measures in opposition to the slave trade, and was advised that colonization on the west African coast by civilized powers, was one of the most effective remedies for that trade. Late in February, 1823, Mercer secured a unanimous vote in the House declaring slave traders pirates.[5]

Indeed, the birth of that settlement which, before the century was half passed, was to become the Republic of Liberia, must be considered the result of the cooperation of the United States Government and the group of colonization philanthropists. The first endeavored to establish an asylum for recaptured Africans. The second hoped to establish a home for those free negroes from America who desired to be free not only from physical but from mental

---

[3] Origin, Constitution, and Proceedings of American Colonization Society, MS., vol. i, p. 33 ff.
[4] African Repository, vol. xviii, p. 129 ff.; Origin, Constitution, and Proceedings of American Colonization Society, MS., vol. i, pp. 116-117.
[5] African Repository, vol. xviii, p. 129 ff.; Minutes of Board of Managers of American Colonization Society, MS., March 4, 1819, Dec. 10, 1819; Origin, Constitution, and Proceedings of American Colonization Society, MS., vol. i, p. 123 ff.

slavery, for nowhere in the United States was the negro really free in 1820; for those slaves whose masters, under the influence of moral suasion, might desire to emancipate; and to establish a colony which would close that part of the African coast to the trader in West Africa negroes. The first direct and tangible steps taken in the colonization enterprise were taken by the Government rather than by the Society. The first vessel sent to the African coast was chartered and paid for by the Government. The first agents received salaries from the government, and the Society was backed by the appropriation of $100,000 contained in the Act of 1819.[6]

Already by 1826 the colony had become so effective a barrier to the slave-trade that a French trader threatened to fit out a piratical expedition and make war on the colony for its interference with his business.[7] In 1827 at the annual meeting of the Society, the powers of Europe and America were called upon to adopt further restrictive measures against an apparently increasing trade. Mercer there called attention to the fact that in 1824 two hundred and eighteen slave vessels had carried away from their homes 120,000 victims. He wished the time to come when the trade would be stamped with "the seal of indelible infamy."[8] At this time Dr. William Thornton, doubtless with the object of making the colony an effective barrier against the trade, was urging the Society to obtain territory for a thousand miles along the coast, even if the width of the territory was not more than a single mile.[9]

Certainly those Americans who were fighting the traffic could have asked for no more effective or energetic colonial agent than was now in the colony, Jehudi Ashmun. Under his administration and, indeed, largely due to his exertion,

---

[6] 27th Cong., 3d sess., H. Rept. No. 283, pp. 247–249.
[7] Minutes of Board of Managers of American Colonization Society, MS., May 23, 1826.
[8] African Repository, vol. ii, pp. 357–358.
[9] Letters of American Colonization Society, MS., Thornton to Gurley, April 11, 1827.

the slave trade had ceased it seemed along the hundred miles of coast over which the Liberian settlers, not over 1200 souls in 1828, assumed jurisdiction. Rev. Leonard Bacon, in his eulogy upon Ashmun in 1828, declared of Cape Montserado that, while a few years ago it was "literally consecrated to the devil" and cursed as a port of entry for the unspeakable slave ship, at the time of Ashmun's death " for a hundred miles no slave trader dares to spread his canvas."[10]

Dr. Randall went out as colonial agent upon the death of Mr. Ashmun. He urged the building and improving of fortifications in the colony in order that it might be effective in its fight against the slave trader. He recommended that a government vessel should cruise for some months along the Liberian coast and watch the movements of the trader. Officers of the Society in this country called upon the President and Secretary of the Navy in order to secure action upon the agent's request.[11] The official effort was seconded by the Philadelphia Quaker, Elliot Cresson, who wrote: "I wish as our friend Key has influence with Old Hickory, thee would occasionally hint to him the advantage which we might derive, from certain welltimed suggestion, such as keeping a sharp lookout on the African Coast by a swift cruiser—or if possible making her a *packet* on her outward voyage."[12]

During the years 1830–1839 the Society was too busy trying to make its resources meet its expenditures and trying to take care of the negroes offered to it, or settled in its colony, or meeting the furious opposition of the Garrisonians, to continue its direct efforts toward the abolition of the slave trade; and in 1839 the general agent reported an alarming increase in the number of African victims taken away from the very vicinity of the colony. The influence of that trade had involved the neighboring tribes in a war which endan-

---

[10] L. Bacon, Funeral Oration on Jehudi Ashmun, New Haven, Conn., 1828.
[11] Minutes of Board of Managers of American Colonization Society, MS., April 13, 1829.
[12] Letters of American Colonization Society, MS., Cresson to Gurley, Philadelphia, Pa., December 7, 1829.

gered the peace of the colony, and Wilkeson pressed the matter before the Secretary of the Navy.[13]

When the Society was reorganized in 1839 there were sent to the colonial governor, Thomas Buchanan, positive instructions urging the passage of a law forbidding "any communication between the citizens of Liberia and the slave traders," and punishing Liberian citizens violating the law "in the same manner as are citizens or subjects of any civilized State, who, are guilty of dealing with or succoring an enemy in time of war." They urged the death penalty for any participation by a Liberian in the business of the trader. The reason for these strict instructions will be understood when it is stated that there were some—there appears no evidence that many were guilty of it—among the Liberians who had themselves been redeemed from the chains of slavery, who were actively engaged in assisting the slave trader; and the Society felt that the whole colonization scheme was jeopardized by such conduct. Indeed, Judge Wilkeson thought that the strongest tie that bound many persons to the colonization cause was their belief that it was the only hope of putting an end to a very unpopular business. Wilkeson commented: "It was natural to suppose that those who had returned to the land of their fathers . . . would urge increasing war against this system of cruelty so long practiced upon their brethren." He thought that if it became known publicly that colonists had aided the slavers, "the colonies would be denounced and execrated from one end of the Union to the other."[14]

The new Governor was another Ashmun in his hatred of the slaver and his energy in routing him from the neighborhood of the colony. During the first year of his administration he brought about the capture of a slaving ship carrying the flag of the United States and sent her to America for trial. She was the schooner Euphrates.[15] He further

---

[13] Ibid., Wilkeson to Secretary of the Navy, February 12, 1839.
[14] Journal of Executive Committee of American Colonization Society, MS., July 25, 1839.
[15] African Repository, vol. xvii, pp. 246-247.

went boldly out with a company of colonists and captured out of their prisons a number of native Africans who were held in waiting for the arrival of the next slaver.[16]

There was not a little difference of opinion as to the most effective means of abolishing the trade. There were those who thought that it would automatically cease as slavery was abolished in the civilized nations that still endured it. There were others who supposed that the iniquity would never be suppressed until the maritime powers jointly and constantly patrolled the waters along the west African coast. But in the early forties the predominating view, it seems, was that the planting of colonies along the west coast would make impossible a traffic between the slave traders and the natives of the interior, and that such colonies, planted by the civilized powers, presented the only efficient remedy for that traffic.

Thomas Foxwell Buxton, who had been so much interested in the abolition of slavery in the West Indies, himself believed that that very abolition had stimulated a disguised form of the slave trade with that colony. The recently emancipated negroes of those Islands refused to work, and the result was the importation of so-called free negro labor from the African coast. Those imported were, many of them, either stolen outright or brought in ignorance to the West Indies, and the result was the legitimating of what had before been illegal.[17] This was also Perry's view.[18] Buxton believed that the only satisfactory remedy was the establishment along the coast of civilized colonies which would not endure the slave trade within their jurisdictions and which would provide an effective barrier between those who operated slave vessels along the coast and those within the interior who were willing to sell their fellow Africans.

In this view the Colonizationists of America heartily concurred.[19] Indeed they had had a practical verification of

---

[16] For an interesting account of the expedition see African Repository, vol. xv, pp. 277-282.
[17] Sir T. F. Buxton, The African Slave Trade and Its Remedy, passim; London Quarterly Review, March, 1839.
[18] African Repository, vol. xvii, pp. 85-86.
[19] Ibid., vol. xvii, pp. 246-247.

the value of this method. Bassa Cove, one of the Liberian settlements, had once been the seat of the slave trade. From five to six thousand natives had been packed into slave vessels and taken from that point annually; after the settlement of that point by the Colonizationists the trade was completely broken up. Cape Montserado itself had once been a depot for the detention of captured natives. Slavers touched there and carried away annually from two to three thousand native Africans into slavery. After the settlement of the cape and its government by the Colonizationists the slave trade ceased.[20]

There is abundant evidence to the value of the colony as a contributor to the suppression of the slave trade. In April, 1842, Secretary of State Webster made inquiries of Captains Charles H. Bell and John S. Paine, both of whom had seen service along the west African coast and were familiar with the influence exerted by the colony of Liberia, as to the length of coast along which the trade was carried on. Those officers replied that the distance from the northernmost to the southernmost points along the coast, where the slave trader put in for slaves was 3600 miles, but that the influence of the British, French, and especially the American settlements was so directly hostile to, and effective against, the trade, that from this extent of coast should be subtracted 600 miles, leaving only 3000 miles of coast along which the slavers actually carried on their work.[21] Captain Arabin, of Her Majesty's Navy, testified: "Wherever the influence of Liberia extends, the slave trade has been abandoned by the natives, and the peaceful pursuits of legitimate commerce established in its place."[22]

M. C. Perry, who had commanded the United States Naval forces on the west coast of Africa, wrote in 1844: "So far as the influence of the colonists has extended, it has been

---
[20] Ibid., vol. xvii, p. 248.
[21] 27th Cong., 3d sess., H. Rept., No. 283, pp. 768–769.
[22] African Repository, vol. xvii, p. 331, Nov., 1841.

exerted to suppress the slave trade, and their endeavors in this respect have been eminently successful; and it is by planting these settlements . . . along the whole extent of coasts, from Cape Verde to Benguela, that the exportation of slaves will be most effectually prevented." He favored appropriations from Congress in aid of the Society for this purpose as well as others.[23] Two years later he declared: "It is useless to talk of destroying this vile traffic in any other way than by belting the whole coast with Christian settlements, unless the European powers should follow the example of the United States and declare it to be piracy, and then faithfully enforce the law," and he thought that at that time the only powers that were in earnest about the destruction of the trade were the United States and Great Britain.[24]

Not only did the colonial governors effectively prohibit the slave trade within the jurisdiction of the colony, but they also provided needed information as to the points along the coast at which the trade was still carried on. Upon several occasions reports were received that certain points along the coast and surrounded by the territory of the colony—for it was years before the colony obtained exclusive jurisdiction over a continuous line of coast—were used as centres of the trade. The Society almost invariably set at once to work to purchase these points.[25] Thousands of dollars were given by Americans for this specific purpose. Governor Roberts in 1843 notified the Society that at a single depot, between Cape Mount and Cape Palmas, both surrounded by Liberian territory, four hundred slaves had but recently been taken away in slavers. At once the question of the purchase of that territory was agitated by the Directors of the Society.[26]

---

[23] African Repository, June, 1844, vol. xx, pp. 167–168; Letter of M. C. Perry to David Henshaw, Secretary of the Navy, January 4, 1844.
[24] African Repository, vol. xxii, pp. 85–86, March, 1846.
[25] Letters of American Colonization Society, MS., Gurley to Rev. S. Cornelius, July 28, 1843.
[26] Ibid., Gurley to Cornelius, July 28, 1843; Journal of Board of Directors of American Colonization Society, MS., vol. iv, p. 24.

By 1845 there were, it seems, but two points along a coast line of seven hundred miles, over which the influence of the colony extended, where the slavers continued to frequent, and they were points which the Society had not had the means to purchase. It should be remembered that twenty years before the whole of that coast line was dotted with depots, slave factories as they were called, where the slaver came to take away hundreds of slaves in a single vessel, scores of the human cargo perishing before the vessel had reached its destination, while there were, in 1845, but two depots that remained, and they without the limits of the Colony. It was probably a fair estimate that the Society made, that it was saving every year, or was the leading instrument in saving from perpetual bondage in some other land or from a horrible death on a slave ship, 20,000 Africans.[27]

If one may venture to estimate the number of native Africans saved from either of these alternatives by the influence of the American Colonization Society, would it be too much to say that not fewer than 100,000 negroes were in this way saved to freedom? When the Garrisonian asked the Colonizationist: "What are you doing to bring about the *immediate* emancipation of the slaves in the United States?" the Colonizationist could and did reply: "We are doing all we can to secure the entire abolition of slavery in the United States as soon as may be consistent with constitutional guarantees, peace, and the preservation of the American Union. What are you doing to bring about the *immediate* abolition of the slave trade?" And the Garrisonian was silent on the efforts of the Society to bring to a speedy end that outlawed and inhuman traffic.

For many years there was active cooperation between the Society and the Government in relation to this trade. In 1844 the Society kept an agent in Liberia whose duty it was to deliver parcels and packages sent to the American squadron patrolling the African coast waters. Also the Govern-

---

[27] *African Repository*, May, 1845, vol. xxi, p. 145 ff.

ment was allowed to land, free of duty, at the port of Monrovia, all provisions, stores, and supplies used by the squadron.[28] It also received hundred of recaptured Africans and settled them in Liberia. The largest single cargo of slaves thus sent to Liberia was that sent in the "Pons" in 1846, for whose support the Government paid the Society thirty-odd thousand dollars.[29]

The Society did not hesitate to investigate cases in which citizens of New York or the New England States were reported to be engaged in operating vessels which were actively engaged in the slave trade.[30] And when there was talk of abrogating that part of the Webster-Ashburton treaty which related to the patrolling of the waters along the African coast, and at other times when there was some discussion of the advisability of either withdrawing or diminishing the size of the squadron kept in those waters, the leaders of the Society consistently protested against such withdrawal or diminution.[31]

It will be of interest to note the opinion of Secretary of State Everett in 1853. Everett said:

Wherever a colony is established on the coast of Africa under the direction of a Christian power in Europe or America, there the slave trade disappears; not merely from the coast of the colony, but from the whole interior of the country which found an outlet at any point on the coast. . . . The last slave mart in that region, the Gallinas, has, within a ⸺t time, I believe, come within the jurisdiction of the American colony of Liberia. Now, along that whole line of coast . . . from every port and every harbor of which the foreign slave trade was carried on—within the memory of man, it has entirely disappeared. . . . And what career is there opened for any colored man in Europe or America, more praiseworthy, more inviting than thus to form as it were, in his own person a portion

---

[28] Journal of Executive Committee of American Colonization Society, MS., June 6, 1844, pp. 381–383.
[29] Ibid., May 1, 1851, p. 187; Minutes of Board of Directors of American Colonization Society, MS., January 16, 1861, pp. 367–368; January 22, 1862, p. 380.
[30] Letters of American Colonization Society, MS., Tracy to McLain, Boston, April 23, 1846; Minutes of Board of Directors of American Colonization Society, MS., January 18, 1855, p. 218.
[31] Minutes of Board of Directors of American Colonization Society, MS., January 20, 1853, p. 120; January 18, 1855, pp. 213–214.

of that living cordon stretching along the coast and barring its whole extent from the approaches of this traffic.[32]

Professor Hart, commenting upon the results of the Colonization movement, says that, with the backing of the Federal Government and its auxiliary societies the Society was yet not able to oversome " distance, malaria, savage neighbors, and a tropical climate."[33] If the positions taken in this study have been successfully maintained, that statement is inadequate. Not only were all those difficulties, except distance, satisfactorily overcome, but, from the point of view of Africa alone, there were brought about two important results: (1) the establishment upon the west African coast of a model republic for Africans, and (2) the salvation of many thousands of natives from the holds of miserable slave ships. If viewed alone in the light of its influence upon Africa, was not this something? Indeed, was it not worth the effort required to bring the Society into being and to preserve it for so many years?

---

[32] Edward Everett, Address at Anniversary of American Colonization Society, MS., January 18, 1853.

[33] Hart, p. 163.

INDEX

Abolitionists, on unhealthfulness of Liberia, 55; leading Garrisonians once Colonizationists, 90-91; rise of Abolition opposition to Colonization, 90, 94-95; effect of opposition, 124, 136-141, 157-166; Garrisonians and radical slaveholders the Colonizationist's bitterest enemies, 125; debates over Colonization, 125-126; two classes of, 126; radical Abolition founded upon a sectional sentiment, 127, 138-139, 166; views on slavery and the Union, compared with views of Colonizationists, 127, 146-149; methods used in criticising Colonization, 128-136; amount of propaganda, 140; Abolitionist and Colonizationist views of slavery contrasted, 142-145, 151; abusive language to slaveholders, 152; injustice of such language, 152-154; confused with Colonizationists in the South, 160; Abolition and the division in the Methodist Church, 163-166; cooperation between Abolitionists and Colonizationists urged, 1828, 166; wherein Abolitionist criticism failed, 171-172; propaganda discourages emancipations, 172-175; Birney on the effects of Abolition upon the South, 174-175; effect of opposition to Colonization on the Middle States, 177; Colonizationists tend to become moderate Abolitionists, 180-214.

American Colonization Society, a national movement, 9-10, 75, 100, 127; influence not to be measured by number of negroes sent to Liberia, 11; motives of organizers, 47-50; slaveholders as presidents of, 74; effect of Pro-Slavery Argument on Colonizationist sentiment in the South, 155-156; effect of Southampton Insurrection on sentiment regarding, in Va. and Md., 92; organization of, 46-47, 50-51, 60; finances of, 57-65, 77-78, 84-85, 88, 90, 101-107, 123-124; geographical distribution of contributions, 65, 123-124; seeks financial aid from Congress, 54, 70-71; investigation of Society's debt, 103-104; auxiliary societies, 61; sentiment toward, in the South, 58-59, 78-88, 92; attitude of New England clergy, 63-64; expeditions sent out, 55, 67, 68; character of emigrants, 89; table of emigrants, 1820-1830, 89; cost to Society per emigrant, 88; attitude of religious denominations, 78-79; attitude of state legislatures, 79-80; Clay's optimism, 77; dissatisfaction of auxiliary societies, 105-106; secession of auxiliaries, 95-101; demand for reorganization, 106; reorganization, 110-122; a new constitution proposed, 115-116; adopted, 120; attitude toward the Union, 145, 150, 166; Birney's and Gerrit Smith's reasons for deserting, 176; Colonization and Abolition confused in the South, 160; opposition to, in North and West, 90; Abolitionist opposition, 90, 94-95; effect of, 136, 157-166; effect of Colonization movement upon emancipations, 180-214; Colonization Society opposes African slave trade, 215-225; number of Africans saved from slavery by, 223. See also

INDEX

Abolition, Emancipation, Garrison, Slavery, Slave Trade, etc.
Anti-Slave-Trade Act of 1819, influence of Colonization Society in securing passage of, 54, 215; President Monroe's interpretation of, 55, 215-216.
Ashmun, Jehudi, sent to Africa, 68; Ashmun and the slave trade, 217-218.
Ayres, Dr. Eli, arrives in Africa as agent, 67; Liberia ceded to Ayres and Stockton, 68; instructed to purchase additional territory in Africa, 69.

Birney, James G., once a Colonizationist, 90, 91; on detaching Virginia from the slave States by a scheme of emancipation and colonization, 174-175; reason given for deserting the Colonizationists, 176; Garrison inquires for, 178.
Breckenridge, Robert J., 167; on relation of Colonizationists to slaveholders, 169; on influence of Colonization Society on emancipations, 187.

Caldwell, E. B., 43-44, 46, 181.
Calhoun, John C., 190.
Carey, Mathew, 161.
Carroll, Charles, of Carrollton, 74.
Church, attitude of Methodist toward slavery and the Society, 10, 79, 163-164; Presbyterian, 78, 91; Friends (Quakers), 78; Episcopal, 79; Dutch Reformed, 79; Congregational, 79; Unitarian, 79; effect of abolition opposition on Colonization sentiment in the churches, 138, 139, 163; slavery and the division in the Methodist Church, 163-166.
Clay, Henry, 51; on the property value of slaves in the South, 21; on the future of slavery, 23-24; attitude toward slavery, 29; on the status of free negroes, 33; on colonization, 39; organization of American Colonization Society, 46; officer in, 51; speech at annual meeting, 1827, urging help from Federal Government, 76-77; on the gradual abolition of slavery through colonization, 76-77; politics and Colonization, 83-84; on danger to Union, from Abolitionist view of slavery, 147-148; on effects of Garrisonian Abolition, 161.
Cocke, General John H., 82-83, 153-154.
Colonization, Maryland House of Representatives on slavery and, 30; Gerrit Smith on, 32; essential to the welfare of the free negro, 37; projects before 1817, 39-44; as the solution of the negro problem, 45-46; a middle state movement, 49; a means of abolishing slavery, 50; effect upon free negro, 52; growth of interest in, 75; Clay's views of effect of, on slavery, 76-77; politics and, 83-84; colonization an aid to emancipation, 90; Birney advocates emancipation and colonization, for Virginia, 174-175; not the solution of the negro problem, 177; effect of, on emancipations, 1817-1850, 180-214; cause of the Colonization Society's influence, 187.
Connecticut, 79.
Cotton, 155.

Delaware, 79.
DeTocqueville, A., on slavery in the U. S., 19-20, 31.
Dew, Thomas, Pro-Slavery Argument, 10-11; effect of, on the South, 155, 156.

Early, Bishop John, 166.
Emancipation, American Colonization Society and, 11, 50, 51, 85, 162, 169, 173-174, 181; effect of Colonization upon, 180-214; Maryland House of Representatives on, 30; attitude of South toward, 30-31; attitude of slaveholders, 38-39; Bishop Meade on effect of Colonization on, 49; legis-

lative acts restricting, 90; views of Garrisonians and Colonizationists compared and contrasted, 127, 142-145; war with Great Britain advocated as a means of emancipating the negro, 134; effect of Abolition on, in New Orleans, 160; slaves offered freedom on condition of their removal to Liberia, 169; Birney advocates general scheme of emancipation and colonization for Va., 174-175; records of, difficult to obtain, 180; Mass. contributes to Society on condition that freed slaves be sent to Liberia, 185; influences discouraging emancipation, 189-194; table of emancipations, 1825-1833, 211-214; estimates of number of emancipated slaves sent to Liberia, 214.
Everett, Edward, 36, 214-225.

Fitzhugh, William H., 48, 57, 59, 85, 195.
Free Negro, Mass. Senate on, 28-29; effect of increase on emancipations, 29; property holdings among, in Virginia, 31; DeTocqueville on, 31; sentiments of various sections toward, 28-37; danger in immediate general emancipation, 142-143; attitude of Colonization Society toward, 143, 182; effect of Colonization enterprise upon, 162; Gerrit Smith accuses Colonization Society of neglecting, 176.
Frelinghuysen, Theodore, 80.
Friends (Quakers), Society of, 64.

Garrison, William Lloyd, 90, 91; hostility to Colonization, 125-179; views on slavery and the Union, compared with those of Colonizationists, 127, 142-149, 150; methods of criticism, 128-136; effect of opposition to Colonization, 136-141, 157-166, 177, 178; sectional basis of Garrisonism, 138-139; Garrisonians in politics, 139; propaganda, 140; resolutions on dissolution of the Union, 149; language to slaveholders, 152-154.
Georgia, 49, 81.
Giles, William B., 83-84.
Grimke, Sarah M., 178.
Gurley, R. R., sent to Liberia, 73; proposes a constitution for Liberia, 74-75; reports on conditions in, 75; influence in Colonization movement, 73-74; on the rise of Abolition opposition, 94-95; on relations between parent and auxiliary societies, 99, 100; views on reorganization of the Society, 117-118; debates with Abolitionists, 126; on the effect of Garrisonian opposition, 137-138; on Abolition and Colonization propaganda, 140; view of the American slave system, 157; on the purchase of freedom for slaves, 183.
Harrison, J. B., reply of, to Pro-Slavery Argument, 11, 155-156; encouragement given by Colonization Society, 11; confers with New Englanders, 75; hopes for abolition of slavery, 167.
Hart, A. B., 225.
Hopkins, Dr. Samuel, 39-41.

Illinois, 162.
Indiana, 79, 80.

Jackson, Andrew, Vice-President of Colonization Society, 51.
Jefferson, Thomas, 40, 41-42.

Kentucky, 79, 173, 187.
Key, Francis Scott, attitude toward slavery, 17-19; and the organization of the Colonization Society, 43-44, 51; agent for Colonization, 57; on effect of Abolitionism on welfare of the negro, 160; on number of slaves whose freedom could be secured on condition of removal to Africa, 169, 186; hope of ultimate abolition of slavery, 175; on Colonization and abolition of slavery, 181.

Latrobe, J. H. B., on slavery, 23; a leader in the Maryland Colonization Society, 61; reason given for secession of Maryland auxiliary society, 97.

Liberator, The, on motives of organizers of Colonization Society, 47; charges against Colonizationists, 100, 169-170; amount of space given to opposition to Colonization, 125, 132; character of criticism, 130; exults over the debt of Colonization Society, 132; language to slaveholders, 152-154.

Liberia, ship line between U. S. and, proposed, 35; healthfulness of, 55-57, 69-70; bad news from, 1820; 66-67; expeditions to, 55, 67; deaths of agents, 67; land purchased, 67; land ceded to Stockton and Ayres, 68; considered as a trust by the Colonization Society, 68; American flag raised, 68; the colony named, 71; discontent among colonists, 71-73; constitution proposed for, 75; Gurley's report on conditions in, 75; number of emigrants and cost per emigrant to, 88-89; table of emigrants sent by Society to, 89; character of emigrants, 89; independent settlements of auxiliary societies, 95; unwise administration in, 102, 107-110; financial difficulties limit expeditions to, 105; recently emancipated slaves make poor colonists, 108; Abolitionist methods of discouraging emigration to, 141, 172, 189; slaves offered freedom on condition of returning to, 169; becomes chief aim of Colonizationists, 177; runaway slaves request to go to, 182; Massachusetts demands that freed slaves be sent to, 185; Key on number of slaves willing to go to, 186; Finley on same, 188; unwillingness of negroes to go to, 191; number of emancipated slaves sent to, 214; Liberia and the slave trade, 216-217; a barrier to the slave trade, 217, 221; U. S. cooperates with Colonization Society in ending slave trade in, 223-224; Edward Everett on influence of Colonization in ending slave trade, 224-225.

Lincoln, Abraham, 145.

Louisiana Colonization Society, 61, 122.

McDonogh, John, 61, 183; bequest to Society, 63; value of his slaves, and his plans for freeing them, 168, 197.

McLane, R. M., 184.

Madison, James, 61, 62, 88.

Manumission, see Emancipation.

Marshall, John, 61, 62, 87.

Maryland, House of Representatives, on slavery, 30; Colonization Society, 61; legislative appropriation, 1831, 62-63; attitude of legislature toward society, 79; effect of Southampton Insurrection in, 92; secession of Maryland Colonization Society from parent society, 95, 96-98; excludes ardent spirits from Cape Palmas, 98; expeditions sent out from Maryland, 98; Maryland colonizationists not controlled by slave holders, 101; influence in bringing about reorganization of the society, 115; effect of abolitionist opposition in, 160; Gurley on the influence of the colonization scheme on slaveholders in Maryland, 170-171.

Massachusetts, 41, 79, 80, 185.

Meade, Bishop William, 34, 49, 57, 58-59.

Mercer, C. F., 16, 34, 54, 57, 61, 75, 215-217.

Methodist Church, 163-166.

Mills, Samuel J., 42, 43, 52, 53.

Mississippi, Colonization Society, 61; sentiment in, 81; effect of reorganization of parent society upon sentiment in, 122; Methodist Church in, 165.

Monroe, James, 52, 55, 90, 188.

New England, 41, 77-78, 137-138.

INDEX

New Jersey, 79.
New Orleans, 160, 210.
New York, 79, 106, 110, 114–115, 117, 120, 177.
North Carolina, 59, 188–189.

Ohio, 61, 79, 81.
Otis, Harrison Gray, 146.

Page, Mrs. Ann R., 152–153.
Paine, Elijah, 60, 186.
Panic of 1837, 191.
Pennsylvania, 80, 98, 114–115, 163, 177.
Perry, M. C., 220, 221–222.
"Pro-Slavery Argument," 10; J. B. Harrison's reply, 11, 155–156; attitude of American Colonization Society toward, 11; influence of, 155, 156.

Rhode Island, 79.
Roberts, Governor, of Liberia, 222.

Sherman, Roger M., 36, 161.
Sierra Leone, 40–41, 42, 52, 67.
Slavery, see American Colonization Society, Emancipation, etc.
Slave Trade, African, 11, 53–54, 70, 177, 215–225.
Smith, Gerrit, attitude toward slaveholders in 1828, 16; on colonization, 32; contributor to American Colonization Society, 60, 62; on the constitutionality of federal aid to the society, 86; attitude of Colonization Society toward slavery, 91; opinion of Colonization Society, 140; reason for deserting the Colonizationists, 176.
South Carolina, 49, 81.
Southwest, effect of economic development on question of slavery, 10–11, 155.
Stiles, Ezra, 39–40.

Stockton, Captain R. F., 67, 68.

Tappan, Arthur, 90, 140, 178.
Tazewell, L. W., 86.
Tennessee, 79.
Thornton, Dr. William, attitude toward slaveholders, 15–16, 21; attitude toward slavery, 28, 181; efforts to colonize the negro, 40–41; and the American Colonization Society, 43–51; and the slave trade, 217.
Tyler, John, 61.

Upsur, Abel P., 61.

Vermont, 79.
Virginia, legislative committee proposes colonization, 1777, 40; 1800, 41–42; Colonization Society of, 61; legislative appropriation for colonization, 63; attitude of legislature, 1820–1830, 70, 82–84; opposition to federal aid to colonization, 82, 85–86, 87–88; effect of the Southampton Insurrection on sentiment in, 92; legislature not representative of the State on question of slavery, 93–94; Virginia Colonizationists not controlled by slaveholders, 101; effect of reorganization of the American Colonization Society upon sentiment in, 122; attitude of, toward slavery, 158–160; effect of abolitionist opposition to Colonization in, 159, 160; constitutional scruples on the subject of slavery, 159.

Washington, Bushrod, 46, 50.
Webster, Daniel, 221.
Weld, Theodore D., 178.
Whittier, J. G., 179.
Whittlesey, Elisha, 94, 117, 148.
Wilberforce, William, 35, 91.
Wilkeson, Samuel, 118–119, 131.